Editor
Walter Kelly

Editorial Project Manager
Karen J. Goldfluss, M.S. Ed.

Editor-in-Chief
Sharon Coan, M.S. Ed.

Illustrators
Ken Tunell
Bruce Hedges

Cover Artist
Cheri Macoubrie Wilson

Art Coordinator
Cheri Macoubrie Wilson

Creative Director
Elayne Roberts

Imaging
Ralph Olmedo, Jr.

Product Manager
Phil Garcia

Publishers:
Rachelle Cracchiolo, M.S. Ed.
Mary Dupuy Smith, M.S. Ed.

Social Studies
Through the Year

PRIMARY

Authors

Deborah P. Cerbus, M.A.
and
Cheryl Feichtenbiner Rice, M.A.

Teacher Created Materials, Inc.
6421 Industry Way
Westminster, CA 92683
www.teachercreated.com

©1999 Teacher Created Materials, Inc.
Reprinted, 2002
ISBN-1-57690-467-9
Made in U.S.A.

Table of Contents

Introduction

Elementary teachers will enjoy organizing their social studies curriculum by using a series of thematic units. Thematic teaching helps children make connections between different areas of the curriculum and provides them with a variety of multilevel learning experiences. Learning with themes is exciting and fun for elementary students.

This book provides a wealth of ideas to link social studies with literature, writing, math, music, creative arts, and technology. A sample weekly schedule is provided as well as detailed instructions for the activities. A blank planning form and a title page are included on pages 5 and 6.

Each section of the book is arranged around a social studies theme appropriate for elementary classrooms. A weekly activities calendar will help teachers in planning their lessons. This calendar can be sent home along with the parent letter to keep parents informed of the children's social studies learning experiences. A blank calendar is also provided to aid teachers in planning additional themes.

The overview pages in each theme unit give complete, easy-to-follow instructions for carrying out the theme during the week. These pages contain suggestions for the following areas of study:

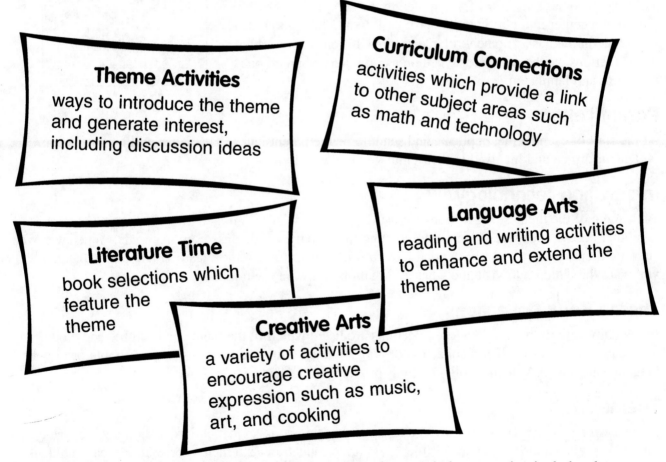

Theme Activities
ways to introduce the theme and generate interest, including discussion ideas

Curriculum Connections
activities which provide a link to other subject areas such as math and technology

Literature Time
book selections which feature the theme

Language Arts
reading and writing activities to enhance and extend the theme

Creative Arts
a variety of activities to encourage creative expression such as music, art, and cooking

In addition to the weekly chart and day-by-day overview plans, each theme section includes the following: a theme sign, a parent letter, a list of journal topics, a mini-book or idea for a class book, and a variety of activity pages. These materials will enable teachers to carry out the theme with minimum preparation time.

The appendix contains other useful materials such as a theme-related bibliography, maps, a journal format, and samples of technology projects.

How to Use This Book

When to Use the Themes

Some of the themes are seasonal, such as the Thanksgiving theme, and need to be started prior to the holiday. Other themes may be used whenever they fit in with your curriculum. Although the themes are designed to be completed in one week, the plans are flexible and should be adapted as needed to fit into your daily schedule.

Using the Theme Signs

A theme sign appears in each section of the book. The sign can be enlarged, colored, and laminated for durability. It may be hung in your classroom, on your door, or displayed with a theme book collection in your language arts area.

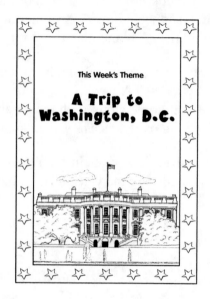

This Week's Theme

A Trip to Washington, D.C.

Learning Centers

The activities for each theme can be easily adapted for use at centers. An activity can be introduced and explained to the whole class first. Then the necessary materials for completing the activity can be placed at a center in a plastic basket or tub. It would be a good idea to include in the basket some written directions for children to refer to. Directions can be written or typed on a computer, mounted on tagboard, and laminated.

Parent Letters

At the start of each theme, duplicate and send home the parent letter. This letter will help to keep parents informed and involved in their child's school experience.

Integrating Technology

With some of the themes, suggestions for using technology are mentioned. If you do not have computer access, ideas are given for completing the activities with classroom materials. Whenever Web sites are mentioned, it is always a good idea for the teacher to visit the sites first and plan what areas you want the children to visit and what information you want them to find.

Theme Book Collections

In the daily activity pages, literature selections are listed which fit the theme and can be read aloud. You may also want to gather a collection of books related to the theme to display on a table or in your language arts area. A theme bibliography is provided at the end of this book.

Theme Journal

A format for a theme journal is provided at the end of this book so that children can integrate writing into their social studies learning. Writing ideas are provided in each theme section. For each student, duplicate the cover on heavy stock paper and add the pages found in the appendix. Include at least five lined pages so children can write about their learning each day. The first page, entitled "What I Know About . . . ," allows teachers to assess students' prior knowledge of the topic.

Weekly Theme Planning Form

Weekly Theme: _____ **Week** _____

	Monday	Tuesday	Wednesday	Thursday	Friday
Date					
Theme Activities					
Literature Time					
Language Arts					
Curriculum Connections					
Creative Arts					

This Week's Theme

Weekly Theme: Look at Me   Week _____

	Monday	Tuesday	Wednesday	Thursday	Friday
Date					
Theme Activities	Describe "me" in positive terms.	Work with names.	Bring in birthday pictures.	Younger or older—which is better?	Set personal goals.
Literature Time	Read *I Like Me* by Nancy Carlson.	Read *Chrysanthemum* by Kevin Henkes.	Read *Birthday Presents* by Cynthia Rylant.	Read *We Are All Alike . . . We Are All Different* by Cheltenham Elementary School Kindergarten.	Read *Muggie Maggie* by Beverly Cleary.
Language Arts	Use the "Me" Star Shape for self-esteem.	Create a name acrostic.	Write about "My Best Birthday Present."	Make lists of "My Likes and Dislikes."	Complete the goal sheet on page 20.
Curriculum Connections	Learn how to write a mini-autobiography.	Create a self-portrait.	Make a seasonal birthday graph.	Develop a "me" time line.	Write a mini-book about "me."
Creative Arts	Make a helping-hands bulletin board.	Design a name tag.	The past—look back at then and now.	Design a birthday cake.	Plan a class birthday celebration.

Overview: Look at Me

Monday

Theme Activities: Discuss how every person is unique and special. Have the students make a list of positive adjectives to describe themselves, such as super, positive, hardworking, friendly, etc.

Literature Time: Read *I Like Me* by Nancy Carlson (Viking, 1998). This is a very positive book which stresses the importance of good self-esteem and seeing the best in oneself.

Language Arts: Talk about the character in the book above and what good self-esteem means. Use the star shape on page 14 for students to list some of the reasons they like themselves.

Curriculum Connections: Write the words "biography" and "autobiography" on the chalkboard or a piece of chart paper. Talk about the meaning of each word and read some examples of biographies from the book *My First Book of Biographies* by Jean Marzollo. A good example of an autobiography would be the book written by Joanna Cole entitled *On the Bus with Joanna Cole* (see the bibliography on page 369). Have each student attempt to write a mini-autobiography during writing time, including some basic information about themselves. They may want to put some of the information from the mini-book found on pages 21–23 in a narrative form.

Creative Arts: Each student is an important member of the classroom community and has a contribution to make to the class. Make a helping-hands bulletin board to illustrate how important it is to be a good helper or citizen. Have the students trace and cut out their handprints on construction paper. On each hand, they can list a way that they help at school. The hands can be displayed on a bulletin board along with photographs of the students helping each other with classroom activities.

Tuesday

Theme Activities: Bring in a baby name book to show the class. Discuss how parents spend a lot of time choosing names for children. Ask the children if they know how their names were chosen. Is anyone named after a relative? After a character from a favorite book?

Literature Time: Today's book selection is *Chrysanthemum* (Greenwillow, 1991) by Kevin Henkes. This book is about how an unusual name can sometimes cause problems.

Language Arts: Let students use their names for acrostic poems. These poems can be written on paper or on the computer using a word processing program such as *ClarisWorks* or a graphics program such as *Kid Pix Studio.* Students start by writing names vertically and then adding words that start with each letter. The added words should tell something about that student.

Overview: Look at Me *(cont.)*

━━━━━━━━━━━━━━━━━━━━━━━━ **Tuesday** *(cont.)* ━━━━━━━━━━━━━━━━━━━━━━━━

Curriculum Connections: Use tempera paints to have students paint self-portraits. Display the portraits with a sentence about each student, written by them.

Creative Arts: Provide the students with a variety of paper, markers, and colored pencils. Have them create name tags for their desks that reflect their interests or favorite things.

━━━━━━━━━━━━━━━━━━━━━━━━━━ **Wednesday** ━━━━━━━━━━━━━━━━━━━━━━━━━━

Theme Activities: Ask students to bring in pictures from a favorite birthday (see the parent letter on page 12). Group the pictures by what birthday it is—first, second, etc.

Literature Time: Read *Birthday Presents* by Cynthia Rylant (Watts, 1987). Display a list of birthstones and flowers so that students can find the ones for their birthday months.

Language Arts: Have students think of a time when they received a really great birthday gift. Write about this special gift, using the present shape on page 15.

Curriculum Connections: There are many possibilities for graphing with birthdays, such as birthstones, flowers, months, or the seasons that the birthdays are in. Complete the seasonal birthday graph found on page 16 or have students create a graph on the computer using a program such as *The Graph Club.*

Creative Arts: Take a look back at the past with the Then and Now activity on page 17. Students draw themselves as they appear now and as they looked when they were babies (to ensure accuracy, they may need to question their parents or look at photographs before doing their baby portraits).

━━━━━━━━━━━━━━━━━━━━━━━━━━━ **Thursday** ━━━━━━━━━━━━━━━━━━━━━━━━━━━

Theme Activities: Today's discussion topic is What are some good things about being the age you are right now? What would be some good things about being older (an adult)?

Literature Time: Read *We Are All Alike . . . We Are All Different* (Scholastic, 1991) which is written by a kindergarten class at Cheltenham Elementary School. Have the students discuss in small groups ways in which they may be alike or different from their friends.

Language Arts: Have students make lists of likes and dislikes, using the form found on page 18. After writing, they can share their lists with partners or in a small group.

Curriculum Connections: Create a "me" time line using information brought in from home. List an important milestone for each year.

Creative Arts: Students can be pastry chefs for a day with this creative activity.

Overview: Look at Me *(cont.)*

Thursday *(cont.)*

Creative Arts *(cont.)*

Duplicate the birthday cake shape on page 19 for each student and have them design a special birthday cake for themselves.

Friday

Theme Activities: Discuss goal setting as a way to improve oneself. Ask students to think of some personal goals they would like to accomplish during the school year.

Literature Time: Today's selection is a chapter book, *Muggie Maggie* by Beverly Cleary (Avon, 1990), and will appeal to older students. This book can be started during this unit and continued with a chapter a day until finished. Younger students may want to read *Leo the Late Bloomer* by Robert Kraus (Dutton, 1971). Both books deal with how difficult it sometimes is to learn new skills.

Language Arts: List the goals discussed during today's theme activity using the goal setting sheet found on page 20.

Curriculum Connections: Have each student create a "mini-book about me" which is found on pages 21–23. The books can be completed over several days and may be sent home or become a part of the classroom library.

Creative Arts: For a culminating activity for this unit, have a class birthday party celebrating everyone's birthday in grand style. Have students form committees to plan decorations and refreshments. Have them design the birthday cakes they wish they could have, using the shape found on page 19. Choose a day for the celebration, sing "Happy Birthday" to us all, and enjoy!

This Week's Theme

Look at Me

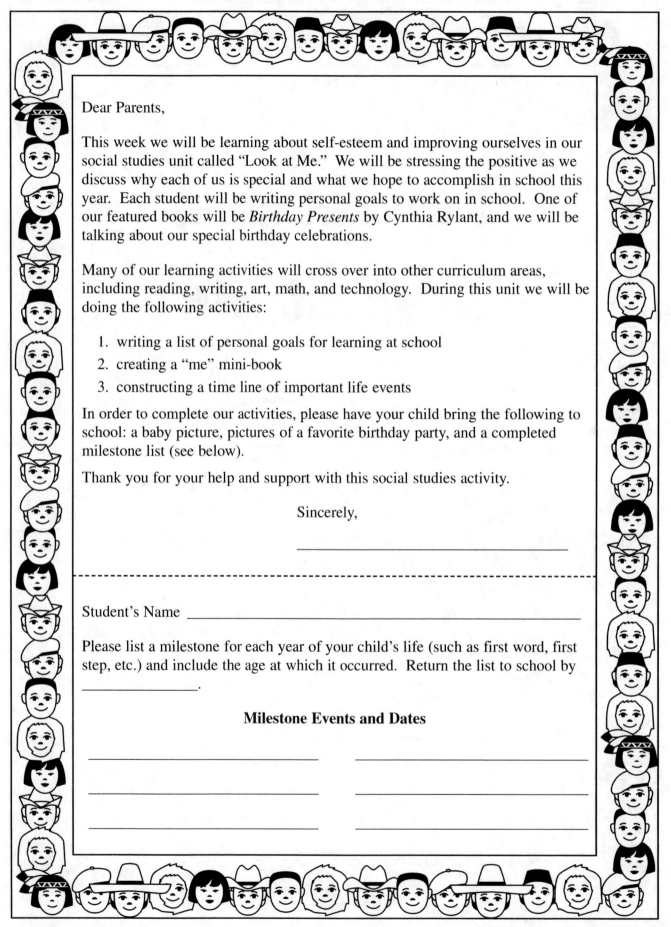

Dear Parents,

This week we will be learning about self-esteem and improving ourselves in our social studies unit called "Look at Me." We will be stressing the positive as we discuss why each of us is special and what we hope to accomplish in school this year. Each student will be writing personal goals to work on in school. One of our featured books will be *Birthday Presents* by Cynthia Rylant, and we will be talking about our special birthday celebrations.

Many of our learning activities will cross over into other curriculum areas, including reading, writing, art, math, and technology. During this unit we will be doing the following activities:

1. writing a list of personal goals for learning at school
2. creating a "me" mini-book
3. constructing a time line of important life events

In order to complete our activities, please have your child bring the following to school: a baby picture, pictures of a favorite birthday party, and a completed milestone list (see below).

Thank you for your help and support with this social studies activity.

Sincerely,

_____

- -

Student's Name _____

Please list a milestone for each year of your child's life (such as first word, first step, etc.) and include the age at which it occurred. Return the list to school by _____.

Milestone Events and Dates

_____   _____

_____   _____

_____   _____

Daily Journal Topics: Look at Me

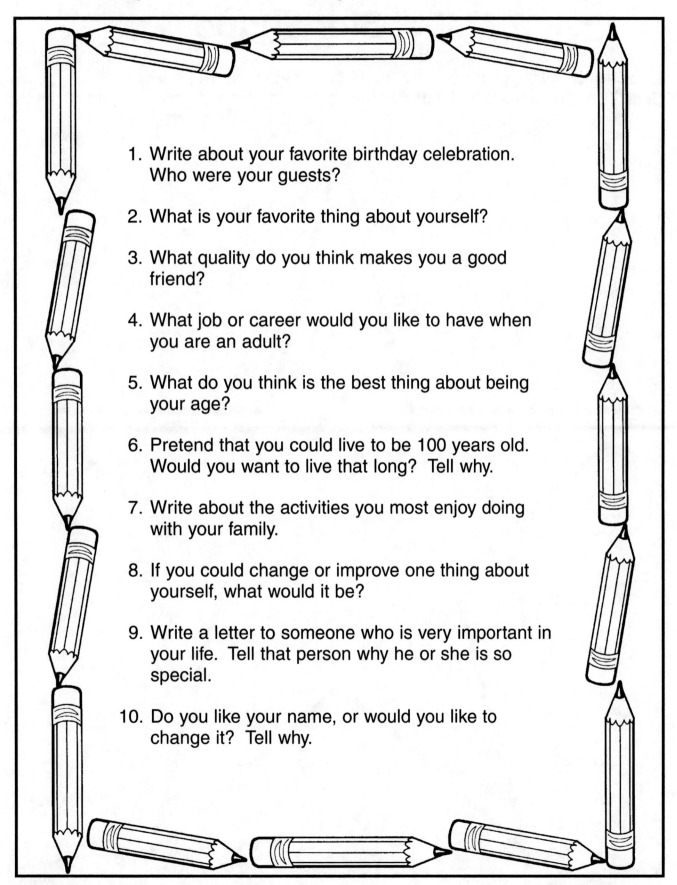

1. Write about your favorite birthday celebration. Who were your guests?

2. What is your favorite thing about yourself?

3. What quality do you think makes you a good friend?

4. What job or career would you like to have when you are an adult?

5. What do you think is the best thing about being your age?

6. Pretend that you could live to be 100 years old. Would you want to live that long? Tell why.

7. Write about the activities you most enjoy doing with your family.

8. If you could change or improve one thing about yourself, what would it be?

9. Write a letter to someone who is very important in your life. Tell that person why he or she is so special.

10. Do you like your name, or would you like to change it? Tell why.

Name _____ Date _____

"Me" Star Shape

Directions: Write your name in the middle of the star. Put a word that describes you on each point of the star.

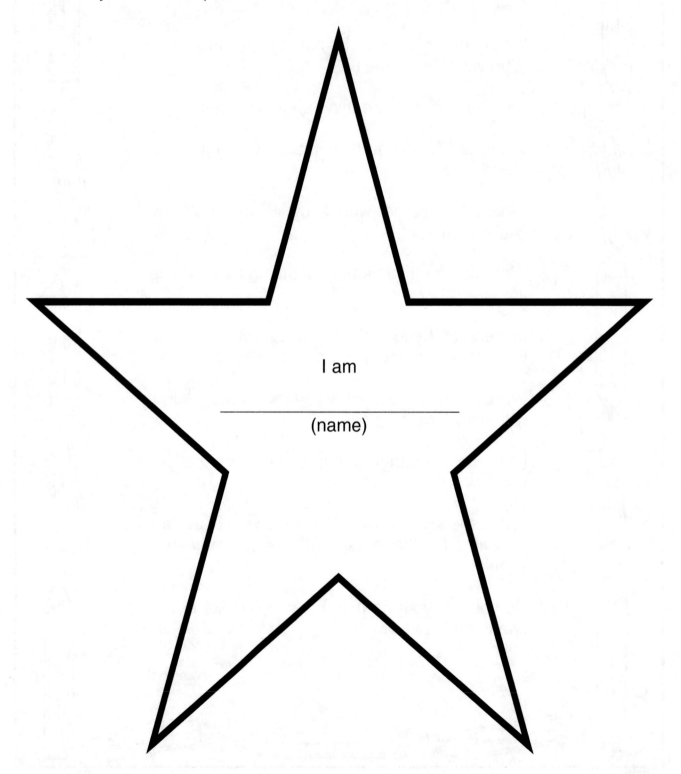

I am

_____
(name)

My Best Present

Directions: Cut out the present shape on the dotted lines and fold on the center line. Decorate the front of the gift box and color the bow. On the inside, draw a favorite birthday present and write about why it is special to you.

My Best Present

Name _____

Name _____ Date _____

Seasonal Birthday Graph

Directions: Create a picture key to use in making this graph. Draw one symbol to represent each season. Survey your class to find out what season each birthday is in. Record the information on the graph, using your symbols.

	spring	summer	fall	winter
12				
11				
10				
9				
8				
7				
6				
5				
4				
3				
2				
1				

Graph Key

spring [ ]   summer [ ]   fall [ ]   winter [ ]

Then and Now

Directions: In the first picture frame, draw a picture of how you looked when you were a baby. In the other frame, draw a picture of how you look today.

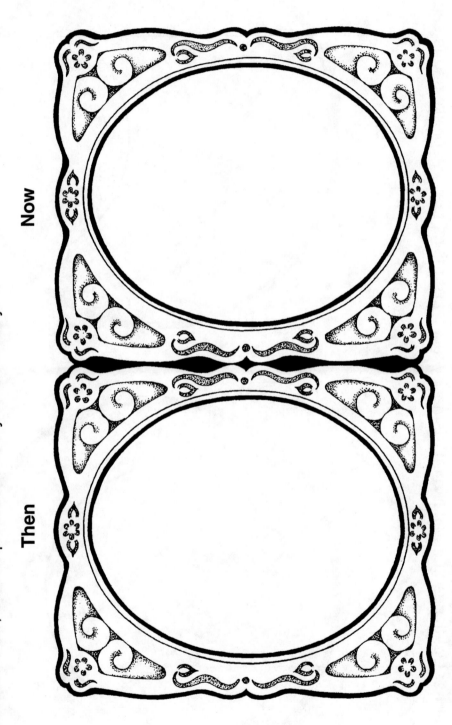

Now

Then

Complete this sentence:

I think the best thing about being a baby was _____

_____

Name _____

Date _____

My Likes and Dislikes

Directions: List things that you like on the happy face. List things that you dislike on the sad face.

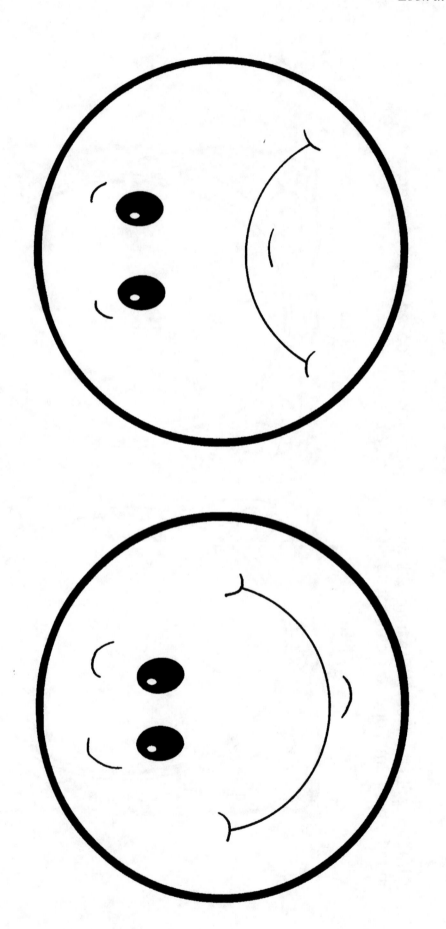

Name _____ Date _____

Happy Birthday to Me!

Directions: Pretend that you are the pastry chef for your birthday party. Use markers, crayons, or colored pencils to design a decorated cake that you would like to have for your birthday.

Name _____ Date _____

My Personal Goals

Directions: Working to achieve a goal is like climbing a mountain—it takes a lot of work to reach the top! Make a list of five to ten goals you want to achieve this year. Put your most important goal at the top of the mountain.

Look at Me Book

Directions: Cut the book on the lines. Put the pages in the correct order and staple to make your own booklet. Fill in the blanks with information about yourself and add illustrations if needed.

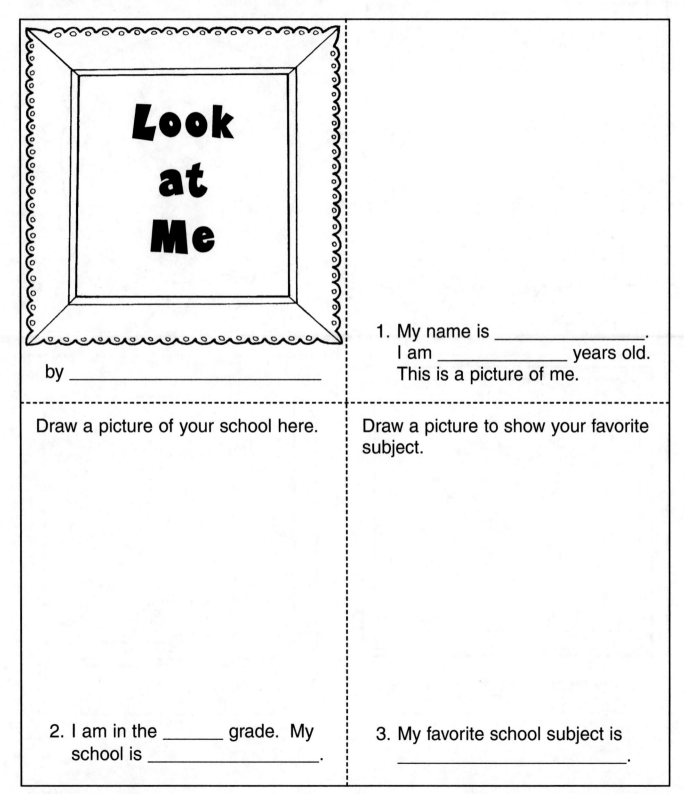

Look
at
Me

by _____

1. My name is _____.
   I am _____ years old.
   This is a picture of me.

Draw a picture of your school here.

Draw a picture to show your favorite subject.

2. I am in the _____ grade. My school is _____.

3. My favorite school subject is _____.

Look at Me Book *(cont.)*

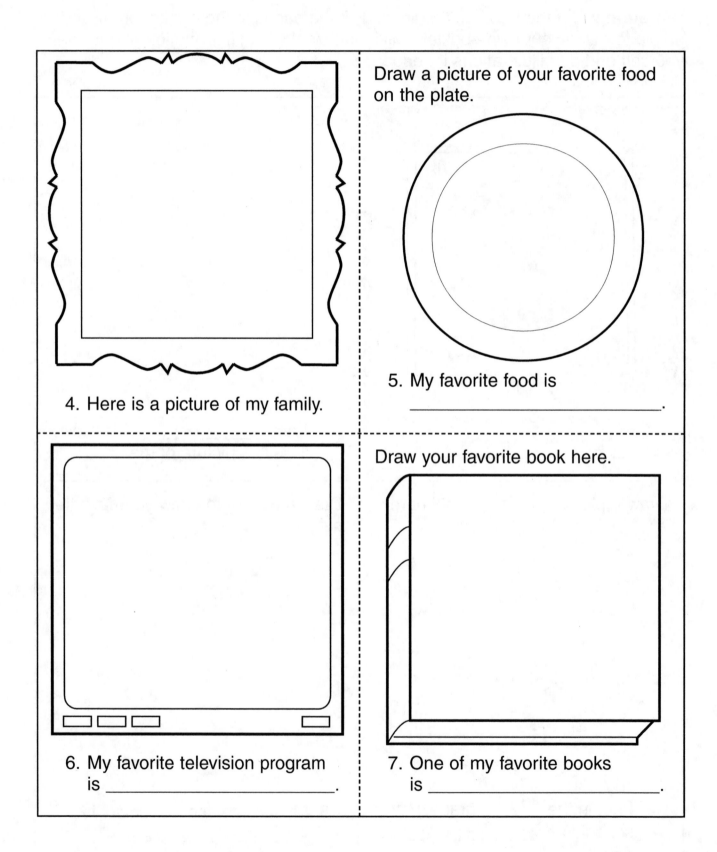

4. Here is a picture of my family.

Draw a picture of your favorite food on the plate.

5. My favorite food is
_____.

6. My favorite television program
is _____.

Draw your favorite book here.

7. One of my favorite books
is _____.

Look at Me Book *(cont.)*

Color the crayon with your favorite color.

8. My favorite color is
_____.

Draw yourself at a future job.

9. For my future job, I would like to be _____.

Draw your friends and write their names.

10. Here is a picture of some of my friends.

Draw yourself when you are happy.

11. The best thing about me is
_____.

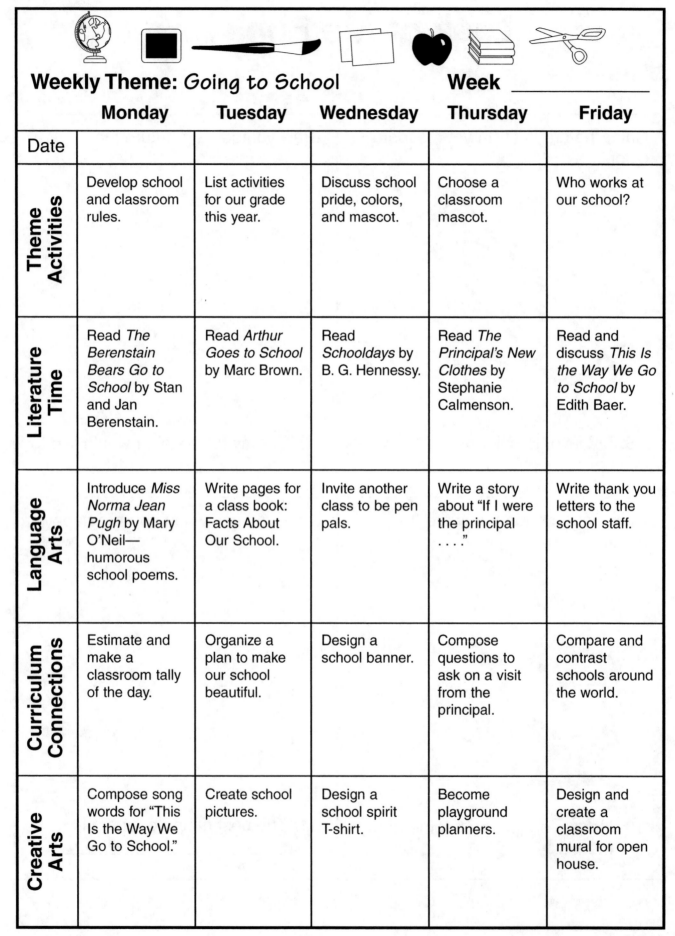

Weekly Theme: *Going to School*   Week _____

	Monday	**Tuesday**	**Wednesday**	**Thursday**	**Friday**
Date					
Theme Activities	Develop school and classroom rules.	List activities for our grade this year.	Discuss school pride, colors, and mascot.	Choose a classroom mascot.	Who works at our school?
Literature Time	Read *The Berenstain Bears Go to School* by Stan and Jan Berenstain.	Read *Arthur Goes to School* by Marc Brown.	Read *Schooldays* by B. G. Hennessy.	Read *The Principal's New Clothes* by Stephanie Calmenson.	Read and discuss *This Is the Way We Go to School* by Edith Baer.
Language Arts	Introduce *Miss Norma Jean Pugh* by Mary O'Neil—humorous school poems.	Write pages for a class book: Facts About Our School.	Invite another class to be pen pals.	Write a story about "If I were the principal . . . ."	Write thank you letters to the school staff.
Curriculum Connections	Estimate and make a classroom tally of the day.	Organize a plan to make our school beautiful.	Design a school banner.	Compose questions to ask on a visit from the principal.	Compare and contrast schools around the world.
Creative Arts	Compose song words for "This Is the Way We Go to School."	Create school pictures.	Design a school spirit T-shirt.	Become playground planners.	Design and create a classroom mural for open house.

Overview: Going to School

Monday

Theme Activities: Discuss why we need rules and ask about rules the class remembers from the previous year. If you have a set of school rules in place, be sure to read and post them. Write some class rules together and have each child sign the rules poster as a pledge or promise.

Literature Time: Read *The Berenstain Bears Go to School* by Stan and Jan Berenstain (Random House, Inc., 1978). Ask the children if they had feelings like Sister Bear when they first came to school.

Language Arts: Introduce some humorous poems about school such as *Miss Norma Jean Pugh, First Grade Teacher* by Mary O'Neil or "The Creature in the Classroom" by Jack Prelutsky (from *The Random House Book of Poetry for Children* selected by Jack Prelutsky, Random House, Inc., 1983).

Curriculum Connections: Choose a common classroom item each day, such as pencils or erasers. Have the children estimate how many of those items are in the classroom (or in a certain area, such as pencils at the art table). Have students work with partners to tally the items.

Creative Arts: To the tune of "Here We Go Round the Mulberry Bush" invent a new song called "This Is the Way We Go to School." A sample line might be "This is the way we write our stories . . . on a bright and early morning."

Tuesday

Theme Activities: List activities that the class thinks will be done this year in their grade. Discuss any work or topics that are different from last year.

Literature Time: Read *Arthur Goes to School* or *Arthur Writes a Story* by Marc Brown. The latter book is a good way to introduce writing workshop time as Arthur struggles to become an author in this delightful story.

Language Arts: Have each student write a page for a class book about your school. First, have students research information about the school and record it on the school fact sheet (found on page 31). Interesting facts such as the number of students, school motto, etc., can then be made into a class book. Cover and page formats are provided on pages 33 and 34.

Curriculum Connections: Take an interest in the environment around school and organize a cleanup of the grounds. If possible, plant a garden or some trees. Observation of plant growth through the year makes a great science lesson.

Creative Arts: Create pictures of your school, using a computer drawing program such as *Kid Pix Studio* (Broderbund Software, Inc., 1995). A sample is provided in the appendix on page 381.

Overview: Going to School *(cont.)*

Wednesday

Theme Activities: Be proud of your school. Discuss why your school is a good place to learn. Display school colors and a picture of your mascot in the classroom or have students choose them if your school does not have any.

Literature Time: Read *Schooldays* by B. G. Hennessy (Viking-Penguin, 1990). Discuss what is best about school.

Language Arts: Contact other teachers in your district and invite a class to be pen pals. Write and send photographs through the year and arrange to meet for a year-end picnic. If you want pen pals from other states, check the listings in *The Mailbox Teacher* magazine (published by the Education Center, Inc.) on the teacher bulletin board page or at their Web site—http://www.themailboxteacher.com

Curriculum Connections: Design a banner about your school and hang it in the hall. The banner can be made with paper, markers, and paint or using a computer program such as *The Print Shop Deluxe* (Broderbund Software, Inc.).

Creative Arts: Using the form found on page 35, design a school spirit T-shirt. Be sure to include school colors and mascot and perhaps write a school motto to go on the shirt.

Thursday

Theme Activities: Choose a class name and mascot. For example, "The Teddy Bear Team of Room Five" might have a stuffed bear as a mascot. Or choose a favorite character like Clifford the big red dog and have a "Clifford's Club."

Literature Time: Invite your principal to read *The Principal's New Clothes* by Stephanie Calmenson (Scholastic) to the class.

Language Arts: Invite children to be "principal for the day" in story form! Make a class book about what they would do if they were the principal.

Curriculum Connections: Before the principal's visit to read today's story, have the class compose a list of questions to ask about the job. Ask the principal to discuss what he or she likes about the job.

Creative Arts: Redesign your playground or outdoor area. Have the children draw their ideas. Ask them what type of equipment they would add and what they would change to create their ideal play space.

Overview: Going to School *(cont.)*

Friday

Theme Activities: Make a list of all workers who help to run your school. Talk about the importance of each job and how all personnel make important contributions to your school.

Literature Time: Launch a discussion of schools around the world with the book *This Is the Way We Go to School: A Book About Children Around the World* by Edith Baer (Scholastic, Inc., 1990). Locate the countries in the story on a globe or world map.

Language Arts: Put the students into small groups and give each group a list of names from this week's theme activity. Have them write thank you letters and be sure to include your principal, office staff, custodial crew, and lunchroom personnel. If you have a large staff, you may need several days to complete the letters.

Curriculum Connections: Using the information in today's literature activity and any other social studies resource material that you have, compare and contrast schools in our country with those in other countries. List similarities and differences on a large piece of chart paper.

Creative Arts: Create a classroom mural for your first open house. Have the children paint or draw favorite classroom activities, subjects, centers, etc., on a long sheet of paper. Add photographs of the children and have them write positive comments about what they enjoy about their grade.

This Week's Theme

Going to School

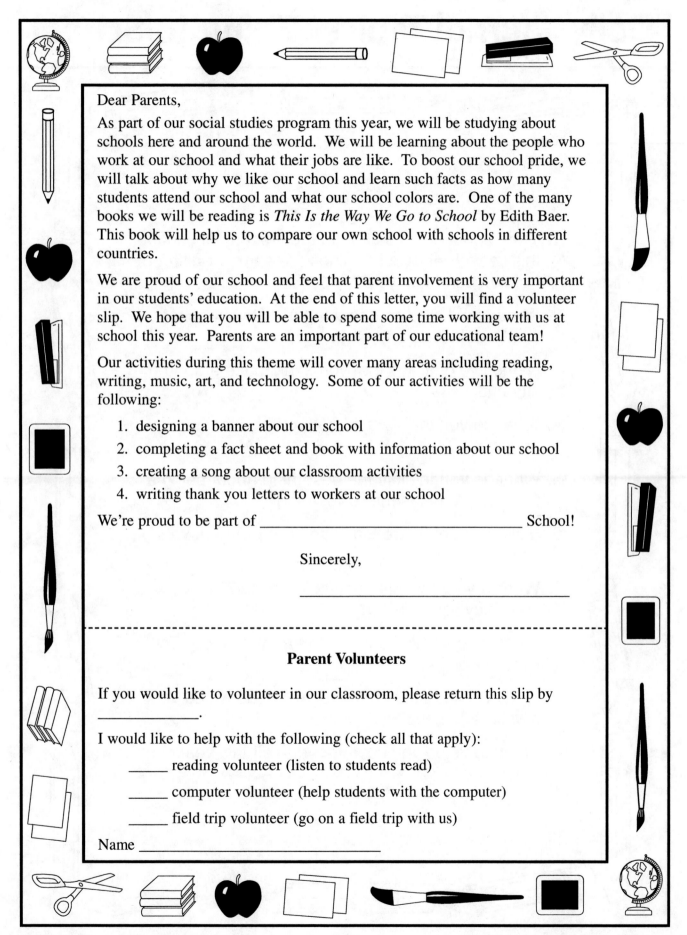

Dear Parents,

As part of our social studies program this year, we will be studying about schools here and around the world. We will be learning about the people who work at our school and what their jobs are like. To boost our school pride, we will talk about why we like our school and learn such facts as how many students attend our school and what our school colors are. One of the many books we will be reading is *This Is the Way We Go to School* by Edith Baer. This book will help us to compare our own school with schools in different countries.

We are proud of our school and feel that parent involvement is very important in our students' education. At the end of this letter, you will find a volunteer slip. We hope that you will be able to spend some time working with us at school this year. Parents are an important part of our educational team!

Our activities during this theme will cover many areas including reading, writing, music, art, and technology. Some of our activities will be the following:

1. designing a banner about our school
2. completing a fact sheet and book with information about our school
3. creating a song about our classroom activities
4. writing thank you letters to workers at our school

We're proud to be part of _____ School!

Sincerely,

_____

- -

Parent Volunteers

If you would like to volunteer in our classroom, please return this slip by _____.

I would like to help with the following (check all that apply):

_____ reading volunteer (listen to students read)

_____ computer volunteer (help students with the computer)

_____ field trip volunteer (go on a field trip with us)

Name _____

Daily Journal Topics: Going to School

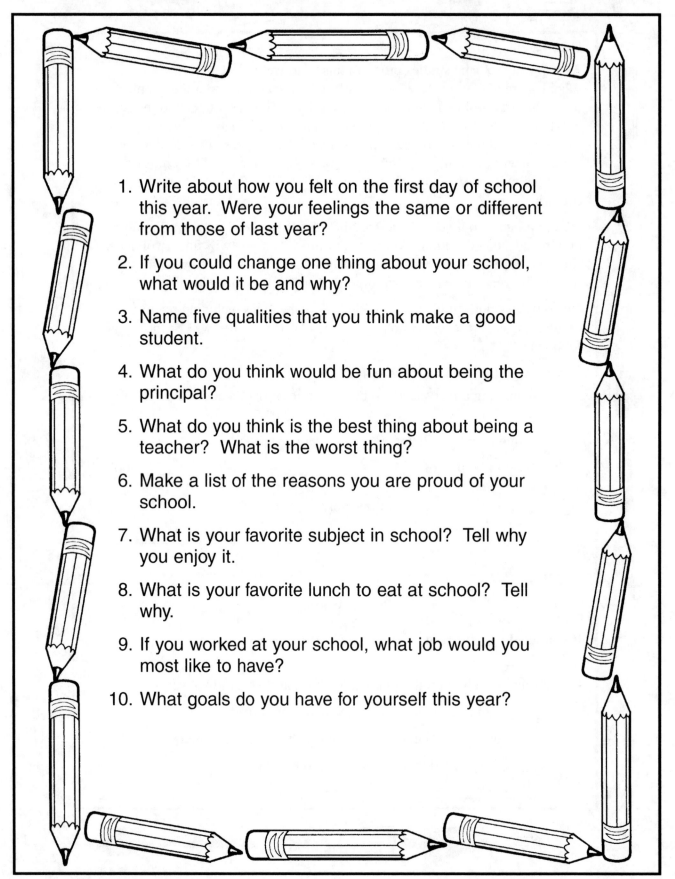

1. Write about how you felt on the first day of school this year. Were your feelings the same or different from those of last year?

2. If you could change one thing about your school, what would it be and why?

3. Name five qualities that you think make a good student.

4. What do you think would be fun about being the principal?

5. What do you think is the best thing about being a teacher? What is the worst thing?

6. Make a list of the reasons you are proud of your school.

7. What is your favorite subject in school? Tell why you enjoy it.

8. What is your favorite lunch to eat at school? Tell why.

9. If you worked at your school, what job would you most like to have?

10. What goals do you have for yourself this year?

School Facts Research

Directions: Be a school detective! Do some research to find out some basic facts about your school. You may want to use materials such as annual reports, school newsletters, or yearbooks to look up your facts. Or try interviewing people who work at your school.

1. Our school was founded in the year _____.

2. This year we have _____ students at our school.

3. We have _____ teachers working at our school.

4. The total number of staff members who work at our school is_____.

5. Our school colors are _____.

6. Our school mascot is _____.

7. Our school motto is_____.

8. We go to school for a total of _____ days each year.

9. Our school's address is_____.

10. Our principal's name is _____.

11. We have _____ classrooms in our school.

12. The number of students who ride the buses at our school is_____.

13. Our school hours are _____.

14. Our school's location is (for example, in a large city, in the country)

    _____.

15. Take a look at the school playground. Tally the different playground equipment.

    • Slides _____   • Teeter-totters _____

    • Swings _____   • Other _____

    • Climbing equipment _____

School Facts

Purpose: Children will each create a page for a class book entitled School Facts. Each page will feature an interesting fact about their school.

Materials

- School Facts Book Cover (page 33)
- School Facts Paper (page 34)
- pencils, markers, crayons
- school annual reports, newsletters, P.T.A. reports, yearbooks

Preparation: Reproduce the school-shaped paper for the children to do their writing. You will need one page for each student (additional pages if you plan on doing a first draft and a final copy). Reproduce one front cover for the class book and color with markers. Mount the cover on a piece of tagboard and cut a back cover in the same school shape. Laminate the covers for durability.

Instructions: Using the school facts paper on page 34, have the class work in pairs to find out facts about the school. They can check school yearbooks, annual reports, school newsletters, or interview school personnel to collect their facts. Have each student then choose a fact to write about for the class book. The space at the bottom of the page will be used for an illustration.

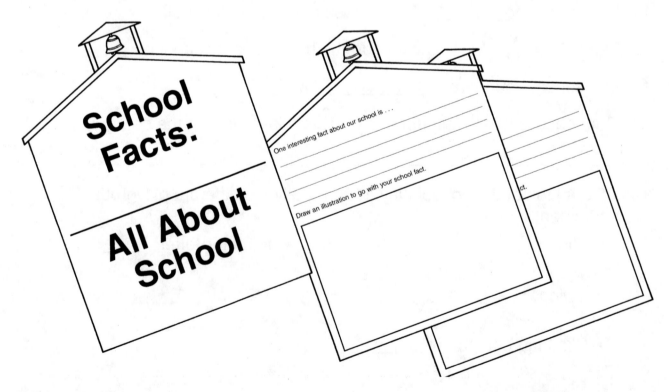

School Facts Book Cover

School Facts:

All About School

School Facts Paper

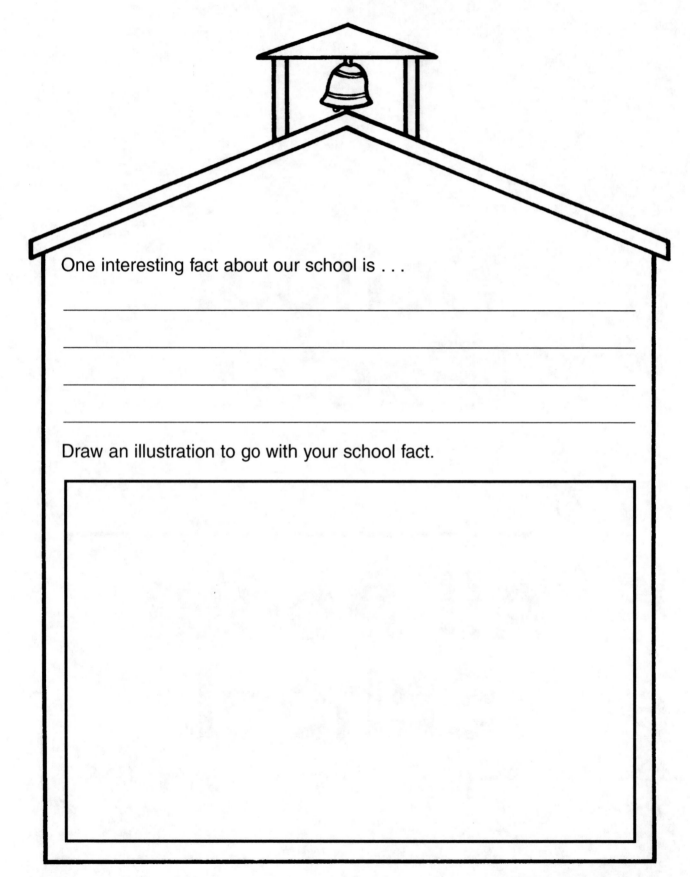

One interesting fact about our school is . . .

_____

_____

_____

_____

Draw an illustration to go with your school fact.

School Spirit T-Shirt

Name _____

Directions: Show your school spirit! Design a shirt that students in your school could wear. Remember to include your school colors and mascot.

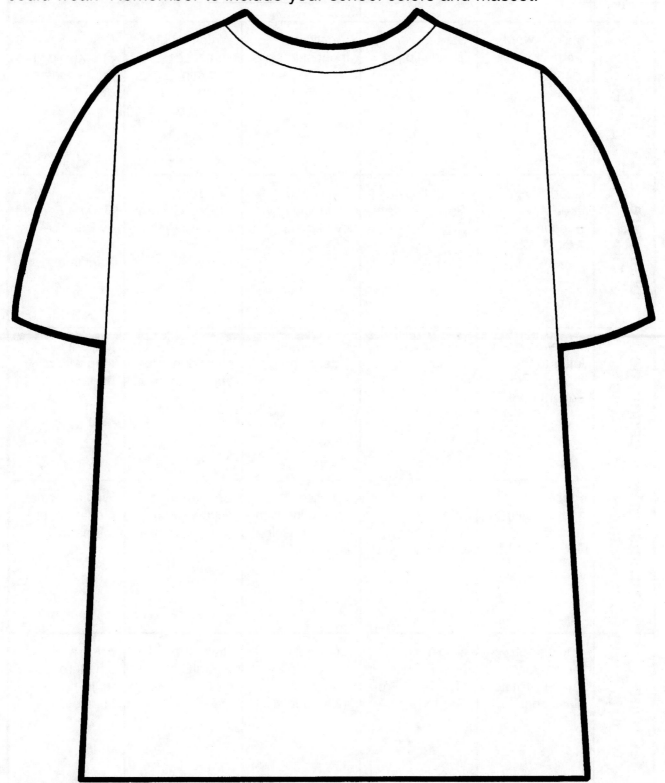

Weekly Theme: *Friends Forever*   **Week** _____

	Monday	**Tuesday**	**Wednesday**	**Thursday**	**Friday**
Date					
Theme Activities	Make a word web about friendship.	Start a friendship jar.	Practice friendship skills.	Write friendly sentences and mini-biographies.	Celebrate Friendship Friday theme day.
Literature Time	Read *Frog and Toad Are Friends* by Arnold Lobel.	Read *We Are Best Friends* by Aliki.	Read *The Rainbow Fish* by Marcus Pfister.	Read *Ira Sleeps Over* by Bernard Waber.	Enjoy *May I Bring a Friend?* by Beatrice Schenk De Regniers.
Language Arts	Write a friendly letter to Frog from Arnold Lobel's book.	Interview friends.	Write a note or letter to a friend.	Create a pocket chart of names and sentences.	Make a story map with a partner.
Curriculum Connections	Practice spelling with partners.	Explore "friendly fractions."	Practice estimating with the friendship jar.	Create friend puppets with *Kid Pix Studio*.	With a partner, create patterns for math.
Creative Arts	Photograph friends for a Friendly Photos class book.	Sing "Make New Friends" or "The More We Get Together."	Create a friendship band with rhythm instruments.	Draw or paint portraits of our class.	Erect a structure with "building buddies."

Overview: Friends Forever

Monday

Theme Activities: Make a word web about the word "friendship." On a piece of chart paper put the word in a circle. Ask the class what words they think of when you mention *friends*. Organize the words around the center circle and look at the children's ideas about friendship.

Literature Time: Read *Frog and Toad Are Friends* by Arnold Lobel (HarperCollins, 1970). Ask the class what friendship qualities they see in these characters (for example, they share and they help each other). After reading all the short stories in this book, vote to see which one is the class favorite.

Language Arts: Have the students write a letter to Frog from the above literature selection. In this letter, tell Frog why he is such a good friend to Toad.

Curriculum Connections: Put each child with a partner during spelling practice time. The partners can practice writing words on a wipe-off board or make the words with magnetic letters. If you do not have a list of words for your grade, use some high frequency words.

Creative Arts: Take photographs of the children working in pairs or small groups during the day. If you have older students, you may want them to take the photos. After the photos are developed, the students can write captions describing the classroom activity pictured. Display the photos at open house with a sign such as "Classroom Friends Learn Together" or put them in a book and let each student have a turn to take the book home.

Tuesday

Theme Activities: Start a friendship jar to acknowledge friendly acts in the classroom. Print the words "Friends Forever" on the front of a small plastic container. Explain that each time you witness a friendly act, you will put a treat in the jar, such as a Hershey chocolate "kiss" or "hug." When the jar is full, the class shares the treat. If you do not wish to use candy, try stickers, tokens to represent extra minutes of recess, or tokens or counters to represent a class goal (for example, when we get 25 tokens, we will do a special art project.)

Literature Time: What happens when your best friend moves away? Read *We Are Best Friends* by Aliki (Mulberry Books, 1982) to find out how two friends cope with being separated and how they stay in touch with each other.

Language Arts: Put the students in pairs to interview each other (see the form for the interview on page 43). Make copies so that students can take home the interview they conducted as well as the one about themselves.

Overview: **Friends Forever** (cont.)

═══════════ **Tuesday** (cont.) ═══════════

Curriculum Connections: Explore "friendly fractions" during math time. Cut out a variety of basic shapes from construction paper (circle, squares, etc.). Have children work in pairs to divide the shapes into common fractions such as $\frac{1}{2}$, $\frac{1}{3}$, and $\frac{1}{4}$, or whatever fractional parts your curriculum covers. Students should label the fractional parts after cutting them. Have a snack such as graham crackers which can easily be divided into fractional pieces.

Creative Arts: Sing some friendship songs such as "Make New Friends" from *Brownies Own Songbook* (Girl Scouts of the U.S.A., 1968) or the classic song "The More We Get Together."

═══════════ **Wednesday** ═══════════

Theme Activities: Practice friendship skills with this simple activity. Have each child cut out thumbs up and thumbs down pictures on page 44. Read one of the sample situations from page 45 and have children display the "thumbs up" if they are hearing about good friendship skills and "thumbs down" if they are not. Discuss how to change the sad situations to happy ones.

Literature Time: Read *The Rainbow Fish* by Marcus Pfister (North-South Books, 1992) to learn why sharing is so important in making friends.

Language Arts: Provide friendly note stationery in your writing center so that the children can write notes to each other during this theme. Emphasize that notes must be positive and friendly. Notes can be posted in the writing center under the caption "Friend to Friend." If you have classroom mailboxes, the notes can also be "mailed."

Curriculum Connections: Use the friendship jar made this week to practice estimating skills. When the jar is almost full, have children estimate how many items are in the jar. Then count the items in groups of 10 to find the true sum.

Creative Arts: Provide the students with instruments such as rhythm sticks or blocks, small drums, and xylophones. Show how the instruments can be used to make a rhythm or song (your music teacher may be helpful here). Have them work in small groups to create their own friendship bands. They can make simple songs or rhythms to present to the group. Older students may enjoy composing a "rap" about friendship.

═══════════ **Thursday** ═══════════

Theme Activities: Draw a few students' names each day to use in writing some "friendly" sentences. On a large piece of poster board, start with a sentence such as "This is our friend Christopher" and then compose a mini-biography. Ask the person to tell a bit about himself or herself and then write sentences such as "His favorite sport is football" or "Christopher has a dog named Bentley."

Overview: Friends Forever *(cont.)*

Thursday *(cont.)*

Literature Time: Read *Ira Sleeps Over* by Bernard Waber. This is a classic story about friends sharing secrets and feelings.

Language Arts: Write the name of each student on a pocket chart strip. Younger students can practice reading and copying the names. Older students might put the names in alphabetical order, or the mini-biographies could be put on sentence strips and read.

Curriculum Connections: Have two classroom friends work together to create puppets representing themselves or perhaps the characters in one of the literature selections this week. The puppets can be made by using art materials you have on hand, such as construction paper or paper bags. Or you may want to integrate some technology and create the puppets using *Kid Pix Studio* (for a sample see page 382).

Creative Arts: Have the students paint self-portraits and write captions about themselves. The pictures can then be assembled into a book with a title such as Fabulous Friends of Room Five.

Friday

Theme Activities: Celebrate your week of friendship with "Friendship Friday." Open the friendship jar and comment on the positive skills developed throughout the week. Do all of today's activities in pairs—partner reading, doing a math paper, practicing spelling words, or any part of your daily classroom routine.

Literature Time: Enjoy a humorous story about friends with *May I Bring a Friend?* by Beatrice Schenk De Regniers.

Language Arts: Have students select a story to read with a partner. After reading, students can work together to respond to the story. They could write about the story, make a story map together (see pages 46–49), or make a poster about what they've read. Younger students could draw a picture and write a sentence or two about their books.

Curriculum Connections: Students can work with friends in the math area to create patterns using whatever materials you have available, such as pattern blocks or unifix cubes. Older students can be challenged to create a symmetrical design with the pattern blocks or a tessellation.

Creative Arts: Challenge the partners to build a structure using plastic interlocking blocks. Integrate this activity with another curriculum area by asking students to reproduce a famous building such as the White House or the Eiffel Tower to tie in with social studies.

This Week's Theme

Friends Forever

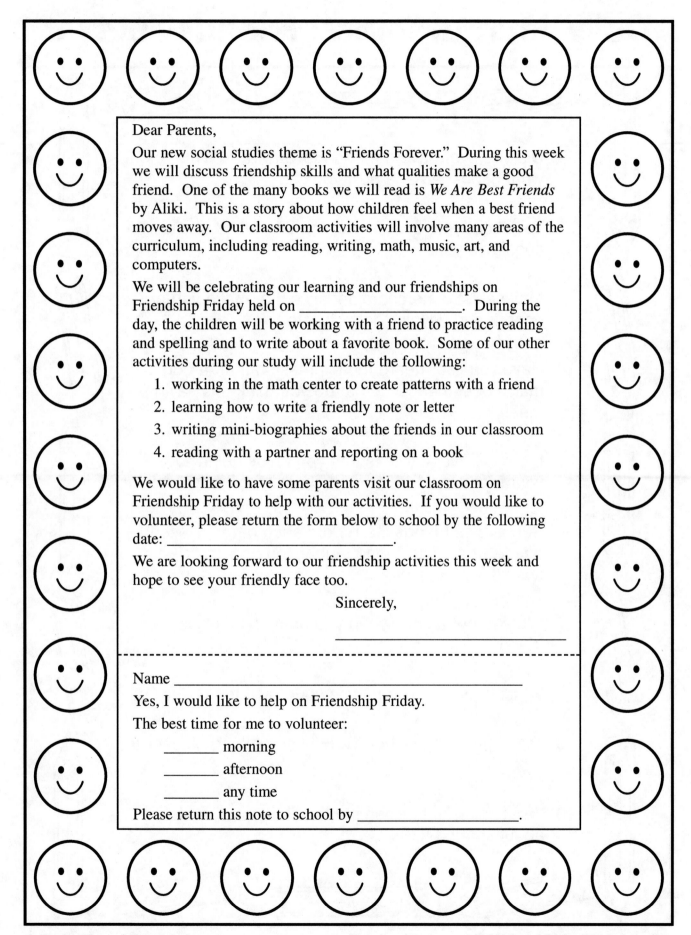

Dear Parents,

Our new social studies theme is "Friends Forever." During this week we will discuss friendship skills and what qualities make a good friend. One of the many books we will read is *We Are Best Friends* by Aliki. This is a story about how children feel when a best friend moves away. Our classroom activities will involve many areas of the curriculum, including reading, writing, math, music, art, and computers.

We will be celebrating our learning and our friendships on Friendship Friday held on _____. During the day, the children will be working with a friend to practice reading and spelling and to write about a favorite book. Some of our other activities during our study will include the following:

1. working in the math center to create patterns with a friend
2. learning how to write a friendly note or letter
3. writing mini-biographies about the friends in our classroom
4. reading with a partner and reporting on a book

We would like to have some parents visit our classroom on Friendship Friday to help with our activities. If you would like to volunteer, please return the form below to school by the following date: _____.

We are looking forward to our friendship activities this week and hope to see your friendly face too.

Sincerely,

_____

- -

Name _____

Yes, I would like to help on Friendship Friday.

The best time for me to volunteer:

_____ morning

_____ afternoon

_____ any time

Please return this note to school by _____.

Daily Journal Topics: Friends Forever

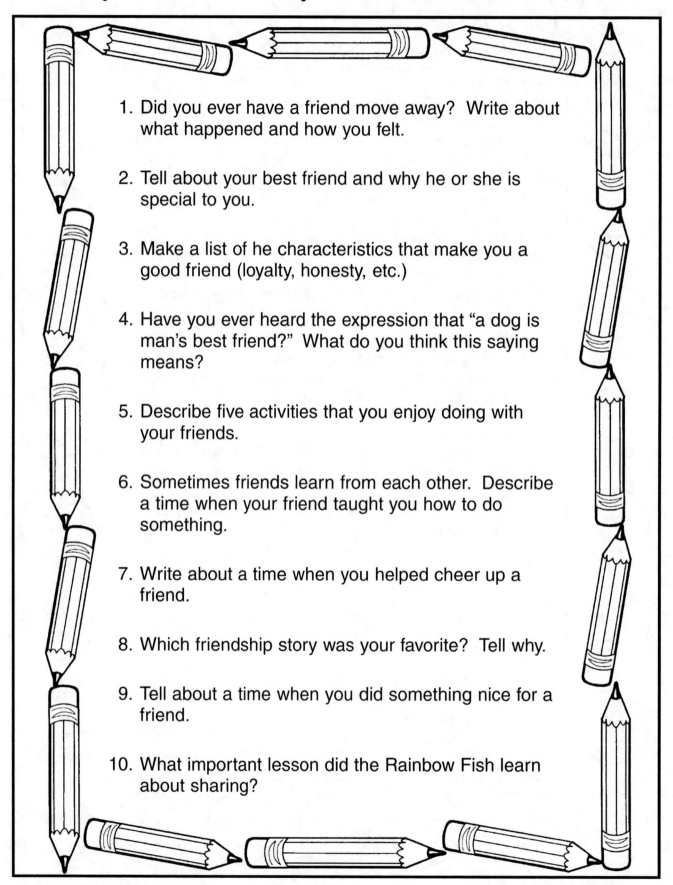

1. Did you ever have a friend move away? Write about what happened and how you felt.

2. Tell about your best friend and why he or she is special to you.

3. Make a list of he characteristics that make you a good friend (loyalty, honesty, etc.)

4. Have you ever heard the expression that "a dog is man's best friend?" What do you think this saying means?

5. Describe five activities that you enjoy doing with your friends.

6. Sometimes friends learn from each other. Describe a time when your friend taught you how to do something.

7. Write about a time when you helped cheer up a friend.

8. Which friendship story was your favorite? Tell why.

9. Tell about a time when you did something nice for a friend.

10. What important lesson did the Rainbow Fish learn about sharing?

Name _____ Date _____

Friendly Interview

Today I interviewed my friend _____.

Here are some favorite facts about my friend:

- favorite book_____
- favorite school subject _____
- favorite food _____
- favorite color_____
- favorite animal _____
- favorite restaurant _____
- favorite song_____
- favorite sport _____
- favorite movie_____
- favorite vacation place _____

Here is a picture of my friend (draw in the space below).

Friendship Skills

Directions: Cut out the thumb pictures and attach them to wooden craft sticks. Read one of the friendship situations on page 45 to the class. (Older students could work in groups and read the page themselves). Have students display the "thumbs up" for good friendship skills and "thumbs down" for negative situations. Discuss how to improve the "thumbs down" situations.

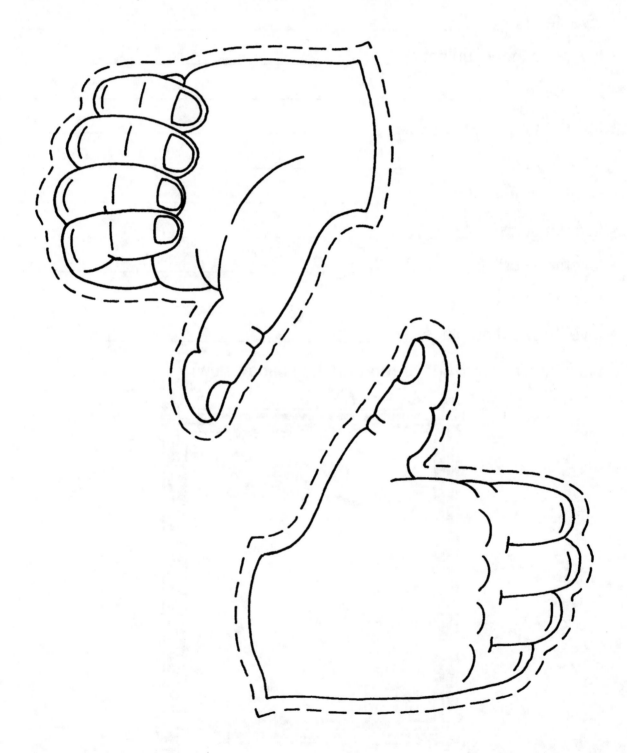

Friendship Skills *(cont.)*

Directions: Read these friendship situations and use the symbols on page 44 to discuss friendship skills.

1. You are playing football with your best friend and another person wants to join you. Your friend tells the other person that he or she can't play with you.

2. Someone from your class is alone on the playground. You invite him or her to join you in a game of tag.

3. You have told your best friend a secret and then you find out that he or she has told several people what you said.

4. In class you are working in a small group on a science experiment. Everyone is arguing about who should have the first turn using a magnifying glass.

5. One of your friends has been sick for several days. You call that person and offer to drop off some important papers from school.

6. One of the other students is working on a drawing in art class. Someone else makes fun of the drawing, but you offer a compliment.

7. Your friend gets mad at you and calls you a name. You get mad and tell your friend that you don't want to be friends anymore.

8. Your friend drops books and school papers on the floor. The class laughs, and your friend is embarrassed. You help your friend pick everything up.

9. You are working on a difficult math problem with a partner. Your partner makes a mistake, and you say that he or she is "stupid."

10. During reading time, one of the students in your group is having difficulty reading a sentence. You offer to help figure out the hard words.

Name _____ Date _____

Story Map

for

_____

book title

The author is _____.

The illustrator is _____.

Draw your book's cover.

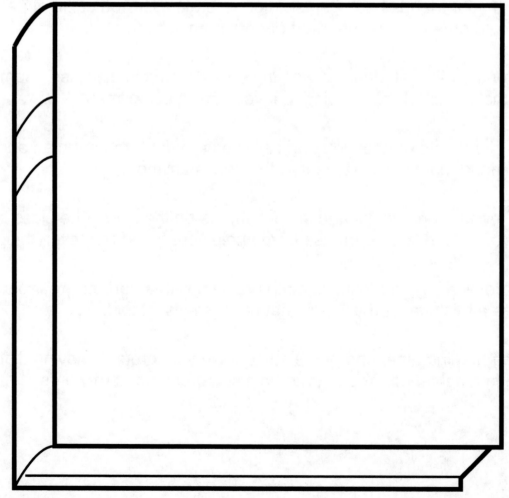

Story Map *(cont.)*

The characters in the story were _____.

Draw a picture of the main character(s).

The setting of the story was _____.

Draw a picture of the setting.

Story Map *(cont.)*

The problem in the story was _____.

Draw a picture of the problem.

The characters solved the problem by_____.

Draw a picture of how the problem was solved.

Story Map *(cont.)*

The theme of the story was _____.

Draw a picture of the theme.

My favorite part of the story was _____.

Draw your favorite part of the story.

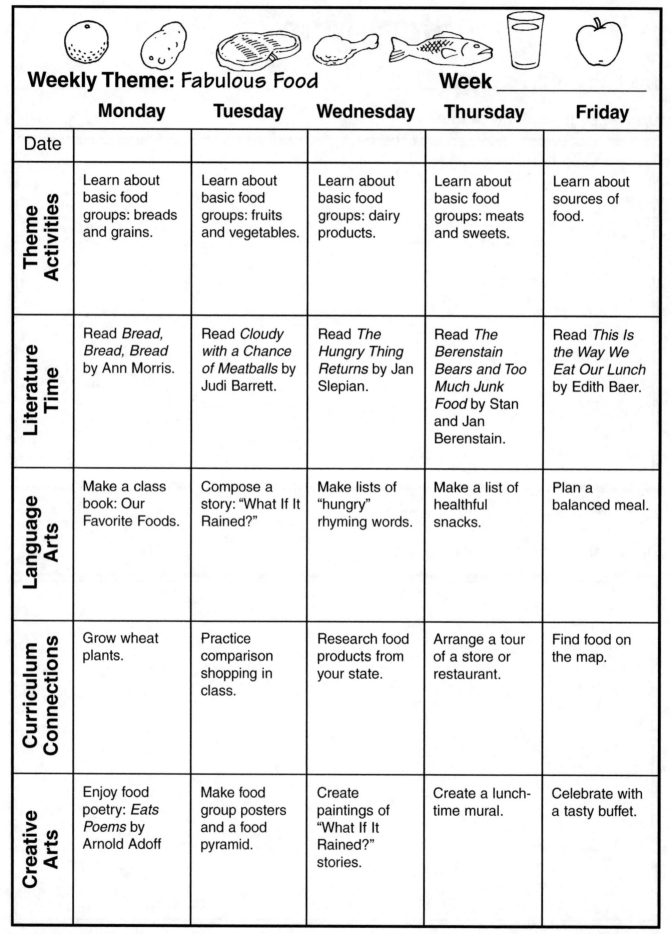

Weekly Theme: *Fabulous Food*   **Week** _____

	Monday	**Tuesday**	**Wednesday**	**Thursday**	**Friday**
Date					
Theme Activities	Learn about basic food groups: breads and grains.	Learn about basic food groups: fruits and vegetables.	Learn about basic food groups: dairy products.	Learn about basic food groups: meats and sweets.	Learn about sources of food.
Literature Time	Read *Bread, Bread, Bread* by Ann Morris.	Read *Cloudy with a Chance of Meatballs* by Judi Barrett.	Read *The Hungry Thing Returns* by Jan Slepian.	Read *The Berenstain Bears and Too Much Junk Food* by Stan and Jan Berenstain.	Read *This Is the Way We Eat Our Lunch* by Edith Baer.
Language Arts	Make a class book: Our Favorite Foods.	Compose a story: "What If It Rained?"	Make lists of "hungry" rhyming words.	Make a list of healthful snacks.	Plan a balanced meal.
Curriculum Connections	Grow wheat plants.	Practice comparison shopping in class.	Research food products from your state.	Arrange a tour of a store or restaurant.	Find food on the map.
Creative Arts	Enjoy food poetry: *Eats Poems* by Arnold Adoff	Make food group posters and a food pyramid.	Create paintings of "What If It Rained?" stories.	Create a lunch-time mural.	Celebrate with a tasty buffet.

Overview: Fabulous Food

Monday

Theme Activities: This week students will become acquainted with the food pyramid and basic food groups. You may want to enlarge the food pyramid on page 60 to poster size. Today's group is breads and grains. Bring in some samples of these foods and discuss how they give us energy.

Literature Time: To learn about many different breads around the world, read *Bread, Bread, Bread* by Ann Morris (Lothrop, 1989). Be sure to locate the countries on a map or globe.

Language Arts: Make a class book about favorite foods. Have students draw and write about what they like. Cover and page formats for this book are found on pages 58 and 59.

Curriculum Connections: Ask students what ingredients are used to make bread. Explain that flour comes from wheat. Plant some wheat seeds in soil in a container with a few drainage holes. Water the plants and track the plant growth. Once a plant sprouts, measure it twice a week. Wheat is fast-growing, so students will be able to make some good growth observations.

Creative Arts: Enjoy food poetry by reading some of the delightful verses from *Eats Poems* by Arnold Adoff. Or how about a serving of "alligator pie" from the poem by Dennis Lee? Children may want to write their own verses of this poem which can be found in the anthology *Dinosaur Dinner*.

Tuesday

Theme Activities: Bring in fruits and vegetables and discuss how important it is to have many servings to be healthy. Find this section on the food pyramid. Ask the children how they can add more fruits and vegetables to their diet.

Literature Time: Read *Cloudy with a Chance of Meatballs* by Judi Barrett (Atheneum, 1978) to find out what happens to a town when they have a very unusual food storm.

Language Arts: After reading today's literature selection, ask students to write an innovation. Have them compose a new story and consider what will rain down in their fictional town, what problems the storm will create, and how the problems will be solved.

Curriculum Connections: Ask students if they know how to compare prices when shopping. Bring in food items for the students to work with in small groups. For example, bring in three to four brands of granola bars and have students compare information on the labels. Have them consider what the price per ounce or gram is on each product and which seems to be a best bargain. Other groups may compare prices on items such as cereal, cookies, and soup.

Overview: Fabulous Food *(cont.)*

Tuesday *(cont.)*

Creative Arts: As the food pyramid is studied this week, put students in small groups. Each group will be assigned one food group and will make a poster highlighting those foods. They should think of a title and a slogan that will make people want to eat foods from that group.

Wednesday

Theme Activities: Bring in some dairy items and ask the class what the items have in common (all come from milk). If you have a dairy farm nearby, it is interesting for students to see the process by which dairy products get from the farm to your store. More information can be found in *The Milk Makers* by Gail Gibbons (see bibliography).

Literature Time: Have some fun with word play and rhyming in *The Hungry Thing Returns* by Jan Slepian (Scholastic, 1990).

Language Arts: Use food words to make some funny rhyming words as the Hungry Thing does. Include some frequently used rhymes such as "-ake" in cake. Students can list real words with the "-ake" ending and then include nonsense words the Hungry Thing might say, such as *shmake* and *trake*.

Curriculum Connections: Each state has certain food products that are important crops. For example, Hawaii produces pineapple, Idaho has potatoes, Michigan has apples and cherries, and California is a large producer of strawberries. Research what food crops are grown in large quantities in your state or area.

Creative Arts: During writing time, the children created "What If It Rained?" stories. Have them create a painting or drawing of their rainstorm. They may want to draw themselves in that storm with an umbrella.

Thursday

Theme Activities: Today's discussion includes the meats and sweets group. Discuss how meats and fish provide protein that gives us energy. Have the students notice that the sweets part of the pyramid is small and that servings from this group should be limited in a healthful diet.

Literature Time: Eating too much junk food can create problems as seen in *The Berenstain Bears and Too Much Junk Food* by Stan and Jan Berenstain (Random House, 1985). How did the bears solve their food problems?

Language Arts: List healthful snacks that can be eaten as part of a nutritious diet. The foods can be listed on the refrigerator shape on page 65 and taken home to share with parents.

Overview: Fabulous Food *(cont.)*

Thursday *(cont.)*

Curriculum Connections: Many restaurant chains offer tours that show how their food is prepared. Arrange a field trip to a restaurant for a behind-the-scenes look at food preparation. Another suggestion would be to visit a grocery store to see how food is delivered, unloaded, and prepared for sale to customers.

Creative Arts: Have students work together to create a mural of favorite lunch foods. Add captions to the pictures to describe the food, such as "Pepperoni Pizza Is the Best!"

Friday

Theme Activities: Ask students to name some favorite foods and to tell you where the foods come from. For example, if the students say "pizza," you can talk about each ingredient (tomato sauce comes from tomatoes, which come from a tomato plant, etc.). Students will quickly discover that food comes from plants or from animals that consume plants. Discuss the importance of farms and how our food is sometimes imported from other countries.

Literature Time: To connect with today's theme activity, read *This Is the Way We Eat Our Lunch* by Edith Baer (Scholastic, 1995). Foods from different cultures and countries are highlighted in this story, and a map is provided in the book.

Language Arts: After studying the food pyramid, students plan a week's worth of well-balanced lunches. Emphasize that foods from each basic group need to be included when planning their meals. Students may also want to take a look at your school's lunch menu to see how foods from each group are included.

Curriculum Connections: Using a large map or a globe, locate each of the countries mentioned in today's literature selection. Write the names of the foods on small cards and attach them to the correct spots on the map.

Creative Arts: As a culminating activity for this unit, celebrate fabulous food with an international buffet. This tasting party will include samples of a variety of foods. Try to include some of the following in your buffet:

- foods that are important crops in your state
- foods from other countries and cultures, especially those that represent children in your class
- foods and recipes featured in the literature selections, such as breads from around the world or the international lunch foods
- unusual or unique foods that the children may not have had, such as star fruit

The parent letter provides an opportunity for families to share foods that reflect their culture backgrounds. Be sure to include some of your favorite foods or recipes too!

This Week's Theme

Fabulous Food

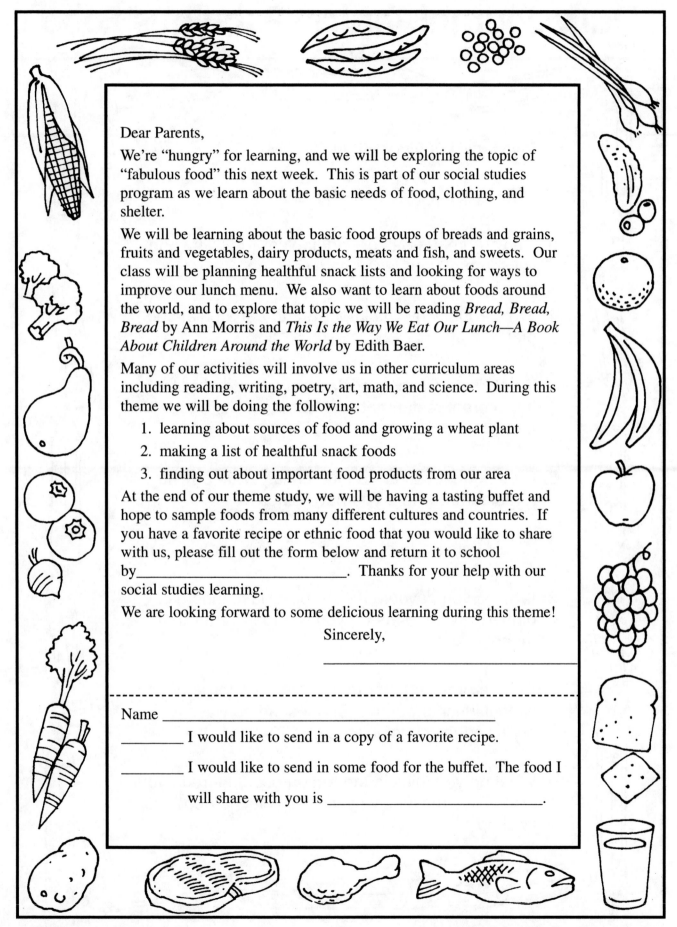

Dear Parents,

We're "hungry" for learning, and we will be exploring the topic of "fabulous food" this next week. This is part of our social studies program as we learn about the basic needs of food, clothing, and shelter.

We will be learning about the basic food groups of breads and grains, fruits and vegetables, dairy products, meats and fish, and sweets. Our class will be planning healthful snack lists and looking for ways to improve our lunch menu. We also want to learn about foods around the world, and to explore that topic we will be reading *Bread, Bread, Bread* by Ann Morris and *This Is the Way We Eat Our Lunch—A Book About Children Around the World* by Edith Baer.

Many of our activities will involve us in other curriculum areas including reading, writing, poetry, art, math, and science. During this theme we will be doing the following:

1. learning about sources of food and growing a wheat plant
2. making a list of healthful snack foods
3. finding out about important food products from our area

At the end of our theme study, we will be having a tasting buffet and hope to sample foods from many different cultures and countries. If you have a favorite recipe or ethnic food that you would like to share with us, please fill out the form below and return it to school by_____. Thanks for your help with our social studies learning.

We are looking forward to some delicious learning during this theme!

Sincerely,

_____

- -

Name _____

_____ I would like to send in a copy of a favorite recipe.

_____ I would like to send in some food for the buffet. The food I

will share with you is _____.

Daily Journal Topics: Fabulous Food

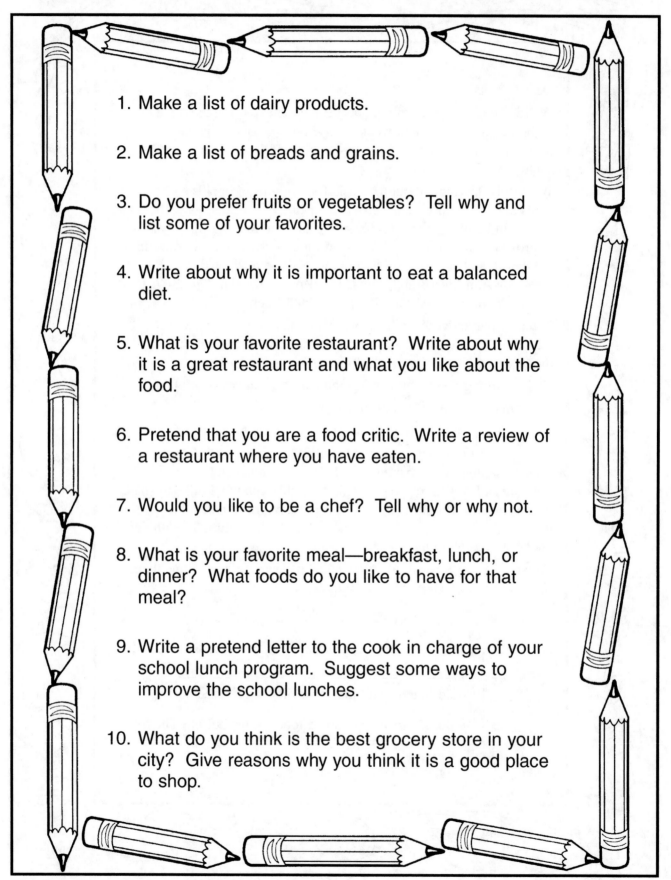

1. Make a list of dairy products.

2. Make a list of breads and grains.

3. Do you prefer fruits or vegetables? Tell why and list some of your favorites.

4. Write about why it is important to eat a balanced diet.

5. What is your favorite restaurant? Write about why it is a great restaurant and what you like about the food.

6. Pretend that you are a food critic. Write a review of a restaurant where you have eaten.

7. Would you like to be a chef? Tell why or why not.

8. What is your favorite meal—breakfast, lunch, or dinner? What foods do you like to have for that meal?

9. Write a pretend letter to the cook in charge of your school lunch program. Suggest some ways to improve the school lunches.

10. What do you think is the best grocery store in your city? Give reasons why you think it is a good place to shop.

Favorite Foods

Purpose: Children will each create a page for a class book entitled Our Favorite Foods. The pages will feature a description of students' favorite foods and why they like them.

Materials

- Favorite Foods Book Cover (page 58)
- Favorite Foods Paper (page 59)
- pencils, markers, crayons

Preparation: Reproduce the plate-shaped paper for the children to write on. You will need one page for each student (additional pages if you plan on doing a first draft and a final copy). Reproduce one front cover on a piece of tagboard and cut a back cover in the same plate shape. Laminate the covers for durability.

Instructions: Have all students choose a favorite food. They can describe the food and write about why they like it. The space at the bottom of the page will be used for an illustration.

Favorite Foods Book Cover

Favorite Foods Paper

My favorite food is

_____

_____

_____

_____

_____

The Food Pyramid

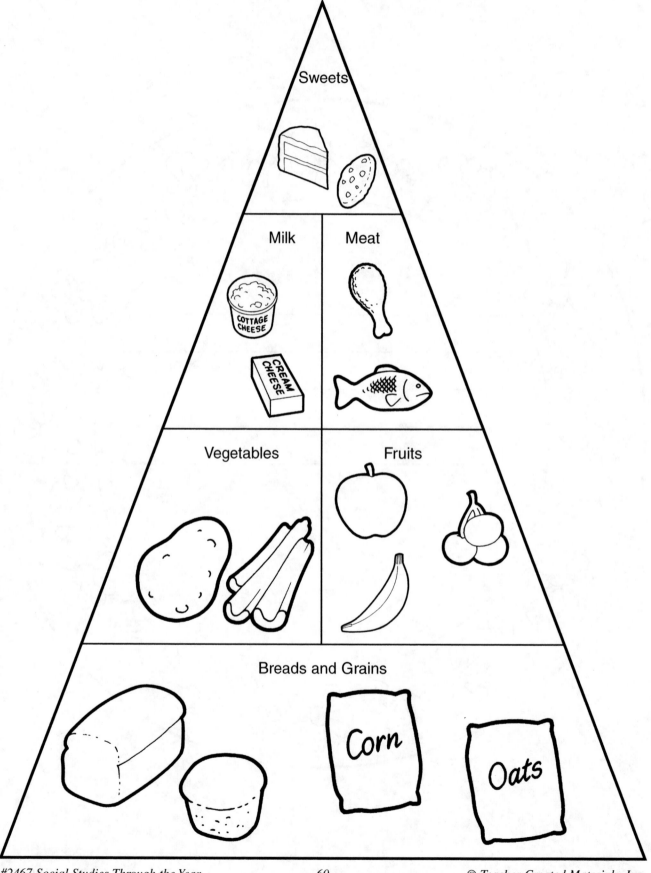

Fruits and Sweets Patterns

Meat and Milk Patterns

Breads and Grains Patterns

Corn

Rye

Wheat

Oats

Rice

Barley

Sorghum

Millet

Vegetable Patterns

Name _____ Date _____

Healthful Snacks List

Make a list of some healthful snacks that you could munch on after school.

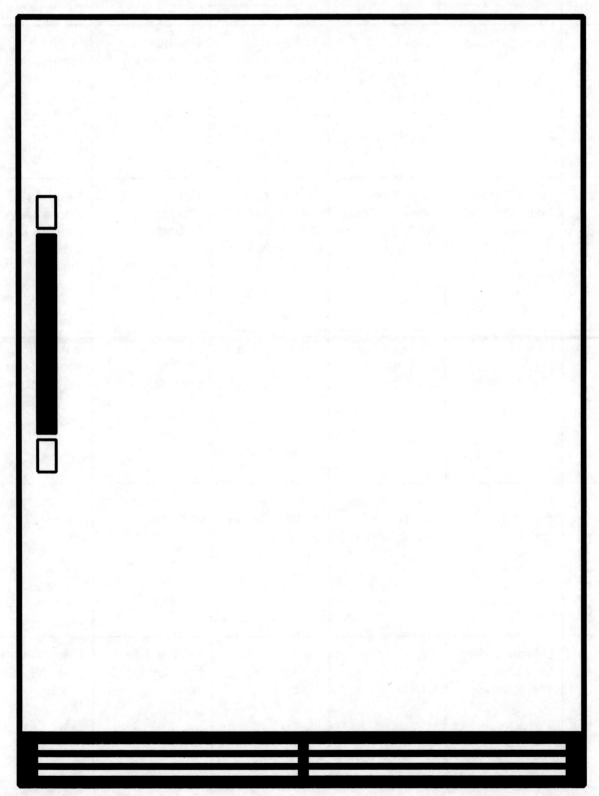

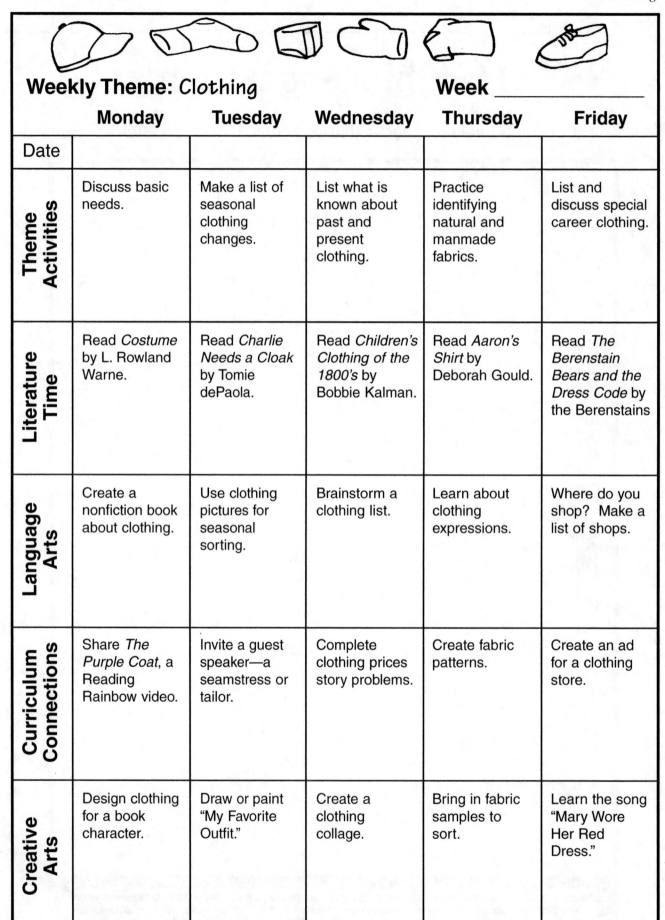

Weekly Theme: *Clothing*   **Week** _____

	Monday	Tuesday	Wednesday	Thursday	Friday
Date					
Theme Activities	Discuss basic needs.	Make a list of seasonal clothing changes.	List what is known about past and present clothing.	Practice identifying natural and manmade fabrics.	List and discuss special career clothing.
Literature Time	Read *Costume* by L. Rowland Warne.	Read *Charlie Needs a Cloak* by Tomie dePaola.	Read *Children's Clothing of the 1800's* by Bobbie Kalman.	Read *Aaron's Shirt* by Deborah Gould.	Read *The Berenstain Bears and the Dress Code* by the Berenstains
Language Arts	Create a nonfiction book about clothing.	Use clothing pictures for seasonal sorting.	Brainstorm a clothing list.	Learn about clothing expressions.	Where do you shop? Make a list of shops.
Curriculum Connections	Share *The Purple Coat*, a Reading Rainbow video.	Invite a guest speaker—a seamstress or tailor.	Complete clothing prices story problems.	Create fabric patterns.	Create an ad for a clothing store.
Creative Arts	Design clothing for a book character.	Draw or paint "My Favorite Outfit."	Create a clothing collage.	Bring in fabric samples to sort.	Learn the song "Mary Wore Her Red Dress."

Overview: Clothing

════ Monday ════

Theme Activities: Discuss the basic needs that all people have for food, clothing, and shelter. Talk about why we need clothing to protect us from the weather. Discuss the differences between needs and wants.

Literature Time: *Costume* by L. Rowland Warne (Alfred A. Knopf, 1992) is an excellent reference book containing valuable information on the history of clothing.

Language Arts: Read the *Clothing* Mini-Book found on pages 73 and 74. Have students color the pages with crayons or colored pencils. They can then discuss facts about clothing in small groups.

Curriculum Connections: Show the Reading Rainbow video *The Purple Coat.* This video describes how the clothing industry in New York's garment district works and features the book by Amy Hest. Look for the video at your local library or your district's instructional media center.

Creative Arts: Make a list of some favorite book characters the class enjoys reading about. Challenge the class by asking them to design a new outfit for one of the characters. The outfit should reflect the character's personality. As an alternative activity, have students design a costume to wear to a party or on Halloween.

════ Tuesday ════

Theme Activities: Clothing needs change as the seasons or weather changes. What are the seasonal weather changes where you live? Make a list of different types of clothing needed in hot, cold, rainy, or snowy conditions.

Literature Time: Read *Charlie Needs a Cloak* by Tomie dePaola (Prentice Hall, 1973) to learn how wool is woven into cloth.

Language Arts: Using the clothing pictures found on pages 75–78, have the class do some seasonal sorting. You may give each student a set of clothing pictures to color and sort, or duplicate several sets and have the students work in small groups. Students may sort the clothing in a number of ways, such as by season or by weather (rainy, snowy, etc.).

Curriculum Connections: Contact a local alterations or tailor shop and invite a seamstress or tailor to your class as a guest speaker. Ask the speaker to talk about the job and perhaps bring samples of clothing in various stages of completion. You might also ask a cobbler to come in to discuss how shoes are made and repaired.

Creative Arts: Have students draw or paint pictures of themselves dressed in a favorite outfit. They can add a sentence or two to the bottom of the picture telling why these are their favorite clothes.

Overview: Clothing *(cont.)*

Wednesday

Theme Activities: Today's topic is how clothing has changed over the years. Assess prior knowledge by listing what the class knows about how clothing was different in the past.

Literature Time: To find out more information about clothing in the 1800's, read *Children's Clothing of the 1800's* by Bobbie Kalman (Crabtree Publishing Company, 1995). This book includes a section on how clothes were cared for and a section on how to create a "clothing museum" as a classroom display.

Language Arts: Brainstorm a list of as many items of clothing as possible. Students may work on their own or with a partner. Compile all the answers into a large list which can then be written on a clothing shape (see pages 75–78 for shapes which can be enlarged and laminated).

Curriculum Connections: Practice math skills with some money and story problems. Have students complete the story problems on page 79.

Creative Arts: Gather catalogs and ads from local clothing stores. Have students cut out pictures which they can then sort in a variety of ways (clothes I like/don't like; winter/summer clothes; clothes/clothing accessories, etc.). The pictures can then be glued onto a piece of construction paper to create a clothing collage.

Thursday

Theme Activities: Show the class some samples of fabric and ask whether they are man-made or natural (from a plant or animal). Some samples of natural fabric are cotton (from a cotton plant), wool (from a sheep), leather (cow), and silk (silkworm). Manmade fabrics include polyester, rayon, and nylon.

Literature Time: Children often have a favorite piece of clothing or a favorite outfit. Read *Aaron's Shirt* by Deborah Gould (Bradbury Press, 1989) in which Aaron finds it difficult to give up his shirt even when he has outgrown it.

Language Arts: On the chalkboard write some clothing expressions that people use. Have students try to figure out what they might mean. Here are a few samples to get you started:

- *The clothes make the man.*
- *I would give you the shirt off my back.*
- *If the shoe fits, wear it.*
- *Walk a mile in my shoes.*
- *She was dressed to the nines.*

Overview: Clothing (cont.)

═══════════════════════ **Thursday** (cont.) ═══════════════════════

Curriculum Connections: Give students some fabric samples that have patterns. Have them figure out the patterns and then create new patterns that could be used for fabric for clothing.

Creative Arts: Bring in a variety of fabric samples and trims (such as lace and rickrack that are used to decorate clothing) for the class to sort into three groups: natural fabric, man-made fabric, and trims. Have the students glue the samples on the fabric sorting sheet found on page 80 and label the samples. To find out about more manmade clothing inventions that were accidental, including Levi's jeans, trouser cuffs, Velcro, and Scotch Guard, read *Mistakes That Worked* by Charlotte Foltz Jones (see bibliography).

═══════════════════════ **Friday** ═══════════════════════

Theme Activities: Some careers, such as being a firefighter or a police officer, require special clothing or a uniform. Make a list of the jobs which require special clothing. Talk about why the clothing is necessary for the job. Some schools have uniforms. Discuss why this might be.

Literature Time: Today's selection, *The Berenstain Bears and the Dress Code* by Stan and Jan Berenstain (Random House, 1994), is a chapter book which could be started today and read one chapter a day until finished. Prior to reading, ask the students if they know what a dress code is and whether or not you have a dress code at your school. Discuss the pros and cons of having a dress code.

Language Arts: Make a list of stores in your community where the students like to shop for clothes. Have the yellow pages of the phone book available for looking up the names of stores.

Curriculum Connections: Check the local newspaper for clothing store ads to bring to school. Talk about the components that an ad might have, such as pictures, a slogan, and words to catch the interest of customers such as "special value" or sale. Students can then create their own ads for stores in your community or for stores that they invent and name.

Creative Arts: Teach the song "Mary Wore Her Red Dress" and ask the students about their favorite colors for clothing. Make new verses for the song by using students' names and the clothing that they are wearing. For example, one new verse might be "Craig wore his brown shoes all day long." This song is available in a big book and cassette set (see bibliography).

This Week's Theme

Clothing

Clothing

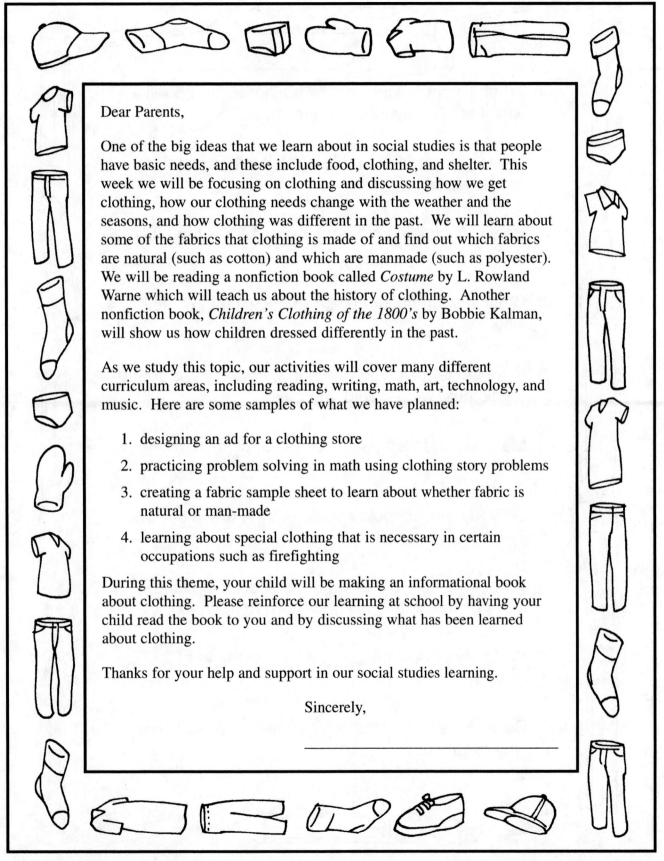

Dear Parents,

One of the big ideas that we learn about in social studies is that people have basic needs, and these include food, clothing, and shelter. This week we will be focusing on clothing and discussing how we get clothing, how our clothing needs change with the weather and the seasons, and how clothing was different in the past. We will learn about some of the fabrics that clothing is made of and find out which fabrics are natural (such as cotton) and which are manmade (such as polyester). We will be reading a nonfiction book called *Costume* by L. Rowland Warne which will teach us about the history of clothing. Another nonfiction book, *Children's Clothing of the 1800's* by Bobbie Kalman, will show us how children dressed differently in the past.

As we study this topic, our activities will cover many different curriculum areas, including reading, writing, math, art, technology, and music. Here are some samples of what we have planned:

1. designing an ad for a clothing store
2. practicing problem solving in math using clothing story problems
3. creating a fabric sample sheet to learn about whether fabric is natural or man-made
4. learning about special clothing that is necessary in certain occupations such as firefighting

During this theme, your child will be making an informational book about clothing. Please reinforce our learning at school by having your child read the book to you and by discussing what has been learned about clothing.

Thanks for your help and support in our social studies learning.

Sincerely,

_____

Daily Journal Topics: Clothing

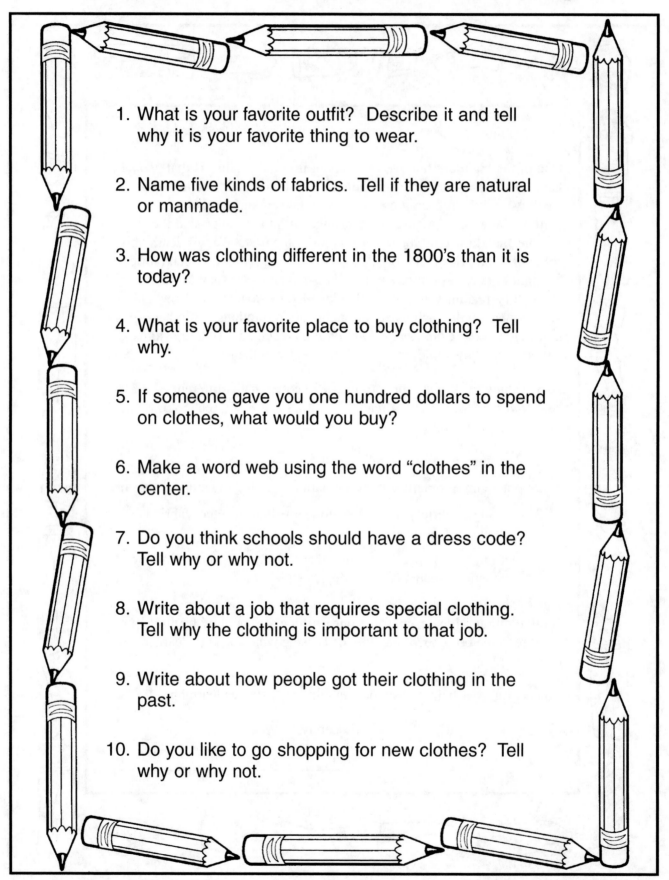

1. What is your favorite outfit? Describe it and tell why it is your favorite thing to wear.

2. Name five kinds of fabrics. Tell if they are natural or manmade.

3. How was clothing different in the 1800's than it is today?

4. What is your favorite place to buy clothing? Tell why.

5. If someone gave you one hundred dollars to spend on clothes, what would you buy?

6. Make a word web using the word "clothes" in the center.

7. Do you think schools should have a dress code? Tell why or why not.

8. Write about a job that requires special clothing. Tell why the clothing is important to that job.

9. Write about how people got their clothing in the past.

10. Do you like to go shopping for new clothes? Tell why or why not.

Clothing Mini-Book

Cut along the solid lines, put the pages in the correct order, and then staple them to make a booklet. Read your clothing book and then color the pictures.

Name _____

My Clothing Mini-Book

1. One of the basic needs that people have is for clothing.

2. We need clothing to protect us from the weather.

3. Different kinds of clothes are needed, depending on the season of the year and the climate or weather where you live.

Clothing Mini-Book *(cont.)*

4. Clothing styles have changed over the years.

5. People wear special clothes for special occasions and for their jobs.

6. Clothes are made of many different types of fabrics. Some fabrics are natural like wool. Some are manmade like polyester.

7. Whether for work or play, it is fun to choose new clothes!

Clothing Patterns

Directions: These clothing pictures can be duplicated and colored with markers or crayons. They can then be sorted by the season in which they are worn. Any of the shapes can be enlarged and laminated for use on a bulletin board, or a list of clothing can be written on the enlarged shape with a transparency pen.

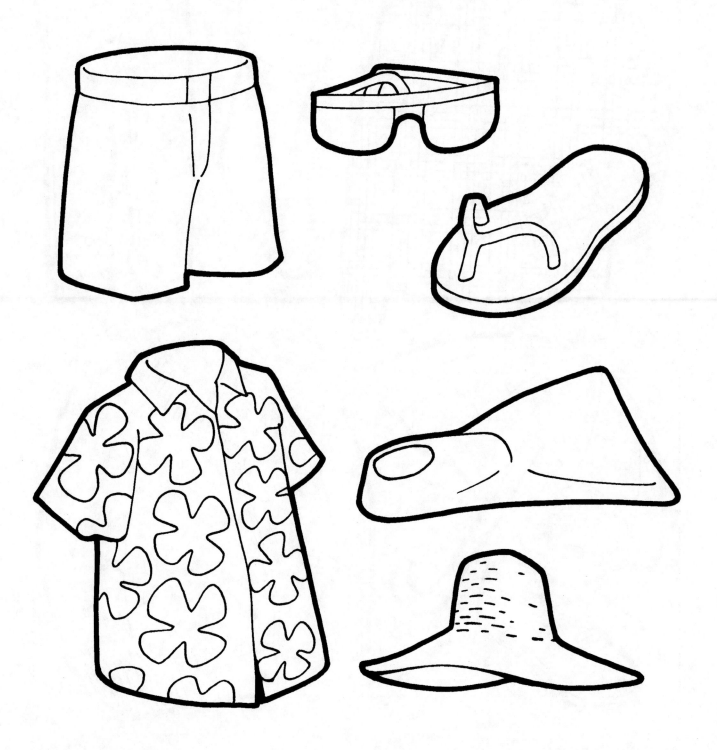

Clothing Patterns *(cont.)*

Clothing Patterns *(cont.)*

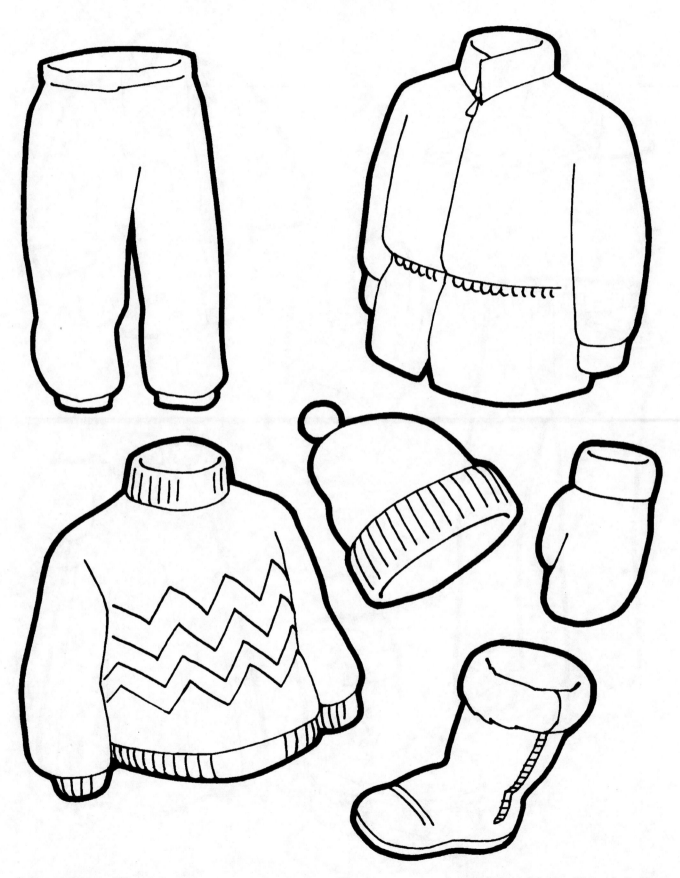

Clothing Patterns *(cont.)*

78

Name _____ Date _____

Clothing Story Problems

Solve these shopping problems. You may need to use computation or a problem-solving strategy.

1. Cameron went to the store to buy a new baseball cap. He had $10.00, and the cap cost $5.99. How much change did he get?

2. The store has five different brands of jeans. Brand A costs less than brand B. Brand C costs twice as much as Brand B. Brand D has a price between brand B and brand A. Which pair of jeans is least expensive?

3. Jenny went shopping and bought three new sweatshirts. Each sweatshirt cost $14.99. How much did she spend altogether?

4. Kevin wanted to buy a Chicago Bears football jersey. The jersey cost $30.00. He has saved $12.89 so far. How much more money will he need in order to buy the jersey?

5. The Midland Mall opened at 9:00 A.M. on Saturday. Helen went to the mall when it opened and shopped for one hour and 45 minutes and then she ate lunch for 30 minutes. After lunch, she shopped for another 40 minutes and then went home. At what time did she leave the mall for home?

6. Tim and Michael went to the toy store to spend some money that their grandma gave them. Tim bought a yo-yo for $2.95. Michael bought a new game for $10.99 and a set of baseball cards for $2.50. How much did the two boys spend together?

Fabric Samples

Trims

Manmade Fabrics

Natural Fabrics

Weekly Theme: *Shelter*   Week _____

	Monday	Tuesday	Wednesday	Thursday	Friday
Date					
Theme Activities	Discuss basic needs: food, clothing, shelter.	Make a list of types of shelters.	Build a house step by step.	Bring in building materials for homes.	Discuss helping the homeless and Habitat for Humanity.
Literature Time	Read *A House Is a House for Me* by Mary Ann Hoberman.	Read *Houses and Homes* by Ann Morris.	Read *Building a House* by Byron Barton.	Read *This Is My House* by Arthur Dorros.	Read *Homes Around the World* by Bobbie Kalman.
Language Arts	Write an innovation from today's literature.	Write about how to build a tree house.	Review steps of how to build a house.	Learn to say *house* in many languages.	Write letters to help the homeless.
Curriculum Connections	Create house paintings.	Make pictures of homes around the world (*Kid Pix*).	Invite a guest speaker: an architect, engineer, or builder.	Be a "house" detective.	Learn about the features of fiction and nonfiction.
Creative Arts	Create a box city.	Erect shelters in the block center.	Post photographs of famous buildings around the world.	Make a welcome sign.	Construct plans for homes of the future.

Overview: Shelter

Monday

Theme Activities: Reinforce the idea that people have basic needs which include the need for food, clothing, and shelter. Discuss what the word "shelter" means and that a shelter protects us from the weather. Talk about a home or house being one kind of shelter. (*Special Note:* When doing a unit on homes, be sensitive to the feelings of children in your room who may be homeless or live in difficult circumstances.)

Literature Time: Explore some different meanings of what a house or home is with this classic book *A House Is a House for Me* by Mary Ann Hoberman (Penguin, 1982). On some of the pages, you may want to read part of the sentence without showing the illustrations to see if the class can predict what the author will say.

Language Arts: Invite the class to write some innovations using the pattern found in today's literature. Write the pattern "A _____ is a house for _____" and discuss a few examples. Then have the students write and illustrate their own ideas.

Curriculum Connections: Have the students create pictures of their own houses. Provide a variety of art materials, including construction paper, paint, color pencils, and chalk and let students make their houses using the medium that they prefer.

Creative Arts: Ask students to bring in a variety of tissue boxes and shoeboxes. Collect some cardboard milk cartons of various sizes. The boxes or cartons can be taped together and covered with construction paper or painted to make a variety of buildings and houses. Have students measure their completed houses and record the height and width of their shelter. Set up an area of your classroom for your "box city." Students can add many other details to the city, such as trees, sidewalks, etc.

Tuesday

Theme Activities: Make a list of many different kinds of shelters such as houses, apartments, tents, etc. Talk about the types of shelters shown in the pictures on pages 88 and 89. Discuss which ones are in your community.

Literature Time: Look at houses around the world with this photographic journey, *Houses and Homes* by Ann Morris (Lothrop, Lee, and Shepard, 1992). On a world map or globe, locate the places mentioned in the book.

Language Arts: There are many different places to live, but one favorite hideaway for children is a tree house. Have students write about how they would design and build a tree house as a special place. They should describe in detail what the house would look like and what would be in it.

Overview: Shelter *(cont.)*

━━━━━━━━━━ **Tuesday** *(cont.)* ━━━━━━━━━━

Curriculum Connections: Make a class book of homes around the world, using the cover and format on pages 91 and 92. Homes can be drawn with crayons or markers, and factual information can be written on the lines. Students may also make pictures on a computer using *Kid Pix Studio* drawing tools. A sample drawing appears on page 381.

Creative Arts: Stock your block center with a variety of building materials including Lego, Lincoln Logs, and wooden blocks for students to build different types of shelters.

━━━━━━━━━━ **Wednesday** ━━━━━━━━━━

Theme Activities: Ask the class if they have ever seen a house being built. What do they think is the first step? Determine whether they know the general order of steps involved in building any house or structure.

Literature Time: Today's book, *Building a House* by Byron Barton (Puffin, 1981), gives a simplified view of the step-by-step process of building a house. Be sure to discuss any steps not included (e.g., putting in cupboards).

Language Arts: Review steps in building a house by using the sequence cards found on page 93. The cards may be used with the whole group and placed in a pocket chart in correct sequence, or a set of cards can be duplicated for each student to cut and glue onto another paper in correct order.

Curriculum Connections: Invite a guest speaker to share information about building occupations (builder, architect, engineer, plumber, electrician). Before the visit, let the students write questions they would like to ask their guest.

Creative Arts: Post photographs of interesting architecture or famed buildings such as the White House or Taj Mahal in your building center so that students can recreate the structures, or in your art center so reproductions of the buildings can be painted or made from clay.

━━━━━━━━━━ **Thursday** ━━━━━━━━━━

Theme Activities: Bring in some materials used in building homes—bricks, pipes, drywall, electrical outlets, etc. Let the students examine the materials and discuss their uses.

Literature Time: Houses around the world contain different types of building materials. Today's book by Arthur Dorros, *This Is My House* (Scholastic, 1992), tours many different shelters in many different countries.

Language Arts: Each page of today's literature selection has the words "This Is My House" written in the language of the featured country. Provide students with index cards and have them copy the sentences from the book. Along with those words, have them write a sentence describing the house from that country. These labels can be placed on a world map on a bulletin board to mark the locations.

Overview: **Shelter** *(cont.)*

Thursday *(cont.)*

Curriculum Connections: For a "house homework" assignment, have students locate some basic features of structures in their own houses. The survey should be adjusted in order to meet the needs of your class. A house detective page is provided on page 94.

Creative Arts: Many homes have a welcome sign to greet visitors. Using the house sign shape found on page 95, students can design signs for their houses. If you have access to some pieces of pine wood, the pattern for the sign can be traced and cut on the pieces of wood. Enlist the aid of parent volunteers in cutting the wood ahead of time with a jigsaw. Students could then complete their signs using paint. A width of $\frac{1}{2}$ inch or 1.3 cm for the pine board works well in craft activities.

Friday

Theme Activities: If it is appropriate for your classroom situation, discuss ways that the class could help people who are homeless. You may want to talk about projects such as Habitat for Humanity, which uses volunteers to build homes.

Literature Time: Read *Homes Around the World* by Bobbie Kalman (Crabtree Publishing Company, 1994). This is a very up-to-date book which addresses the fact that people live in many different kinds of circumstances.

Language Arts: Have students write to community, state, and government leaders with their concerns and ideas of how to help people who are homeless.

Curriculum Connections: Using today's literature, discuss the features common to nonfiction books. Find the following parts of the book: table of contents, featured vocabulary (in boldface type), words to know, and the index. Put the students in small groups and provide each group with a set of books, some fiction, some nonfiction, some a mixture of both styles (Magic School Bus® books are good examples of fiction that includes some informational text). Have students look for the components of fiction and decide what group their books fit into best. An additional feature to look for (not found in today's selection) is the use of diagrams and labels.

Creative Arts: What will homes of the future look like? Ask the class to draw or paint their ideas of what homes might look like 100 years from now. They could also create pictures of cities of the future. Encourage them to think about and include many details, such as what the transportation might look like, what kinds of special building materials might be used, and how the designs of buildings might be different in the future.

This Week's Theme

Shelter

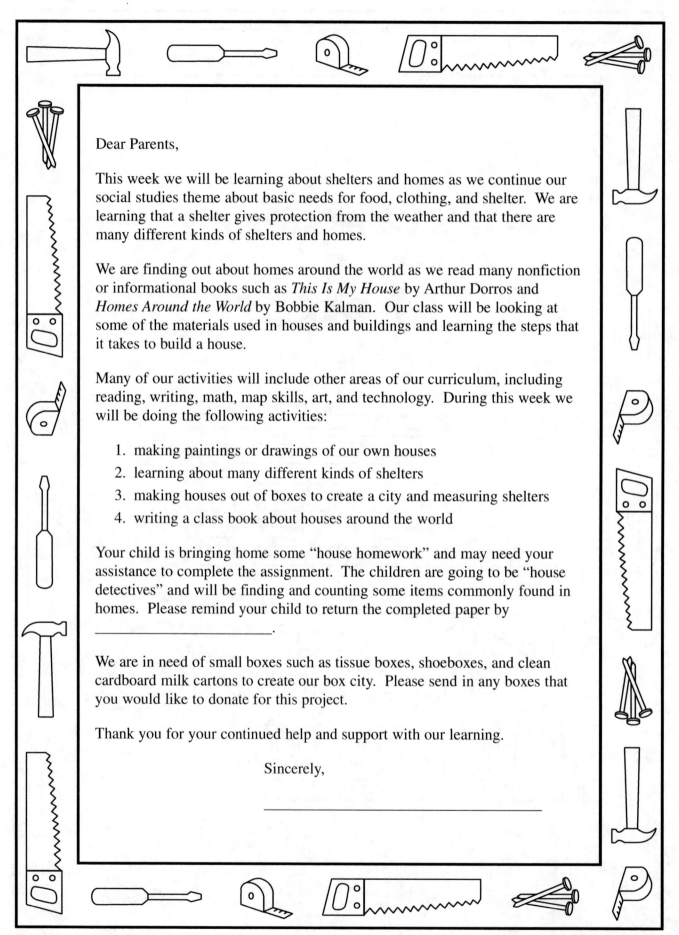

Dear Parents,

This week we will be learning about shelters and homes as we continue our social studies theme about basic needs for food, clothing, and shelter. We are learning that a shelter gives protection from the weather and that there are many different kinds of shelters and homes.

We are finding out about homes around the world as we read many nonfiction or informational books such as *This Is My House* by Arthur Dorros and *Homes Around the World* by Bobbie Kalman. Our class will be looking at some of the materials used in houses and buildings and learning the steps that it takes to build a house.

Many of our activities will include other areas of our curriculum, including reading, writing, math, map skills, art, and technology. During this week we will be doing the following activities:

1. making paintings or drawings of our own houses
2. learning about many different kinds of shelters
3. making houses out of boxes to create a city and measuring shelters
4. writing a class book about houses around the world

Your child is bringing home some "house homework" and may need your assistance to complete the assignment. The children are going to be "house detectives" and will be finding and counting some items commonly found in homes. Please remind your child to return the completed paper by

_____.

We are in need of small boxes such as tissue boxes, shoeboxes, and clean cardboard milk cartons to create our box city. Please send in any boxes that you would like to donate for this project.

Thank you for your continued help and support with our learning.

Sincerely,

_____

Daily Journal Activities: Shelter

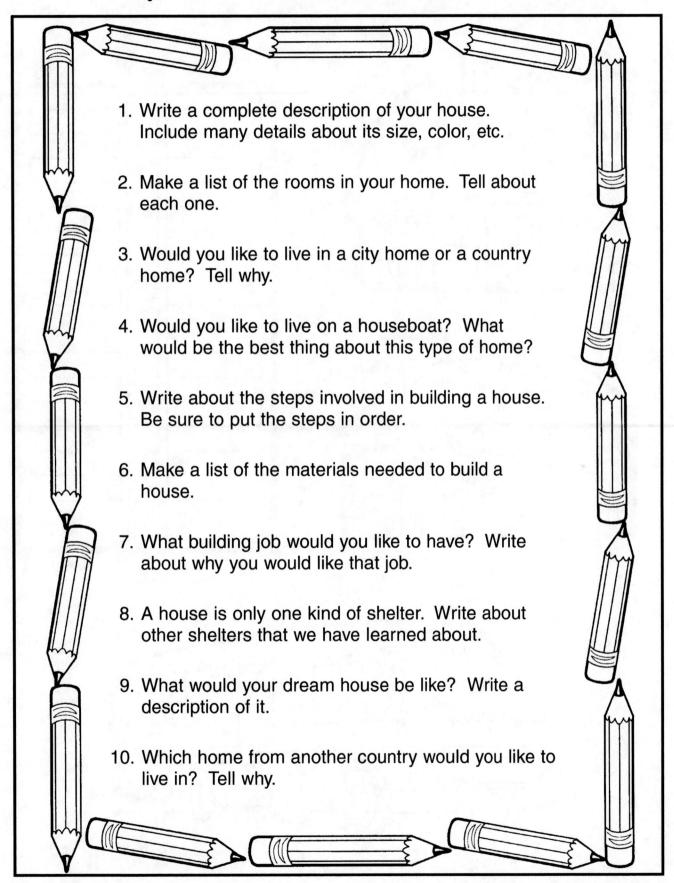

1. Write a complete description of your house. Include many details about its size, color, etc.

2. Make a list of the rooms in your home. Tell about each one.

3. Would you like to live in a city home or a country home? Tell why.

4. Would you like to live on a houseboat? What would be the best thing about this type of home?

5. Write about the steps involved in building a house. Be sure to put the steps in order.

6. Make a list of the materials needed to build a house.

7. What building job would you like to have? Write about why you would like that job.

8. A house is only one kind of shelter. Write about other shelters that we have learned about.

9. What would your dream house be like? Write a description of it.

10. Which home from another country would you like to live in? Tell why.

House Patterns

House Patterns *(cont.)*

Houses of the World

Purpose: Children each create a page for a class book titled Houses of the World. They will draw a home found in another country and then write about the home and what it is like.

Materials

- Homes Around the World Book Cover (page 91)
- Homes Around the World Paper (page 92)
- pencils, markers, crayons (or pictures may be created using *Kid Pix Studio* and then glued on the page)

Preparation: Reproduce the shaped paper for the children to write on. You will need one page for each student (additional pages if you plan on doing a first draft and a final copy). Reproduce one front cover for the class book and color it with markers. Mount the cover on a piece of tagboard and cut a back cover in the same globe shape. Laminate the covers for durability.

Instructions: Have each student select a home from one of the literature selections read during the week. They can draw the picture of the house in the space below or glue on a picture made by using *Kid Pix Studio* on the computer. They will then write about the home selected, telling what country it is found in, what it is made of, and other information that they have learned.

Homes Around the World Book Cover

Homes Around the World Paper

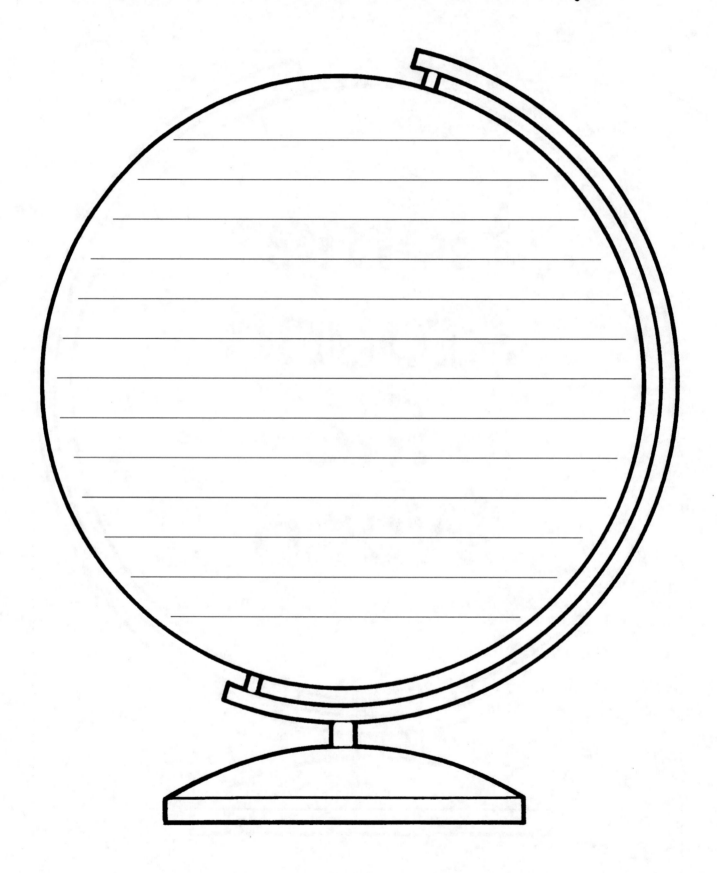

How to Build a House

Cut the cards apart on the dotted lines. Put them in order to show the steps involved in building a house.

Draw a blueprint or design for the house.

Clear a place for the house and dig a hole for the foundation.

Make a cement foundation.

Build the floor using wood.

Construct the walls and the roof.

Add any brickwork, including a chimney and a fireplace.

Install plumbing and electrical work.

Complete the inside of the house with drywall and finish work.

Put in the windows and doors. Paint the house and move in.

Be a House Detective

Directions: Look around the place where you live. Find the following items and record them on this sheet.

House Item	Number Found	Location
1. doors	_____	_____
2. windows	_____	_____
3. electrical outlets	_____	_____
4. stairs	_____	_____
5. sinks	_____	_____
6. bathtubs	_____	_____
7. cabinets	_____	_____
8. lights	_____	_____
9. telephones	_____	_____
10. doorknobs	_____	_____

A Welcome Sign

Make a welcome sign for your home. Put your family name on the sign and include the date you moved into your home. Decorate your sign with pictures that tell about your family (for example, a heart to show love).

Welcome

to the

_____

Home

Established in _____

Weekly Theme: Fabulous Families   Week _____

	Monday	**Tuesday**	**Wednesday**	**Thursday**	**Friday**
Date					
Theme Activities	Introduce the concept of "family."	Discuss how families function.	Diagram families through the generations.	Discuss conflicts in families.	Discuss the concept of a family reunion.
Literature Time	Read *Families Are Different* by Nina Pellegrini. Read *All Kinds of Families* by Norma Simon.	Read *Family Pictures* by Carmen Lomas Garza and *Mama, Do You Love Me?* by Barbara M. Joosse.	Read *The Keeping Quilt* by Patricia Polacco.	Read *My Rotten Redheaded Older Brother* by Patricia Polacco and *Potato: A Tale from the Great Depression* by Kate Lied.	Read *The Relatives Came* by Cynthia Rylant and *Tanya's Reunion* by Valerie Flournoy.
Language Arts	Use multiple copies of *The Berenstain Bears Are a Family* by Stan and Jan Berenstain.	Introduce the poem called "Families."	Complete My Family Keepsake.	Discuss how families can solve problems.	Write a reunion invitation.
Curriculum Connections	Graph the number of people in each family.	Help students read My Mini-Book About an Inuit Family.	Trace the immigration of Patricia Polacco's family.	Learn about Patricia Polacco.	Develop a shopping list for a reunion.
Creative Arts	Paint and display family portraits.	Begin making My Family Pop-Up Book.	Continue making My Family Pop-Up Book.	Continue My Family Pop-Up Book.	Make plans and posters for a reunion.

Overview: Fabulous Families

Monday

Theme Activities: Lead your class in a discussion of what the word "family" means. Organize your students' thoughts with a word web with "family" in the center and their suggestions surrounding "family." (Be sure that children point out different sizes of families, who might be in a family, what families do, etc.)

Literature Time: Read the book *Families Are Different* by Nina Pellegrini (Holiday House, 1991) to your class. This book is also available as a big book from Scholastic if you would like your students to join in reading the book with you during a shared reading time. You might read the book *All Kinds of Families* by Norma Simon (Albert Whitman, 1976) as an alternate selection for older students.

Language Arts: Use multiple copies of *The Berenstain Bears Are a Family* by Stan and Jan Berenstain (Random House, 1991) at your reading center or during guided reading time to give children the opportunity to read independently a rhyming, beginning reader text about families.

Curriculum Connections: Have students create a graph of the number of people in each of their families. You should explain to students that for the purposes of this graph they should consider only the family members who live with them. Each child then draws a picture of his or her family with crayons on a 3" x 5" or 4" x 6" (8 cm x 13 cm or 10 cm x 15 cm) index card. Cards are then graphed by the number of people in each family.

Creative Arts: Have students paint portraits of their families by using tempera paints on 12" x 18" (30 cm x 46 cm) sheets of white construction paper. Display these in your classroom or hallway during your study of families.

Tuesday

Theme Activities: Discuss how families work together and help each other. You might want to read the emergent reader book called *Families Share* by Rozanne Lanczak Williams (Creative Teaching Press, 1996) to your young students or provide multiple copies for students to read independently.

Literature Time: Read the books *Family Pictures* by Carmen Lomas Garza (Children's Book Press, 1990) and *Mama Do You Love Me?* by Barbara M. Joosse (Chronicle Books, 1991) to explore how people live in an Hispanic family and Inuit family, respectively.

Language Arts: Enlarge the poem "Families" (page 103) onto a chart or use an overhead transparency. As you read the poem with students, have them identify what families do together, as well as noting the rhyming words used in the poem.

Overview: Fabulous Families (cont.)

Tuesday (cont.)

Curriculum Connections: Reproduce My Book About an Inuit Family (pages 104–107). Help your students read the text to learn about the life of an Inuit family, assemble the book, and take it home to share with their families.

Creative Arts: Students will begin making pop-up books about their families. Assemble the books before you begin this project. Today children will draw a picture of their families with crayons on white paper cut to fit onto the construction paper cover. For the cover, fold a sheet of 12" x 18" (30 cm x 46 cm) construction paper in half. The fold will become the top of the book. Reproduce one copy of page 108 for each student to tell about himself or herself, and reproduce one copy of page 109 for each of the other members of the child's family. Finally, reproduce one copy of page 110 for each child to conclude the book with the entire family. Each page is folded in the middle and then cut on the solid lines (as shown in the diagram below) to make the middle pop up. The pages are then glued together in the correct order (student page, family pages, together page) and then glued into the cover. Cut blank index cards into strips on which children may draw individual family members. These individuals are glued onto the appropriate page in the book.

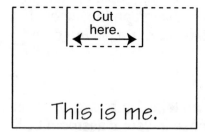
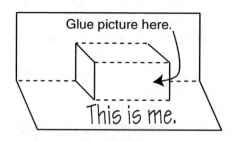
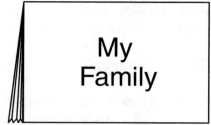

Wednesday

Theme Activity: Draw a diagram for your students (similar to a family tree, but with boxes) as you discuss how families are related. Use words such as *me, brother, sister, mother, father, aunt, uncle, grandmother, grandfather, great-aunt, great-uncle, great-grandmother, great-grandfather,* etc.

Literature Time: Read the book *The Keeping Quilt* by Patricia Polacco (Simon & Schuster Books for Young Readers, 1998). Discuss how the characters are related.

Language Arts: Discuss how the quilt from *The Keeping Quilt* was a special family keepsake and what other things might be family keepsakes. Have students complete My Family Keepsake on page 111 to tell about a keepsake they would like to pass from generation to generation in their own families.

Curriculum Connections: Use a world map or globe to trace the immigration of Patricia Polacco's family from Russia.

Creative Arts: Students will continue work in their family pop-up books that were begun yesterday.

Overview: Fabulous Families *(cont.)*

========================= **Thursday** =========================

Theme Activities: Lead a discussion with your students about the problems, conflicts, or difficulties that families may face. Write these on a chart for your students to use in a later activity.

Literature Time: Read and discuss two true recounts of family problems that were faced by real families: *My Rotten Redheaded Older Brother* by Patricia Polacco and *Potato: A Tale from the Great Depression* by Kate Lied.

Language Arts: Help your students brainstorm a list of solutions to family problems that were recorded on the chart during the Theme Activity. Students may work individually or in small groups. Reproduce page 112 for students to complete Family Problem-Solving Logic.

Curriculum Connections: Learn about the author Patricia Polacco by reading her autobiography, *Firetalking* (Richard C. Owen, 1994). Reproduce the mini-book on page 113 for students to read independently.

Creative Arts: Students will continue the work in their family pop-up books.

========================= **Friday** =========================

Theme Activities: Discuss what a family reunion is and ask students to share their experiences if they have attended a family reunion.

Literature Time: Read *The Relatives Came* by Cynthia Rylant (Bradbury Press, 1985) and *Tanya's Reunion* by Valerie Flournoy (Dial Books for Young Readers, 1995) to help develop your students' knowledge of family reunions.

Language Arts: Students will write an invitation to a family reunion. Direct them to include the basic information (who? what? where? when? why?), plus any details that they feel would encourage relatives to attend.

Curriculum Connections: Students will list food items that they plan to serve at their reunion on a shopping list. Then have students group their items according to the basic food groups. Have they included items for each of the basic food groups? If not, direct them to add items to help relatives eat nutritious meals.

Creative Arts: Students will make posters on construction paper with information about their reunions. They may use markers for their words and illustrations. They may cut pictures from magazines to provide additional illustrations.

This Week's Theme

Fabulous Families

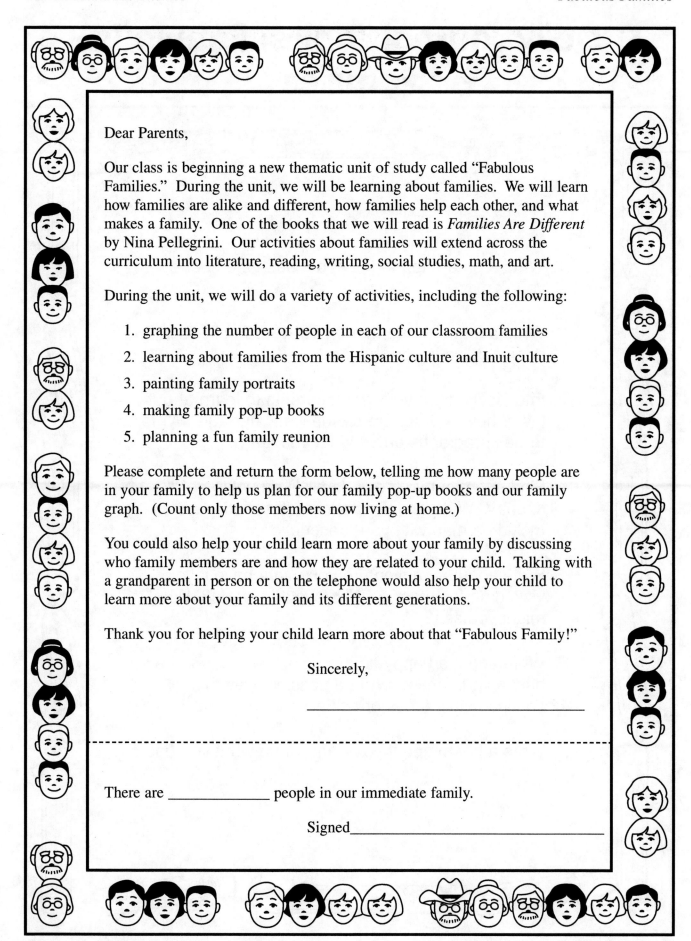

Dear Parents,

Our class is beginning a new thematic unit of study called "Fabulous Families." During the unit, we will be learning about families. We will learn how families are alike and different, how families help each other, and what makes a family. One of the books that we will read is *Families Are Different* by Nina Pellegrini. Our activities about families will extend across the curriculum into literature, reading, writing, social studies, math, and art.

During the unit, we will do a variety of activities, including the following:

1. graphing the number of people in each of our classroom families

2. learning about families from the Hispanic culture and Inuit culture

3. painting family portraits

4. making family pop-up books

5. planning a fun family reunion

Please complete and return the form below, telling me how many people are in your family to help us plan for our family pop-up books and our family graph. (Count only those members now living at home.)

You could also help your child learn more about your family by discussing who family members are and how they are related to your child. Talking with a grandparent in person or on the telephone would also help your child to learn more about your family and its different generations.

Thank you for helping your child learn more about that "Fabulous Family!"

Sincerely,

_____

- -

There are _____ people in our immediate family.

Signed_____

Daily Journal Topics: Fabulous Families

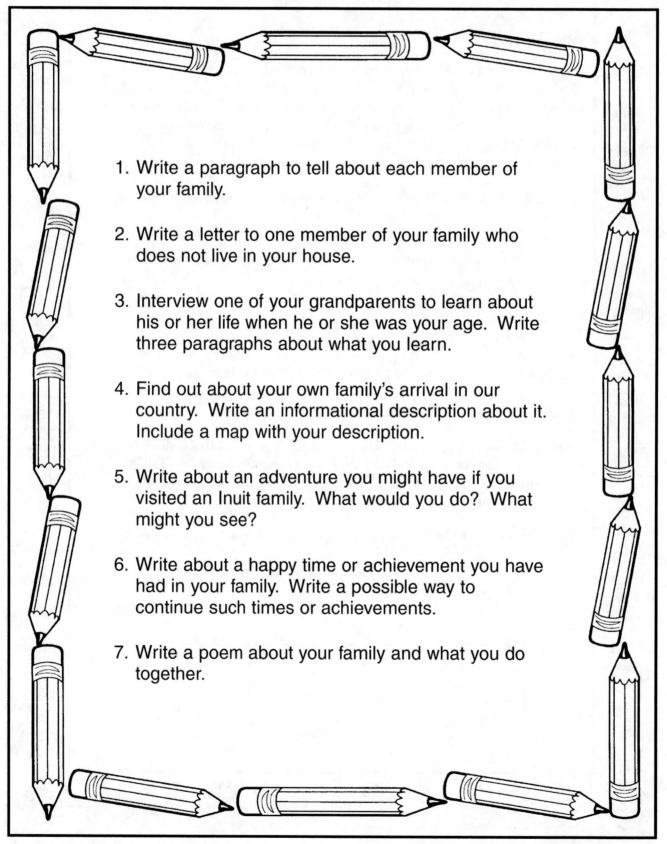

1. Write a paragraph to tell about each member of your family.

2. Write a letter to one member of your family who does not live in your house.

3. Interview one of your grandparents to learn about his or her life when he or she was your age. Write three paragraphs about what you learn.

4. Find out about your own family's arrival in our country. Write an informational description about it. Include a map with your description.

5. Write about an adventure you might have if you visited an Inuit family. What would you do? What might you see?

6. Write about a happy time or achievement you have had in your family. Write a possible way to continue such times or achievements.

7. Write a poem about your family and what you do together.

Families

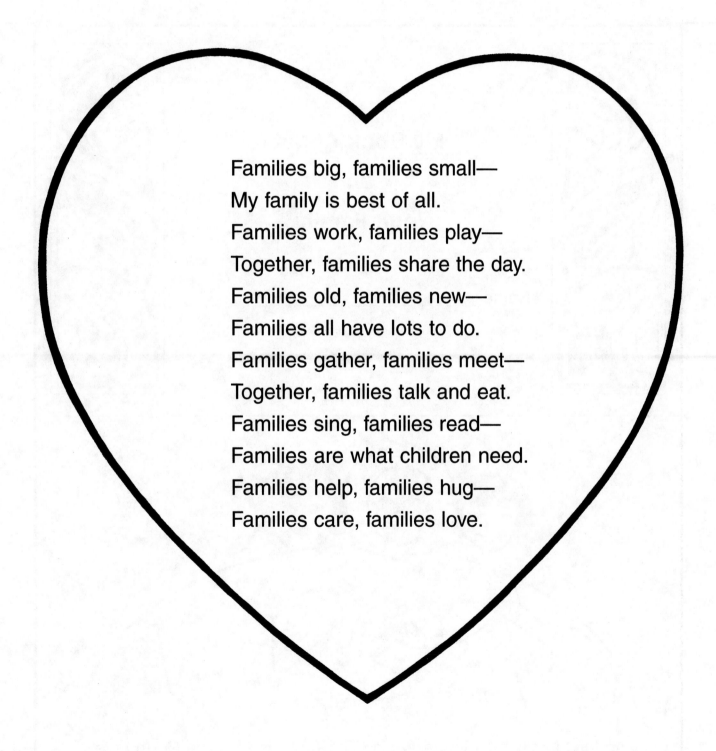

Families big, families small—
My family is best of all.
Families work, families play—
Together, families share the day.
Families old, families new—
Families all have lots to do.
Families gather, families meet—
Together, families talk and eat.
Families sing, families read—
Families are what children need.
Families help, families hug—
Families care, families love.

My Book About an Inuit Family

Directions: Read the information about Inuits. Cut on the lines. Put the pages in order and staple to make your own booklet. You may color the illustrations.

My Book About

an

Inuit Family

Name _____

An Inuit family lives in the Arctic. The Arctic is near the North Pole.

1

My Book About an Inuit Family *(cont.)*

Noon   **Midnight**

For a few days in winter, the sun never rises. For a few days in summer, the sun never sets.

2

It is very cold in the Arctic. The Inuit wear parkas, mittens, and mukluks to stay warm.

3

My Book About an Inuit Family *(cont.)*

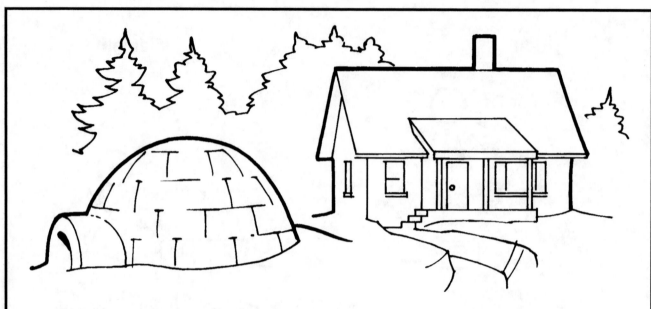

Some Inuit used to live in igloos, but now they live in houses that are raised above the ground.

4

The Inuit used to travel by dogsleds. Now they may use snowmobiles.

5

My Book About an Inuit Family *(cont.)*

Many animals share the Arctic with the Inuit. Polar bears are the most dangerous of these animals. There are salmon, ravens, and ptarmigan, too.

6

An Inuit family works and plays together in the Arctic.

7

My Family Pop-Up Book

Directions: See page 98.

This is me. My name is _____.

My Family Pop-Up Book *(cont.)*

This is _____.

My Family Pop-Up Book *(cont.)*

Together we are a family.

My Family Keepsake

Name _____ Date _____

Directions: Use the sentence frame below to write about a family keepsake that you would like to pass from one generation to the next in your family. Draw a picture of your family keepsake in the box below.

If my family had a special family keepsake, it would be _____.

It would be special to our family because _____.

My _____ would give the keepsake to me when I become

_____ years old. I would keep the keepsake in a safe place.

I would probably keep it in my _____.

Since it would pass from one generation in my family to the next, I would give it

to my_____next.

My Family Keepsake

Family Problem-Solving Logic

Name _____ Date _____

Dad, Mom, Christina, Jenna, and Baroness the puppy each want to do something different on a Sunday afternoon. No two family members want to do the same thing. This is a problem. First, find out which family member wants to do each choice. Then decide how they can spend the afternoon together and each still enjoy the afternoon. They might need to compromise!

Use the clues below to determine which choice belongs to each person. Use the grid to guide your thinking. Put an "O" in the box of the choice you know to be correct for each family member. Put an "X" in the boxes of choices you eliminate. Once a choice has been determined as one family member's favorite, it is no longer a possibility as another family member's choice and should be eliminated. (*Note:* Family members' names are arranged in the grid list in order of age, from oldest at the top to youngest at the bottom.)

1. This four-legged family member wants to go for a walk.
2. This male family member wants to watch sports on TV.
3. The youngest daughter wants to practice shooting baskets.
4. The oldest female family member wants to have a picnic.
5. The oldest daughter wants to shop at the mall.

	basketball	TV	picnic	shopping	walk
Dad					
Mom					
Christina					
Jenna					
Baroness					

What do you think they could do to spend the afternoon together and still enjoy the afternoon?_____

_____

Meet Patricia Polacco

Directions: Cut on the solid lines below. Fold on the dotted lines to make a mini-book about Patricia Polacco, the author of *The Keeping Quilt, My Rotten Redheaded Older Brother,* and *Firetalking.* Read the book and color the illustrations.

3

It is about her older brother.
She wrote My Rotten
Redheaded Older Brother.
Patricia Polacco writes
about her childhood.

2

family and their special quilt.
It told a true story about her
She wrote The Keeping Quilt.
Patricia Polacco writes and
illustrates books for children.

Patricia Polacco likes to
write about her family.
She has written many
books about them.

What is your favorite
Patricia Polacco book?

_____

_____

_____

4

Meet the Author

Patricia Polacco

My name is _____.

Weekly Themes: *My Community*   Week _____

	Monday	**Tuesday**	**Wednesday**	**Thursday**	**Friday**
Date					
Theme Activities	What is a community? Discuss the question.	Cities, towns, and villages—discuss the terms.	Locate our city on a state map.	Discuss our neighborhood and school area.	Discuss advantages of city vs. country life.
Literature Time	Read *Apt. 3* by Ezra Jack Keats.	Read *Alphabet City* by Stephen T. Johnson.	Read *Abuela* by Arthur Dorros.	Read *Visiting a Village* by Bobbie Kalman.	Read *Town and Country* by Alice and Martin Provensen.
Language Arts	Complete the City Facts sheet.	Read city poems to the class.	Make a class book: Our Community.	Make lists of things about our city, A to Z.	Create a comparison chart of town and country.
Curriculum Connections	Take a trip to city hall and other community places.	Study a map of our neighborhood.	Celebrate city cultures.	Investigate community resources.	Take a photo tour of our neighborhood.
Creative Arts	Design a new park for our city.	Make an alphabet book for our own city.	Make a cities, suburbs, and farms bulletin board.	Promote our city.	Make up a song about our city.

Overview: My Community

Monday

Theme Activities: Before starting this unit, gather a collection of fiction and nonfiction books about cities. There are many books written about larger cities like New York, and you may want to select books that would be of interest to your class. Start this theme by discussing what the word "community" means. *The American Heritage Dictionary* (Houghton Mifflin, 1969) defines a community as "a group of people living in the same locality and under the same government."

Literature Time: Take a look at city life in an apartment building in the classic story by Ezra Jack Keats, *Apt. 3* (Macmillan, 1971). Compare the setting to the city or town that you live in.

Language Arts: Gather some information about your city or town. You may need to write to your city hall or city council to find information. Complete the city facts sheet (page 121) as you find out data about your city.

Curriculum Connections: Arrange for the class to visit your city hall or attend a meeting of your city council. Talk about how the council is the governing branch of a city and the mayor is the executive in charge of decisions. Visit other points of interest in your community such as the courthouse or police station.

Creative Arts: Talk about some of the parks in your area. What features do they have that the students like, such as picnic areas, playground equipment, ponds, etc.? List some of the areas or features that might be included in a park. Give each student a 18" x 24" (46 cm x 61 cm) piece of white construction paper and have them design a dream park.

Tuesday

Theme Activities: Discuss the different terms used in describing locations, such as *city*, *town*, and *village*. These terms denote a difference in size, with *city* being the biggest and *village* being the smallest. Which one do you live in?

Literature Time: Take an unusual look at a city through the eyes of a photographer in *Alphabet City* by Stephen T. Johnson (Viking, 1995). This Caldecott Honor book has photographs of city things which look like letters of the alphabet.

Language Arts: Share some poems about big cities with the class. Try reading "City" by Langston Hughes and "Sing a Song of People" by Lois Lenski which are found in *The Random House Book of Poetry for Children* (Random House, 1983).

Overview: My Community (cont.)

━━━━━━━━━ **Tuesday** (cont.) ━━━━━━━━━

Curriculum Connections: Obtain a map of your neighborhood from your city hall. Put the map on a bulletin board and have each student locate his or her street. Younger children may want to practice saying their addresses. You can put each student's name on a self-adhesive piece of paper and place it on the correct street.

Creative Arts: Make a class photo alphabet book based on today's literature selection. Bring in a camera and have the students look around your school or neighborhood for things that look like the letters of the alphabet.

━━━━━━━━━ **Wednesday** ━━━━━━━━━

Theme Activities: Take out a state map and locate the city or area that the students live in. Talk about the location of the city in your state—is it in the north, south, east, or west? What major cities are located nearby?

Literature Time: Follow a girl and her grandmother as they take a magical trip over New York City in *Abuela* by Arthur Dorros (Dutton, 1991). This book contains some Spanish phrases as the "abuela" or grandmother describes the city.

Language Arts: Make a class book about the community in which you live. A book cover and format are found on pages 123 and 124. Students can write facts about their community and add an illustration with crayon or colored pencils.

Curriculum Connections: Many communities are a wonderful blend of different cultures. Celebrate the city cultures found in today's book by learning the Spanish phrases that Abuela says. Duplicate the Spanish mini-book found on pages 125–127 for each student. Practice reading the words and color the illustrations before students take the books home.

Creative Arts: Besides a big city setting, many students live in a suburban or a rural area. Talk about these communities and compare and contrast them. Divide a bulletin board into three sections and put lettering at the top for city, suburb, and country or farm (use labels that would be appropriate for your area). Have the students draw pictures of what neighborhoods might look like in each community and place the drawings on the board.

━━━━━━━━━ **Thursday** ━━━━━━━━━

Theme Activities: Discuss how cities and towns may be divided into neighborhoods. Talk about the neighborhood around your school and what type of area it is (city block, suburb, rural, etc.).

Literature Time: For a look into the past when people lived in small villages, read *Visiting a Village* by Bobbie Kalman (Crabtree Publishing Co., 1990). This nonfiction book describes the details of daily life in an historic village.

Overview: My Community (cont.)

━━━━━━━━━━━━━━━━━━━━━━━ **Thursday** (cont.) ━━━━━━━━━━━━━━━━━━━━━━━

Language Arts: Give each student the A to Z sheet found on page 128. Have the students work in small groups to try to list things about their city that start with each letter. The ideas can then be compiled into several alphabet class books called Our City: A to Z. One idea would be written about and illustrated on each page.

Curriculum Connections: Each community has many resources that its residents use in their daily lives. Investigate the resources found in your community by having the students look in local newspapers and phone books for agencies and groups that serve your community, such as the Salvation Army, police and fire stations, a community center or YMCA, the Red Cross, etc. Have students write the name of the agency and how it serves the community.

Creative Arts: Cities often have a chamber of commerce or a public relations department to promote them. Offer students the chance to be your city's public relations person for a day. Have them design posters, sayings, contests, etc.—any idea that would promote the good points of your city so that people would want to move there.

━━━━━━━━━━━━━━━━━━━━━━━━━ **Friday** ━━━━━━━━━━━━━━━━━━━━━━━━━

Theme Activities: Discuss the differences between city life and country life. What type of area do you live in? What are the advantages and disadvantages of each place?

Literature Time: Read *Town and Country* by Alice and Martin Provensen (Crown Publishers, Inc., 1984) to take a closer look at life in urban and rural America.

Language Arts: Compare and contrast life in the city and country, using the chart found on page 129. The chart may be done with the whole group or a chart can be duplicated for each student. Encourage students to use what they have learned this week as well as from today's literature selection for facts for the chart.

Curriculum Connections: What features are there in your neighborhood? What kinds of houses and structures are near your school? If at all possible, take a walk in your neighborhood with the class and take photographs of what you can find in your neighborhood. Put the photos in a class book and have the students write a caption for each picture.

Creative Arts: Encourage students to make up a song about your city. Use a familiar tune like "Mary Had a Little Lamb" or "The Muffin Man" and compose verses that tell about your city.

This Week's Theme

My Community

Dear Parents,

We will be exploring the world around us this week as we learn all about our community. Our class will be discussing what a community is and talking about related words such as *city*, *town*, and *village*. Students will gather information about our city and compare modern life with village life of long ago.

During this theme, we will read many books, including *Apt. 3* by Ezra Jack Keats, which tells about life in a big city. To help us to compare city and country life, we will read *Town and Country* by Alice and Martin Provensen. Our class will be using the library to locate other nonfiction books about cities.

Our activities this week focus on social studies but also cross over into other areas of our curriculum. Some of our work this week will include these activities:

1. completing a fact sheet about our city
2. making a comparison chart of city life and country life
3. designing a new park for our city
4. looking at a map of our neighborhood and locating our homes

One of the topics we will discuss this week is that communities have many resources such as the Salvation Army and the police station that help its residents. Please help your child to look in the newspaper and phone book to locate one community resource that is important in your community. The information can be written on the slip below and returned to school by_____.

Thank you for participating in your child's social studies learning.

> Sincerely,
>
> _____

Name _____

One of our community resources is _____.

Please return this homework by _____.

Daily Journal Topics: My Community

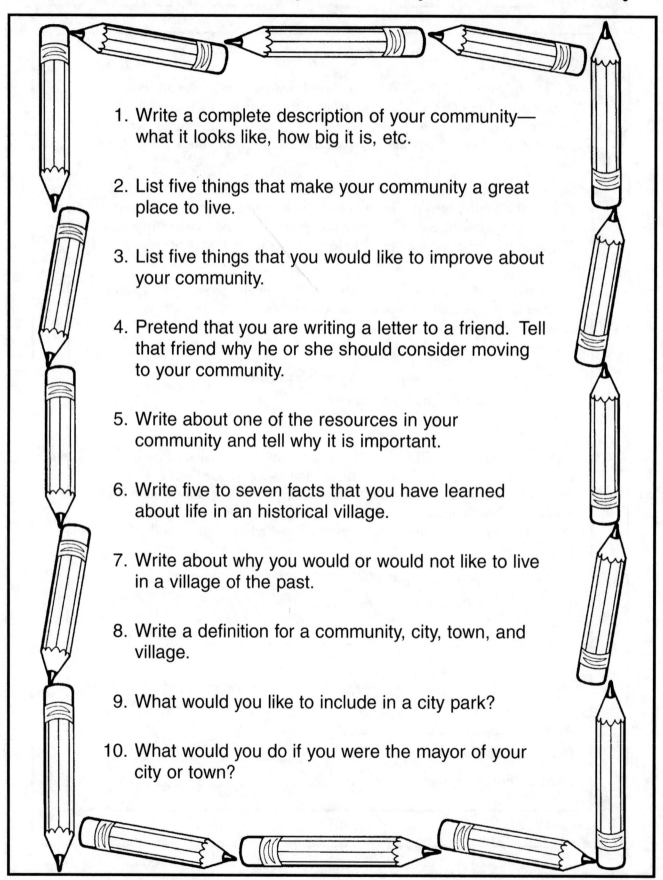

1. Write a complete description of your community—what it looks like, how big it is, etc.

2. List five things that make your community a great place to live.

3. List five things that you would like to improve about your community.

4. Pretend that you are writing a letter to a friend. Tell that friend why he or she should consider moving to your community.

5. Write about one of the resources in your community and tell why it is important.

6. Write five to seven facts that you have learned about life in an historical village.

7. Write about why you would or would not like to live in a village of the past.

8. Write a definition for a community, city, town, and village.

9. What would you like to include in a city park?

10. What would you do if you were the mayor of your city or town?

Name _____ Date _____

City Facts

1. The name of my city or town is _____.

2. It was established in the year _____.

3. The area that includes my city is (circle one): **urban   suburban   rural**.

4. The current population of my city is _____.

5. The mayor of my city is_____.

6. The location of our city hall is _____.

7. Our city motto is _____.

8. Some of our important businesses and industries are _____.

9. Our city has the following (circle all that apply): ***hospital, movie theater***, ***police station***, ***fire station***, ***radio station***, ***post office***.

10. The major city closest to us is _____.

11. Some cities have special yearly events like parades or fairs. In our city we have _____.

12. My favorite place in my city is _____. Draw your favorite place in the space below.

Our Community

Purpose: Children will each create a page for a class book titled Our Community. Each page will feature an interesting fact about the community.

Materials

- Our Community Book Cover (page 123)
- Our Community Book Paper (page 124)
- pencils, markers, crayons
- information gathered about the community from the city council, city hall, and other sources

Preparation: Reproduce the lined paper for the children to write on. You will need one page for each student (additional pages if you plan on doing a first draft and a final copy). Reproduce one front cover for the class book and color with markers. Mount the cover on a piece of tagboard and cut a back cover in the same shape. Laminate the covers for durability.

Instructions: Each student will write an interesting fact about the community on the lined paper. An illustration is then added in the space below the lines.

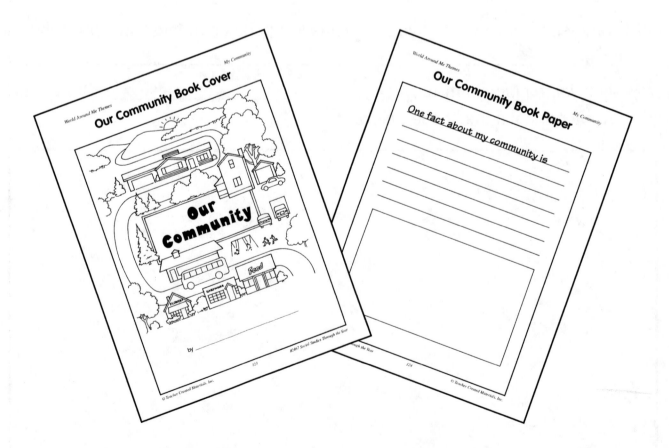

Our Community Book Cover

by _____

Our Community Book Paper

<u>One fact about my community is</u>

_____

_____

_____

_____

_____

Spanish Word Book

Duplicate the word book. Cut on the lines, assemble the pages in order, and staple.

Mi Libro de Palabras de la Ciudad

(*My Book of City Words*)

Mi nombre es (*My name is*)

_____

1. mi abuela (*my grandmother*)

2. el parque (*the park*)

3. el autobús (*the bus*)

Spanish Word Book *(cont.)*

4. la bandada de pájaros (*the flock of birds*)

5. el taxi (*the taxicab*)

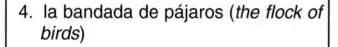

6. la calle (*the street*)

7. los carros (*the cars*)

Spanish Word Book *(cont.)*

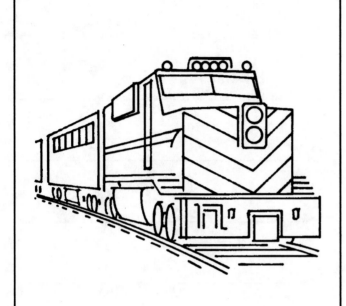

8. el tren (*the train*)

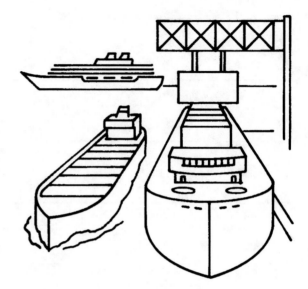

9. los barcos (*the ships*)

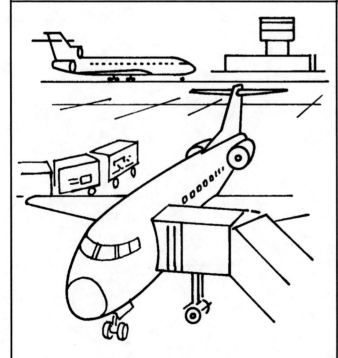

10. el aeropuerto (*the airport*)

11. la tienda (*the store*)

Our City: A to Z

Directions are provided on page 117.

A _____   N _____

B _____   O _____

C _____   P _____

D _____   Q _____

E _____   R _____

F _____   S _____

G _____   T _____

H _____   U _____

I _____   V _____

J _____   W _____

K _____   X _____

L _____   Y _____

M _____   Z _____

City vs. Country

Directions: Use this chart to compare a city (suburban or urban) with a country (rural) area.

Country	City

California Washington Arizona

Weekly Theme: My State   Week _____

	Monday	Tuesday	Wednesday	Thursday	Friday
Date					
Theme Activities	Where do we live? Identify our city and state.	What do we know about our state? Use a K-W-L list.	Display and discuss our state flag.	Our state and region: Discuss and locate state landmarks.	Learn about our state government.
Literature Time	Read from *Wish You Were Here—Emily's Guide to the 50 States* by Kathleen Krull.	Read from *Wish You Were Here—Emily's Guide to the 50 States* by Kathleen Krull.	Read from *Wish You Were Here—Emily's Guide to the 50 States* by Kathleen Krull.	Read from *Fabulous Facts About the 50 States* by Wilma S. Ross.	Read from *Fabulous Facts About the 50 States* by Wilma S. Ross.
Language Arts	Write a letter to the tourism board.	Assemble a book of facts about our state.	Create a postcard: Wish you were here in our state.	Compose and post trivia questions of the day.	Arrange a trip to the state capital.
Curriculum Connections	Create state outlines using *ClarisWorks*.	Create a travel brochure.	Find out about early settlers in our state.	Create a "stately" slide show.	Make a class book of state capitals.
Creative Arts	Set up an information booth.	Write a travel review: Visiting Favorite Places.	Create a mural representing our state.	Make state trading cards.	Design a new state flag and motto.

Overview: My State

Monday

Theme Activities: Ask students to name their city and state. Locate the city on a state map and locate your school. Find your state on a United States map. Younger children tend to confuse city, state, and country, so be sure to talk about this topic many times throughout the week. Show older students envelopes with addresses, noting the city, state, zip code, and what the state abbreviation is.

Literature Time: For the first three days of the theme, read to the class from *Wish You Were Here—Emily's Guide to the 50 States* by Kathleen Krull. Emily takes a cross-country trip with her aunt, and there are pages for each state with information about landmarks and other characteristics. Find your state on Emily's map and read that section of the book.

Language Arts: The appendix of *Wish You Were Here* lists addresses for each state's board of travel and tourism. Have students compose a friendly letter to the board, requesting information and brochures about your state. To extend this activity, each student may choose a different state to research.

Curriculum Connections: Create state maps on a computer, using the draw or paint programs in *ClarisWorks*. Outlines of a United States map as well as outlines of individual states can be found under "file" in the "library" section. Go to the library section and click on USA maps. Students can then add text and details to their maps. Or you may use a U.S. map to enlarge the shape of the state needed.

Creative Arts: Using information gathered from reference books, the board of tourism, and brochures or magazines from travel agencies, plan an "information booth" for your state. Ask students to bring in any information that they have about your state, including photographs, newspaper articles, maps, and souvenirs from trips around the state.

Tuesday

Theme Activities: To assess the students' knowledge about your state, do a **K-W-L** exercise. List "what you **K**now" about your state on a large piece of tagboard or chart paper. Then ask the students "what they **W**ant to know about their state," listing any questions they have. Finally, start a list of "what we've **L**earned" for facts already gathered.

Literature Time: Look up some facts about your state on the chart in *Wish You Were Here*. The state bird, flower, tree, and nicknames are all listed.

Language Arts: Create a book of facts about your state, listing basic information gathered from your reading. A format for a mini-book is found on pages 137–140. Provide students with pictures so that they will be able to draw accurate illustrations for the bird, flower, etc.

Overview: My State *(cont.)*

═══════════════════════ **Tuesday** *(cont.)* ═══════════════════════

Curriculum Connections: Advertise your state with a class travel brochure. This brochure can be created by using a drawing program such as *Kid Pix Studio*. Complete directions for a tri-fold brochure can be found in *Kid Pix for Terrified Teachers* (Grades 3–5) by Marsha Lifter and Marian E. Adams (see the sample on page 382).

Creative Arts: If students have visited landmarks or traveled around the state, have them write reviews of their trips. Read or show travel reviews from newspapers and travel books to help them. If they have not traveled much, have them write about a destination they would like to visit.

═══════════════════════ **Wednesday** ═══════════════════════

Theme Activities: Bring in your state flag. Talk about the colors and the significance of the pictures and words found on it. Display the flag with your state information booth.

Literature Time: Read about states which are neighbors to yours. Compare and contrast your state with one nearby.

Language Arts: Bring in postcards from various places in your state. Ask students to examine the postcards—the illustrations or photographs, captions on the fronts and backs, and information written on the backs of the postcards. Have the students create postcards for one of your state's landmarks. Students may then write on them and send the postcards to their families, telling them what they have been learning during this social studies theme. A postcard format appears page 379.

Curriculum Connections: Research the history of your state, including the year it was founded, the order in which it joined the United States, and how it got its name. Use the *Wish You Were Here* book as one reference. Find out about the early settlers and explorers of your state, including Native American tribes that may have lived there.

Creative Arts: Make a large mural representing your state. Have students work in small groups so each may contribute to a part of the mural. Be creative and use a variety of materials, including some of these items: a computer-generated banner for the title, photographs and travel brochures, souvenirs from state landmarks, student drawings and paintings, a branch from your state tree, pictures of your state flower and bird, etc. Encourage your students to think of as many different items as they can.

═══════════════════════ **Thursday** ═══════════════════════

Theme Activities: Discuss prominent landmarks or historical attractions your state has, such as the Mackinac Bridge in Michigan or Mount Rushmore in South Dakota. Find landmarks on your state map. Discuss the region of the U.S. your state is located in (Midwest, South, Southwest, etc.).

Overview: My State (cont.)

=== **Thursday** (cont.) ===

Literature Time: Read the section about your state from *Fabulous Facts About the 50 States* by Wilma S. Ross (Scholastic, 1997). This book contains maps and information about state population, products, and points of interest.

Language Arts: To review information about your state, make up some state trivia-of-the-day questions. Post one every day for students to try to answer. Continue these questions after the theme is complete to enhance students' retention of the material covered.

Curriculum Connections: At the end of this theme, students could use *ClarisWorks* or *Kid Pix Studio* to create a computer slide show about their state. Both slide shows are extremely easy to use and directions are included with both of these programs. Complete directions for a *Kid Pix Studio* slide show can be found in the *Kid Pix for Terrified Teachers* reference mentioned earlier in this theme section.

Creative Arts: Children love to collect and swap trading cards. Make some trading cards for your state and other states, using the card format found on page 141.

=== **Friday** ===

Theme Activities: Learn about your state's government. Discuss where the state capital is located and who your governor is. Talk about the branches of your state government—legislative, executive, and judicial.

Literature Time: In *Fabulous Facts About the 50 States,* read about the states in your region. Compare the products of the other states to those of your own state. Are they the same or different?

Language Arts: If possible, arrange a trip for your students to tour the state capitol. Be sure to allow sufficient time for a complete tour, and have your students formulate some questions prior to the trip.

Curriculum Connections: Study a map that has the state capitals listed. Encourage the students to learn the capitals of as many states as possible. Make a class book of state capitals, having each student write about and illustrate one or two.

Creative Arts: Earlier in the week, students studied their state flag and motto. Ask students what kind of flag they would design for their state and what motto or saying they think best represents their state. Using the flag outline found on page 142, have students create and draw their flag, using crayons, markers, or colored pencils. They can then add their new state motto at the bottom of the page.

California   Washington   Arizona

Colorado

Nebraska

TEXAS

Georgia

This Week's Theme

My State:

_____

Wisconsin

Mississippi

New York   Connecticut   ALASKA

California　　Washington　　Arizona

Colorado

Nebraska

Dear Parents,

During our new social studies theme, we will be learning all about our state. Some of the basic information we will research will include our state motto, state flag, state bird, and state flower. We will find out about important landmarks in our state and the types of products our state is known for. We will improve our map skills as we study state and United States maps and learn about the region of the country that we live in.

Good learning involves making connections with other subject areas. Some of our activities will involve reading, writing, map skills, research skills, and technology. During this week, the students will participate in the following activities:

1. creating a travel brochure about great places in our state
2. learning about the history of our state and its early settlers
3. writing a letter to the tourism board for information about our state
4. making a book of facts about our state

One of the main nonfiction books we will be using to learn about our state is *Wish You Were Here—Emily's Guide to the 50 States* by Kathleen Krull. This book contains a wealth of information about all the states as Emily travels across the country.

We would like to set up an information booth about our state. If you have any items that will help us to learn about our state, we would like to have you send the items in this week. Some possibilities are these:

• souvenirs from trips around our state
• photographs, especially of our state's landmarks or travel destinations
• travel brochures or books about our state

Please take a few minutes each day to discuss what your child is learning during this theme and to read our state fact book when it comes home. Thanks so much for your continued help and support.

Sincerely,

_____

TEXAS

Georgia

Wisconsin

Mississippi

New York　　Connecticut　　ALASKA

Daily Journal Topics: My State

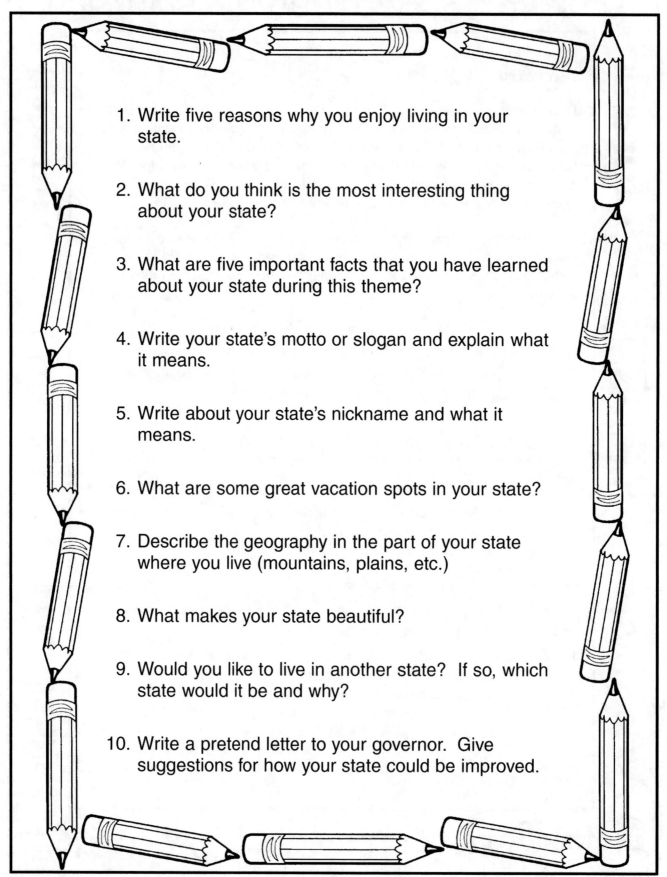

1. Write five reasons why you enjoy living in your state.

2. What do you think is the most interesting thing about your state?

3. What are five important facts that you have learned about your state during this theme?

4. Write your state's motto or slogan and explain what it means.

5. Write about your state's nickname and what it means.

6. What are some great vacation spots in your state?

7. Describe the geography in the part of your state where you live (mountains, plains, etc.)

8. What makes your state beautiful?

9. Would you like to live in another state? If so, which state would it be and why?

10. Write a pretend letter to your governor. Give suggestions for how your state could be improved.

State Facts Book

My Book of State Facts

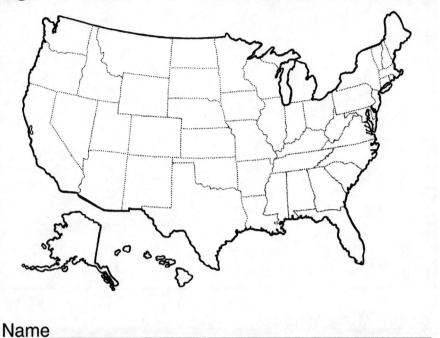

Name_____

Draw an outline of your state. Mark the location of the capital city.

1. I live in the state of _____.

   The capital city is _____.

State Facts Book *(cont.)*

Draw your state flag.

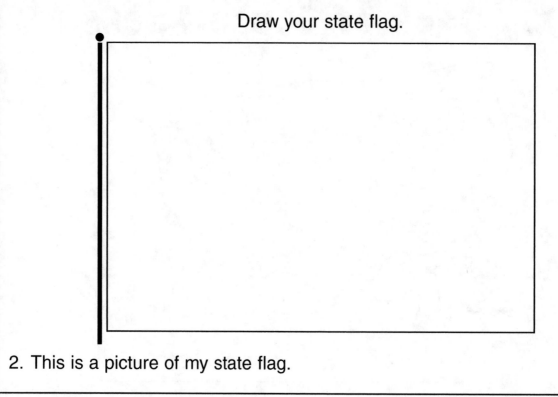

2. This is a picture of my state flag.

Draw your state flower.

3. My state flower is _____.

State Facts Book *(cont.)*

Draw your state bird.

4. My state bird is _____.

Draw your state tree.

5. My state tree is _____.

State Facts Book *(cont.)*

Write your motto on the banner. Decorate the banner to match the motto.

6. My state motto is _____.

Draw an illustration to go with your sentence.

7. My favorite thing about my state is _____.

Great State Trading Cards

Create a trading card featuring important facts about your state. You might also want to try designing cards for other states. Trade them with your classmates! When you have completed both sides, glue the card together.

state snapshot

Here is a picture of _____

_____ which is a landmark of this state.

State Statistics

State Capital: _____

Year Established: _____

State Tree: _____

State Flower: _____

State Bird: _____

back of card

The Great State of

_____
(name of state)

State Motto: _____

_____

_____

_____

front of card

Design a State Flag

Study your state's flag. Design a new flag that will promote the best features of your state. Write a new slogan or state motto that would make tourists want to come and visit your state.

My new state motto: _____

_____

_____

_____

_____

_____

Weekly Theme: Maps and Globes   Week _____

	Monday	Tuesday	Wednesday	Thursday	Friday
Date					
Theme Activities	What is a map? What do we use it for?	Learn about using a globe.	Learn about using an atlas.	Compare different types of maps.	Learn how to use a map key.
Literature Time	Read from *Maps and Globes* by Ray Broekel.	Read *Me on the Map* by Joan Sweeney.	Read *Atlas of Countries* by Gallimard Jeunesse.	Read *Letters from Felix: A Little Rabbit on a World Tour* by Annette Langen and Constanza Droop.	Read *Mouse Views—What the Class Pet Saw* by Bruce McMillan.
Language Arts	Learn about maps and globes—a nonfiction book.	Where in the world am I? Write an innovation.	Review vocabulary words for maps and globes.	Write "Dear Felix" letters to a world traveler.	Pose some travel riddles.
Curriculum Connections	Set up a travel writing center.	Explore *Where in the World Is Carmen Sandiego?*	Complete the atlas research sheet.	Learn about miles and kilometers.	Practice map skills.
Creative Arts	Play the travel alphabet game.	Make a bulletin board of "suitcase students."	Create a photo album.	Design and create a mural of Felix's travels.	Draw a classroom map.

Overview: Maps and Globes

Monday

Theme Activities: Start this week's theme by asking students to define a *map*. The definition should suggest that a map is a drawing or a picture representation of a place. Discuss the fact that maps help us find certain locations and have special features such as a map key to help us use them.

Literature Time: Today's nonfiction selection, *Maps and Globes* by Ray Broekel (Children's Press, 1983), contains a wealth of information about different types of maps and how to use them. The book can be read in its entirety, but you may want to review certain sections throughout the week.

Language Arts: Make a mini-book with some basic facts about maps and globes. Duplicate a copy of the book found on pages 150–153 for each student. Read and discuss the information in the book and then have students take it home to share with their families.

Curriculum Connections: Travelers often write to friends, telling about their experiences. Set up a writing center in your classroom so that students can practice this type of writing. Include a variety of materials such as postcards, stationery, and cards. Encourage students to pretend that they are writing from a travel destination of their choice. They can write to a friend, telling all about their travels.

Creative Arts: Play a traditional game to practice the names of cities and countries. In the travel alphabet game, the first player makes up a sentence using a place that starts with letter Aa. For example, *A: My name is Angelica, and my husband's name is Alex. We come from Alaska and we sell apples*. The next player does letter Bb and so on.

Tuesday

Theme Activities: Today's topic is learning about globes. Discuss the definition of a globe and how it is different from a map. You can find an excellent description of globes on page 42 in Monday's literature selection.

Literature Time: Read *Me on the Map* by Joan Sweeney (Crown Publishers, Inc., 1996) for a personal view of maps as the girl in the book finds her special street address, city, state, country, continent, and planet.

Language Arts: Students can write about themselves as they write an innovation on today's literature selection. Include house address—city, state, country, continent, and planet.

Curriculum Connections: One of the best educational series about geography for children is *Where in the World Is Carmen Sandiego?*, seen on public broadcasting television. Also available for classroom use is the board game *Where in the U.S.A. Is Carmen Sandiego?* (University Games Corporation, 1993) which focuses on learning about U.S. landmarks and capitals. A software version is available from Broderbund Software Inc.

Overview: Maps and Globes *(cont.)*

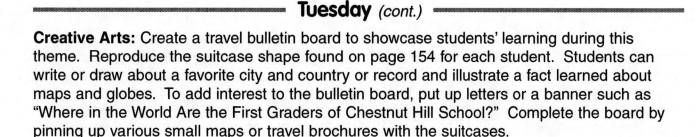

═══════════════════ **Tuesday** *(cont.)* ═══════════════════

Creative Arts: Create a travel bulletin board to showcase students' learning during this theme. Reproduce the suitcase shape found on page 154 for each student. Students can write or draw about a favorite city and country or record and illustrate a fact learned about maps and globes. To add interest to the bulletin board, put up letters or a banner such as "Where in the World Are the First Graders of Chestnut Hill School?" Complete the board by pinning up various small maps or travel brochures with the suitcases.

═══════════════════ **Wednesday** ═══════════════════

Theme Activities: Today's map topic is all about atlases. An atlas is a collection or book of maps. The name "atlas" is taken from a Greek legend (see *Maps and Globes* by Ray Broekel for more information on this story). Show the class several different kinds of atlases (see bibliography).

Literature Time: Read the *Atlas of Countries* by Gallimard Jeunesse (Scholastic, 1994). This book contains data about all continents, including how they may have been formed.

Language Arts: The study of maps and globes includes many vocabulary words which may be unfamiliar to students. As new words and definitions are used, write the words on cards and post them on a bulletin board or wall. Review a few words daily as you work on this theme.

Curriculum Connections: Make available a number of atlases for the students to practice map research skills. For this activity, you will need an atlas which includes picture representations of each country's products and features. Students choose a country to find information about, using the atlas research sheet provided on page 155.

Creative Arts: Have students choose a country that is of interest to them. They can use the library or media center to locate books or information about the country. Once the information is gathered, they can then create a page for a "photo album" to describe what it is like to travel to that country. A photo album format can be found on page 156.

═══════════════════ **Thursday** ═══════════════════

Theme Activities: Bring in many different kinds of maps to discuss, compare, and contrast. Types of maps to include are neighborhood, city, state, country, continent, and world. Take a look at a map of the moon's surface too!

Literature Time: Read about the many travels of a rabbit in *Letters from Felix: A Little Rabbit on a World Tour* by Annette Langen and Constanza Droop (Abbeville Press, 1994). A unique feature of this book is that it contains real letters and envelopes plus travel stickers for Felix's suitcase. (At some specialty bookstores, you can also find a stuffed rabbit like the character in the book.)

Overview: Maps and Globes *(cont.)*

═══════ Thursday *(cont.)* ═══════

Language Arts: After reading today's literature selection, ask the class to respond to Felix's letters. Talk about correct letter form, including the parts of a letter (greeting, body, closing, and signature). Find the places that Felix is visiting and trace his route on a world map.

Curriculum Connections: Using the scales of miles or kilometers on maps is an important skill. Bring in multiple copies of your state map and have the students practice with a partner. Ask them to figure out how far it would be to travel from your city to other cities in your state. To include more math, have them figure out how long it takes to travel to the destination at a certain rate of speed such as 60 miles (or 100 kilometers) per hour.

Creative Arts: Make a mural of Felix's travels and show the famous landmarks and locations he visits. Use a large sheet of blue paper for the background and add outlines of the countries. Other pictures can be drawn or made with construction paper and added to the mural. Don't forget to include a picture of Felix with his suitcase!

═══════ Friday ═══════

Theme Activities: Spend some time discussing the use and importance of map keys. Display pictures of some common map key pictures, such as a plane to represent an airport or a tree to represent a state park. Discuss the meanings of the pictures and locate some of these symbols on your state map.

Literature Time: Today's book selection is *Mouse Views—What the Class Pet Saw* by Bruce McMillan (Holiday House, Inc., 1993). This book has closeup photography of common classroom objects as seen by the escaped class pet. The book contains a classroom map which provides a nice bridge to the creative arts activity for today (see below).

Language Arts: Practice geography skills with some daily travel riddles. Pose questions about familiar places in your state or country.

Some examples might be these:

1. Where is the Statue of Liberty located?
2. What is the capital of Michigan?
3. Name the continent that France is located in.
4. Name the southernmost continent.

Tailor questions to your social studies curriculum.

Curriculum Connections: During this theme, students have been learning many different map skills. Have them practice map skills using the map provided on page 157.

Creative Arts: Students can work in pairs to create a classroom map similar to the one found in the book *Mouse Views.* Have students look at a map of your school building if one is available.

This Week's Theme

Maps and Globes

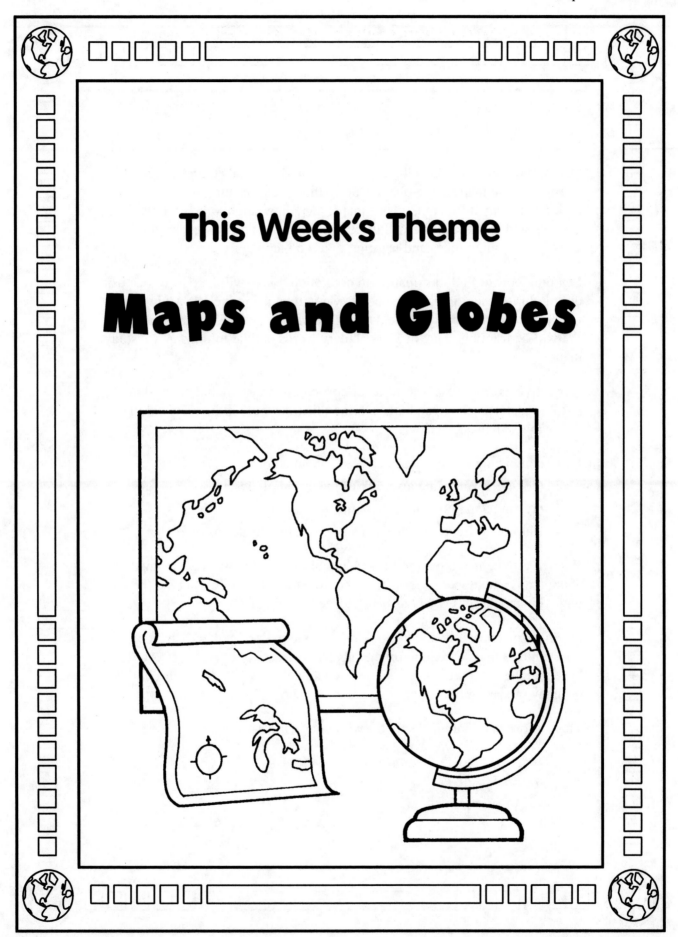

Dear Parents,

One of the important skills that we work on in our social studies program is learning to use maps and globes. During this week, the children will be looking at many different kinds of maps, including neighborhood, city, state, country, and continent. We will discuss how globes and atlases are used, and we will be reading maps and learning to use a map key.

Learning how to find information in nonfiction books will be part of our work during this theme. Some of the books we will be using include *Maps and Globes* by Ray Broekel and the *Atlas of Countries* by Gallimard Jeunesse. We will be learning many new vocabulary words and definitions as we study maps.

Our activities will cross over to other curriculum areas, including reading, writing, math, research, and art. During this time we will be involved in the following activities:

1. completing an atlas research sheet about a country
2. looking at and using a variety of maps and globes
3. drawing a map of our classroom
4. learning to figure out distances between two locations on a map

We will also be making a mini-book summarizing what we have learned about maps and globes. Please take the time to have your child read the book with you and discuss what has been learned at school.

For more practice at home, try looking at some maps together. Challenge your child to find something on the map, such as a city or river. If you don't have a globe or an atlas at home, they would be great gifts for your child on a birthday or special occasion.

Thanks for your continued support with your child's learning.

Sincerely,

_____

Daily Journal Topics: Maps and Globes

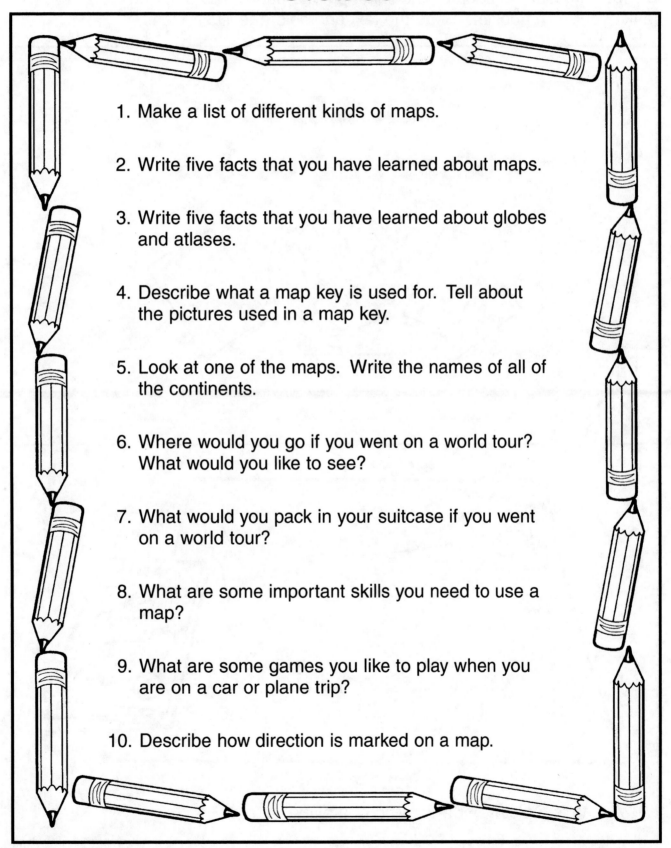

1. Make a list of different kinds of maps.

2. Write five facts that you have learned about maps.

3. Write five facts that you have learned about globes and atlases.

4. Describe what a map key is used for. Tell about the pictures used in a map key.

5. Look at one of the maps. Write the names of all of the continents.

6. Where would you go if you went on a world tour? What would you like to see?

7. What would you pack in your suitcase if you went on a world tour?

8. What are some important skills you need to use a map?

9. What are some games you like to play when you are on a car or plane trip?

10. Describe how direction is marked on a map.

Maps and Globes Book

Directions: Cut the book on the lines, put the pages in order, and staple to make your own booklet. Read the text and color the illustrations.

All About
Maps and Globes

Name _____

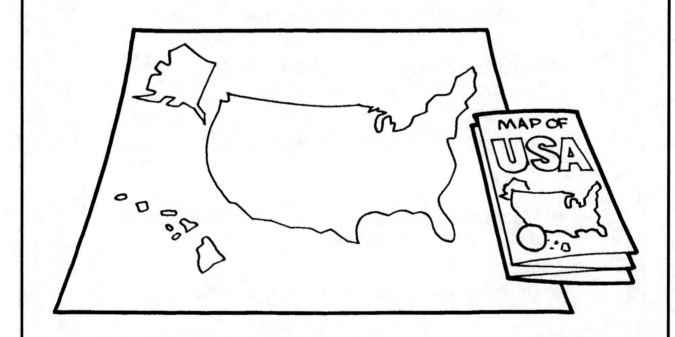

1. A map is a picture or a drawing of a place.

Maps and Globes Book *(cont.)*

2. There are many different kinds of maps. Outline maps mark boundaries of an area. Physical or topographic maps help us to see land and water forms.

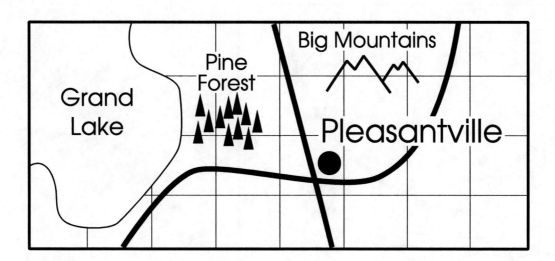

3. A map shows many features of land, such as roads, bodies of water, and mountains.

Maps and Globes Book *(cont.)*

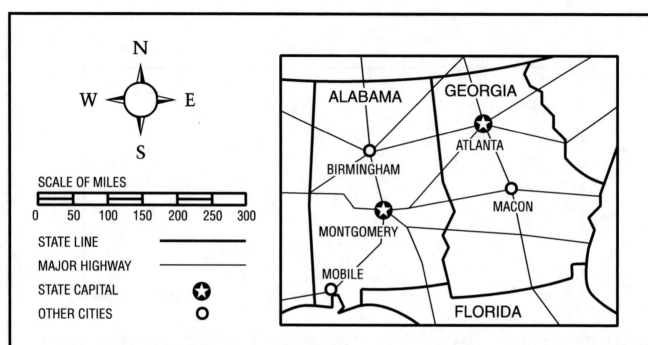

4. A map key explains what the pictures or symbols on a map stand for. A map scale helps us to figure out the distances on the map.

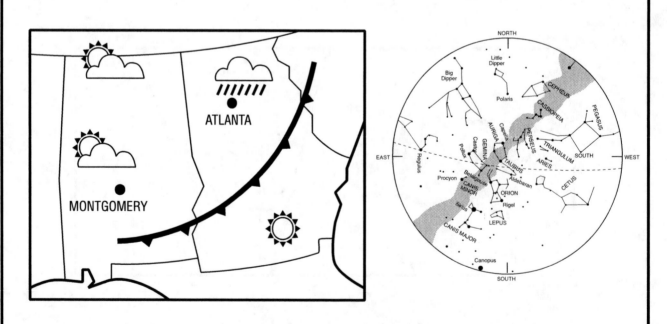

5. There are weather maps that we can see on daily news programs. There are even moon maps and maps of the sky called star charts.

Maps and Globes Book *(cont.)*

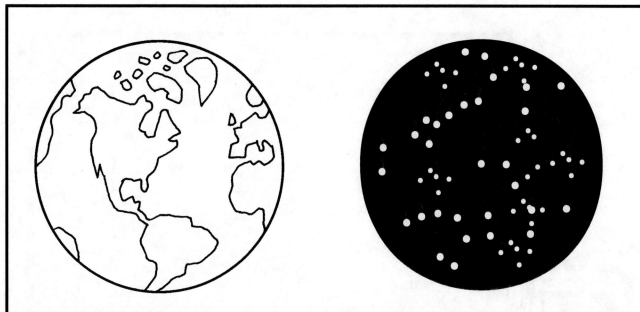

6. A special representation, or three-dimensional model, of our Earth is called
   a globe. Another type of globe is the celestial globe, which shows the
   position of the stars, moon, and planets.

7. Maps and globes are useful tools that help us to find locations. How have
   maps and globes helped you?

Suitcase Shape

See directions for use on page 145.

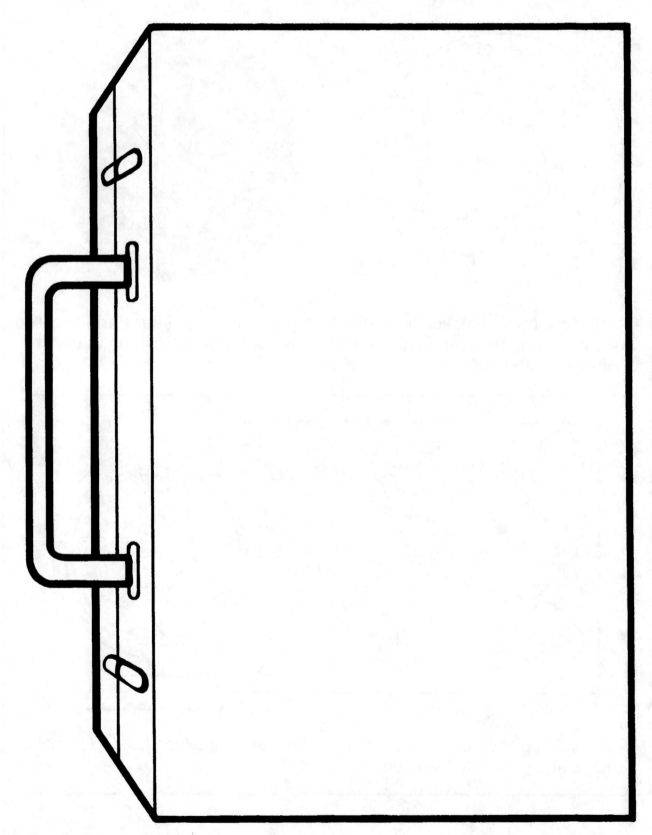

World Traveler

Using an Atlas

I used the world atlas today.

I found the country of_____.

It is in the continent of _____.

I found out that this country has . . .   (draw a picture and write about what
you saw on the map).

I would like to travel to this country because _____

_____

_____

_____.

Photo Album Page

Use with the Creative Arts Activity found on page 145.

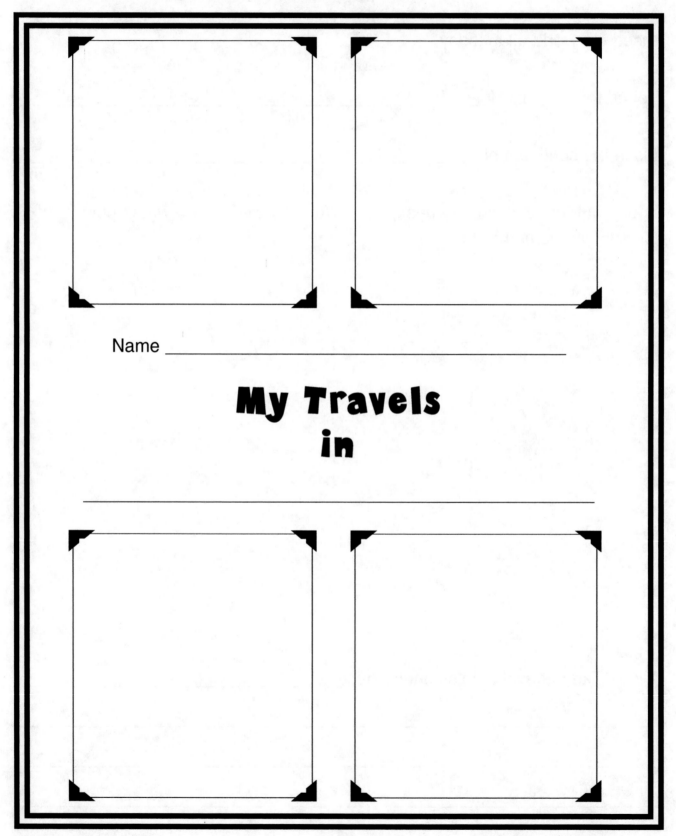

Name _____

My Travels in

_____

Name _____   Date _____

Practicing Map Skills

Pretend that you are going on a field trip from the school. Use the map of the area to answer the questions.

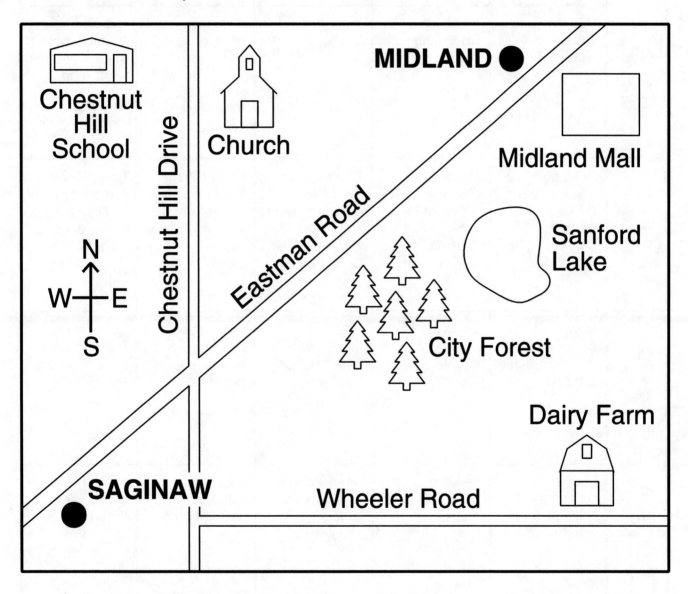

1. The dairy farm is located on _____ Road.

2. The church is N S E W (circle one) of the school.

3. Sanford Lake is N S E W (circle one) of the mall.

4. _____ Road runs between Saginaw and Midland.

5. The road which travels in a north/south direction is _____.

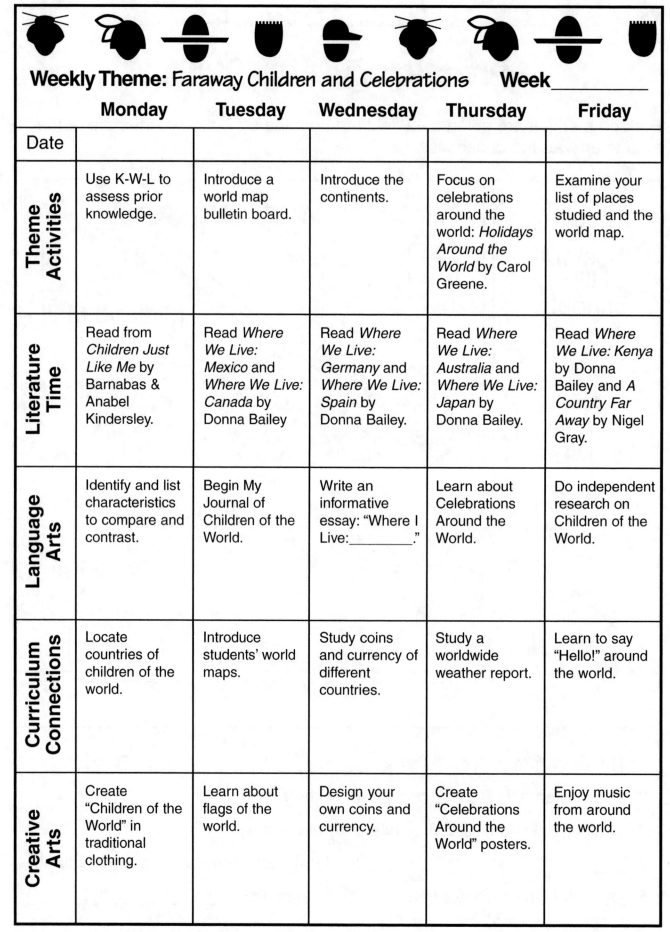

Weekly Theme: Faraway Children and Celebrations   **Week**_____

	Monday	**Tuesday**	**Wednesday**	**Thursday**	**Friday**
Date					
Theme Activities	Use K-W-L to assess prior knowledge.	Introduce a world map bulletin board.	Introduce the continents.	Focus on celebrations around the world: *Holidays Around the World* by Carol Greene.	Examine your list of places studied and the world map.
Literature Time	Read from *Children Just Like Me* by Barnabas & Anabel Kindersley.	Read *Where We Live: Mexico* and *Where We Live: Canada* by Donna Bailey	Read *Where We Live: Germany* and *Where We Live: Spain* by Donna Bailey.	Read *Where We Live: Australia* and *Where We Live: Japan* by Donna Bailey.	Read *Where We Live: Kenya* by Donna Bailey and *A Country Far Away* by Nigel Gray.
Language Arts	Identify and list characteristics to compare and contrast.	Begin My Journal of Children of the World.	Write an informative essay: "Where I Live:_____."	Learn about Celebrations Around the World.	Do independent research on Children of the World.
Curriculum Connections	Locate countries of children of the world.	Introduce students' world maps.	Study coins and currency of different countries.	Study a worldwide weather report.	Learn to say "Hello!" around the world.
Creative Arts	Create "Children of the World" in traditional clothing.	Learn about flags of the world.	Design your own coins and currency.	Create "Celebrations Around the World" posters.	Enjoy music from around the world.

Overview: Faraway Children and Celebrations

Monday

Theme Activities: Do a **K-W-L** (What we already **K**now—What we **W**ant to learn—What we have **L**earned) with your class to assess students' prior knowledge about children and holidays around the world. You might want to organize the information in two lists, one list including what students already know about children and the other list including what students already know about holidays around the world.

Literature Time: Read selected excerpts from *Children Just Like Me* by Barnabas and Anabel Kindersley (Dorling Kindersley, 1995), a lengthy but valuable resource for information about children around the world. (You may choose to read a few excerpts each day during this unit.)

Language Arts: Have your students identify ways that children around the world may be compared. (You may want to identify these characteristics yourself with categories such as *country, food, clothing, shelter, language, holidays,* and *climate.*) Organize and record the information your students learn on a chart that lists the name of each country and the categories you plan to compare and contrast.

Curriculum Connections: Use a globe to locate the countries where the children you read about live.

Creative Arts: Students may make their own "Children of the World" wearing traditional clothing. Refer to the photographs in *Children Just Like Me* and other related materials to keep the clothing authentic looking.

Tuesday

Theme Activities: Post a world map to use in locating the countries where the children you read about live. You might want to label each country with its name so that you will be able to locate it easily throughout the unit. Discuss how the location of each country affects its climate.

Literature Time: Read two informational books today about the closest neighbors to the United States—*Where We Live: Mexico* and *Where We Live: Canada*, both by Donna Bailey (Steck-Vaughn, 1992). (Add the information you learn to the comparison chart and identify the locations of these countries on your world map.)

Language Arts: Use the format on pages 165 and 166 to begin My Journal of Children of the World. Write about how people live in each of the countries.

Curriculum Connections: Reproduce the world map found on page 378 for each of your students. Students will locate and label each country about which you read. These maps will become a part of each individual student's Journal of Children of the World.

Overview: Faraway Children and Celebrations *(cont.)*

═══════════════════════ **Tuesday** *(cont.)* ═══════════════════════

Creative Arts: Students will use reference materials to learn about flags of the world. (*My First Atlas* by Bill Boyle (Dorling Kindersley, 1994) is an excellent source for this material.) Individual students will use tempera paints to paint the flag of a different country on 12" x 18" (30 cm x 46 cm) white construction paper. Attach a strip of 2" x 18" (5 cm x 46 cm) black tagboard at the left-hand side for a flagpole. Display these in your classroom or hallway during your unit.

═══════════════════════ **Wednesday** ═══════════════════════

Theme Activities: Introduce the concept of "continent" to your students. Use the world map or globe to show students where the seven continents are located.

Literature Time: Read *Where We Live: Germany* and *Where We Live: Spain*, both by Donna Bailey (Steck-Vaughn, 1992). Add the information you learn to the comparison chart, and identify locations of the countries on your world map. Students will also add the information to their Journal of Children of the World books and maps.

Language Arts: Reproduce the sentence frame on page 167 for students to use in writing their own informative essay, "Where I Live:_____" (inserting the title of your home country in the blank) to tell about their own countries.

Curriculum Connections: Learn about the currency and coins of different countries. Ask students to bring in samples of money from other countries for examination or visit a local bank to learn more about foreign currency.

Creative Arts: Use the basic shape patterns found on page 168 to create your own currency and coins.

═══════════════════════ **Thursday** ═══════════════════════

Theme Activities: Focus on celebrations held around the world. You might read *Holidays Around the World* by Carol Greene (Childrens Press, 1982) to your class to provide them with a broad overview of the world's holidays.

Literature Time: Read *Where We Live: Australia* and *Where We Live: Japan,* both by Donna Bailey (Steck-Vaughn, 1992). Add the information you learn to the comparison chart and identify locations of these countries on your world map. Students will also add the information to their Journal of Children of the World books and maps.

Language Arts: Reproduce pages 169–172 for your students to read and learn about Celebrations Around the World.

Overview: Faraway Children and Celebrations (cont.)

Thursday (cont.)

Curriculum Connections: Watch the Weather Channel or check the Internet (http://groundhog.sprl.umich.edu/) to see what the weather is like today in different locations around the world. Decide if the weather is suitable for an outdoor celebration today in each of the countries you check.

Creative Arts: Students may use watercolor markers to create posters of "Celebrations Around the World." Share these with classmates and then display them in your classroom.

Friday

Theme Activities: Examine your list of countries studied and your world map. Group the countries according to the continent where they are located. Are all continents represented? If not, try to learn about those.

Literature Time: Read *Where We Live: Kenya* by Donna Bailey (Steck-Vaughn, 1992) and *A Country Far Away* by Nigel Gray (Orchard Books, 1988). Add the information you learn to the comparison chart and identify the locations of these countries on your world map. Students will also add the information to their Journal of Children of the World.

Language Arts: Students will use resource materials to read independently about children around the world. Design a page for each student to use in recording the information. Use the pages for a class book or display in your classroom.

Curriculum Connections: Use the chart below to teach students to say "Hello!" in a variety of different languages.

Hola . . . Spanish   *Shalom* . . . Yiddish

Guten Tag . . . German   *Zdrasdvitche* . . . Russian

Bon Jour . . . French   *Nin Hau* . . . Chinese

Buon Giorno . . . Italian   *Ghja Sas* . . . Greek

Aloha . . . Hawaiian   *Hujambo* . . . Swahili

Namaste . . . Hindi   *Assalamoo Ahlaykum* . . . Arabic

Koneechewa . . . Japanese

Creative Arts: Sing "It's a Small World" by Richard M. Sherman and Robert B. Sherman from the *New Illustrated Disney Songbook* (Harry N. Abrams, Inc. 1986). Enjoy music from around the world, such as the folk songs and dances in *The Magic of Music* (Cherry Lane Music Company, 1998).

This Week's Theme

Faraway Children and Celebrations

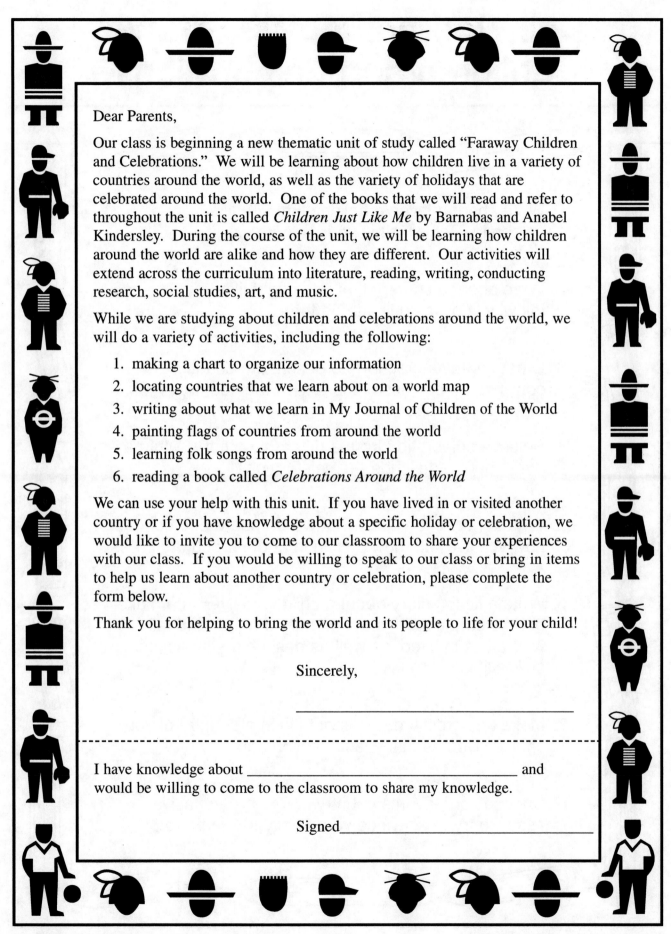

Dear Parents,

Our class is beginning a new thematic unit of study called "Faraway Children and Celebrations." We will be learning about how children live in a variety of countries around the world, as well as the variety of holidays that are celebrated around the world. One of the books that we will read and refer to throughout the unit is called *Children Just Like Me* by Barnabas and Anabel Kindersley. During the course of the unit, we will be learning how children around the world are alike and how they are different. Our activities will extend across the curriculum into literature, reading, writing, conducting research, social studies, art, and music.

While we are studying about children and celebrations around the world, we will do a variety of activities, including the following:

1. making a chart to organize our information
2. locating countries that we learn about on a world map
3. writing about what we learn in My Journal of Children of the World
4. painting flags of countries from around the world
5. learning folk songs from around the world
6. reading a book called *Celebrations Around the World*

We can use your help with this unit. If you have lived in or visited another country or if you have knowledge about a specific holiday or celebration, we would like to invite you to come to our classroom to share your experiences with our class. If you would be willing to speak to our class or bring in items to help us learn about another country or celebration, please complete the form below.

Thank you for helping to bring the world and its people to life for your child!

Sincerely,

_____

- -

I have knowledge about _____ and would be willing to come to the classroom to share my knowledge.

Signed_____

Daily Journal Topics: Faraway Children and Celebrations

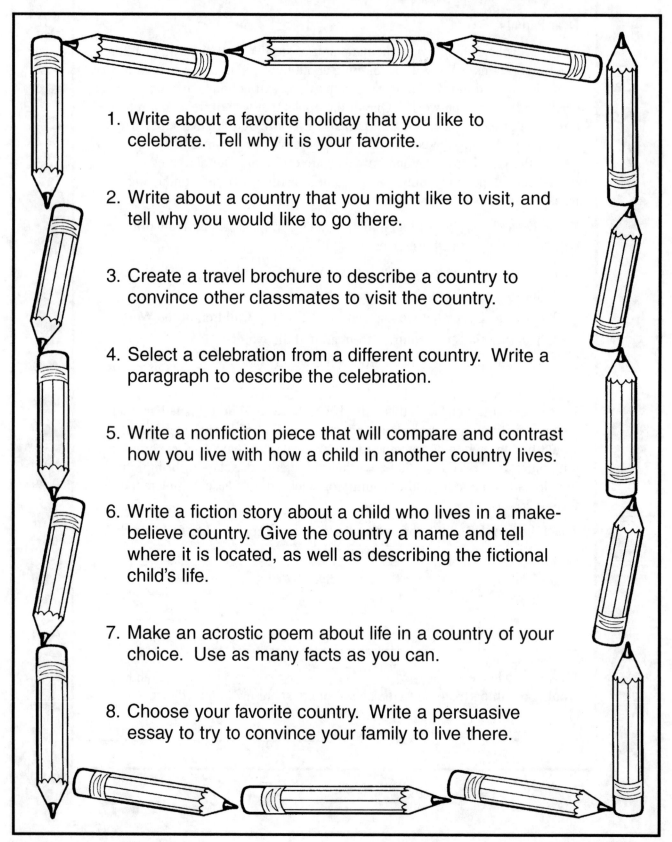

1. Write about a favorite holiday that you like to celebrate. Tell why it is your favorite.

2. Write about a country that you might like to visit, and tell why you would like to go there.

3. Create a travel brochure to describe a country to convince other classmates to visit the country.

4. Select a celebration from a different country. Write a paragraph to describe the celebration.

5. Write a nonfiction piece that will compare and contrast how you live with how a child in another country lives.

6. Write a fiction story about a child who lives in a make-believe country. Give the country a name and tell where it is located, as well as describing the fictional child's life.

7. Make an acrostic poem about life in a country of your choice. Use as many facts as you can.

8. Choose your favorite country. Write a persuasive essay to try to convince your family to live there.

Journal of Children of the World

Directions: Reproduce one cover for each student. Reproduce one format page for each country that students will write about.

My Journal
of
Children of the
World

by _____

Journal of Children of the World *(cont.)*

1. This is a drawing of a child who lives in the country called _____.

2. The country of _____ is on the continent called _____.

3. The people in this country speak a language called _____.

4. The weather in this country is _____.

5. People in this country eat foods such as _____, _____, _____, and _____.

6. Children in this country like to _____.

7. One holiday that is celebrated in this country is called _____.

A Snapshot of This Country

Where I Live

This is a drawing of me in my country.

[drawing box]

My country is called _____. It is on the continent

called _____. The people in this country speak a

language called _____.

The weather in this country is _____.

People in this country eat foods such as _____,

_____, and _____. Children in

this country like to _____. One holiday that is

celebrated in this country is called _____. I especially

like living in my country because _____.

By_____

Currency and Coins

Name _____ Date _____

Directions: Use the shapes below to create your own unique design for currency and coins for a country of your choice.

Celebrations Around the World

Directions: Read the information about celebrations. Cut on the lines, put the pages in order, and staple to make your own booklet. You may color the illustrations.

People all around the world have special celebrations.

1

Celebrations Around the World *(cont.)*

New Year's Day is celebrated all around the world. It is celebrated on several different dates. The Chinese New Year comes in January or February.

2

Cinco de Mayo is a Mexican holiday celebrated with a fiesta on May 5.

3

Celebrations Around the World *(cont.)*

Hanukkah is celebrated by people who are Jewish. It lasts for eight days in November or December.

4

Christmas is a Christian holiday that is celebrated on December 25.

5

Celebrations Around the World *(cont.)*

Kwanzaa is a holiday to honor African Americans and their history. It begins on December 26 and ends on January 1.

6

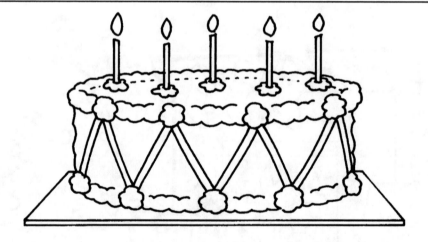

Happy Birthday

Birthdays are each person's special day to celebrate. My birthday is _____.

7

Weekly Theme: Thanksgiving   Week _____

	Monday	**Tuesday**	**Wednesday**	**Thursday**	**Friday**
Date					
Theme Activities	Make a word web for Thanksgiving.	Make a list of holidays.	Discuss the first Thanksgiving.	Brainstorm a list of "We are thankful for . . . ."	Locate holiday dates on a year calendar.
Literature Time	Read *Thanksgiving Day* by Gail Gibbons.	Read *If You Sailed on the Mayflower* by Ann McGovern.	Read *Sarah Morton's Day* or *Samuel Eaton's Day* by Kate Waters.	Read *Oh, What a Thanksgiving* by Steven Kroll.	Read *Thanksgiving at the Tappeltons'* by Eileen Spinelli.
Language Arts	Create a nonfiction book about the first Thanksgiving.	Develop a class book of turkey recipes.	Learn Thanksgiving words.	Make a comparison chart of then and now Thanksgivings.	Create a Venn diagram of past and present Thanksgivings.
Curriculum Connections	Try some Thanksgiving problem solving.	Make a tally of favorite foods.	Complete shopping list math.	Do a science study of real turkeys.	Organize a food drive.
Creative Arts	Create a "thankful" headband.	Play old-fashioned games.	Make a paper-plate feast collage.	Try baking bread and pies.	Plan a classroom sharing feast.

Overview: Thanksgiving

Monday

Theme Activities: Introduce the theme using a graphic organizer to record the class ideas. Make a word web by putting the word "Thanksgiving" in a circle on the middle of a sheet of tagboard or chart paper. Ask the class to think of words which relate to Thanksgiving. Then draw lines from the center circle and put the words in other circles. As you draw, related circles can be used to organize the ideas.

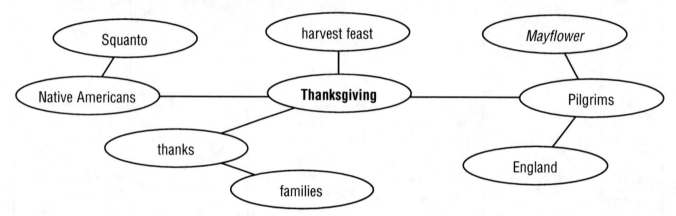

Literature Time: Read *Thanksgiving Day* by Gail Gibbons (Holiday House, 1983). This book explains the origins of the holiday and the many customs and traditions that people have developed. Discuss how the children's celebration may be the same or different from the ideas in the book.

Language Arts: Make a nonfiction book of facts about the first Thanksgiving shared by Pilgrims and Native Americans. Complete the mini-book found on pages 180–183. Read and discuss the book with the class before sending it home.

Curriculum Connections: One technique used in math problem solving is to make an organized list. Show the Thanksgiving math problems on page 184 to the class. Explain how a list will help them find all the possible combinations in a problem. If the students are unfamiliar with problem solving, you may want to do the problems together.

Creative Arts: Using the shape on page 185, create a headband to celebrate the holiday. The students will cut out and decorate the headband by using markers, crayons, or colored pencils. Have them draw and write about three to five things that they are thankful for on the headbands.

Tuesday

Theme Activities: Many other holidays are celebrated in our country and around the world. Have the class make a list of other holidays and discuss the reasons each is celebrated.

Literature Time: What would it be like to have lived in the 1600s? Find out by reading *If You Sailed on the Mayflower* by Ann McGovern (Scholastic, 1969). This book may be read over a week, covering and discussing a few facts each day.

Overview: Thanksgiving *(cont.)*

Tuesday *(cont.)*

Language Arts: Have the class pretend they are the chefs in charge of Thanksgiving dinner. Ask the students to write recipes to prepare the turkey with step-by-step directions. They can also write about other foods they would serve with the turkey, telling how to prepare them for a Thanksgiving feast. Type the recipes and make copies of the book for students to take home.

Curriculum Connections: Make a list of foods served at a traditional Thanksgiving dinner. Use tally marks to find out which food is the class favorite. If you have students who don't celebrate Thanksgiving, ask them to name their favorite foods for a holiday celebration or special occasion.

Creative Arts: At the first Thanksgiving, the Pilgrims and Native Americans played games of skill. At recess, try some "old-fashioned" games such as footraces, marbles, and tag.

Wednesday

Theme Activities: Discuss the first Thanksgiving, when it occurred and why, who was there, and how the celebration was the same or different from Thanksgiving today. Some children may not be aware that other countries do not celebrate Thanksgiving, so you may want to discuss this.

Literature Time: To find out how a Pilgrim child lived, read *Sarah Morton's Day* or *Samuel Eaton's Day.* Both books are written by Kate Waters (Scholastic, 1989 and 1993).

Language Arts: Choose some important vocabulary words related to this holiday, such as *Thanksgiving, Pilgrims, Native Americans, feast,* and *Mayflower.* Enlarge and laminate the turkey shape found on page 189 and list the words on the shape, using an erasable transparency pen. The vocabulary word cards on pages 186 and 187 can be placed in a pocket chart and used for spelling practice, writing sentences or stories, or for writing definitions.

Curriculum Connections: Using ads from your local grocery stores, have students find the prices of foods they would have at their Thanksgiving dinners. Students can create shopping lists of the foods they would buy and calculate the cost of dinner by using the format on page 188.

Creative Arts: Make a paper-plate collage to represent the plentiful foods of a feast. Give each student a large paper plate. Cut out pictures of favorite foods from magazines and glue them to the plate to create a delicious collage.

Thursday

Theme Activities: We have many things to be thankful for in our daily lives. Discuss what it means to be thankful and brainstorm a list of what the students are thankful for.

Overview: Thanksgiving *(cont.)*

=========================== **Thursday** *(cont.)* ===========================

Literature Time: Read the classic story *Oh, What a Thanksgiving* by Steven Kroll (Scholastic, 1988). In this book, David imagines what it would be like to be a Pilgrim.

Language Arts: Divide a piece of large chart paper into two halves. On one half write "The First Thanksgiving." On the other half write "Thanksgiving Today." Make a chart comparing past and present.

Curriculum Connections: To link to a study of life science, read some nonfiction books about real turkeys. Research for facts about this bird, such as its size, what it eats, and what different types of turkeys there are.

Creative Arts: Try some baking activities with the class. Bake some bread or pumpkin pie, using your favorite recipe. Baking activities provide good learning experiences in reading and following directions and measuring skills.

=============================== **Friday** ===============================

Theme Activities: Provide the students with a year-long calendar. Have them work in small groups to find out the dates when various holidays are celebrated. Add the dates to the holiday list generated on Tuesday.

Literature Time: Today's selection is *Thanksgiving at the Tappleton's* by Eileen Spinelli. This is a comical story of a Thanksgiving where everything goes wrong.

Language Arts: Using information learned during the week, have students show what they learned by creating a Venn diagram comparing the first Thanksgiving with Thanksgiving in the present (see page 380).

Curriculum Connections: Organize a food drive in your school. Collect canned foods and other nonperishable items. Donate them to a shelter or charitable organization before the holidays.

Creative Arts: As a culminating activity for this unit, plan a class sharing feast. Students may bring a food to share, and you can include the foods that the class baked together. Younger students may want to wear paper Pilgrim or Native American hats or the "thankful headbands" created at school. Parents can be invited to come in after the feast, and students may present some of the projects completed during the unit, such as the Venn diagrams and comparison charts. Some of the facts from the nonfiction books could be made into posters and presented as part of the program. Students can also do a choral reading using some of the delightful poetry found in Jack Prelutsky's book *It's Thanksgiving Day* (Scholastic, 1982).

This Week's Theme

Thanksgiving

Dear Parents,

As part of our social studies curriculum, we will be studying the holiday of Thanksgiving. During our theme, we will discuss the first Thanksgiving and compare it to how we celebrate Thanksgiving today. We will explore history as we learn about how Pilgrims and Native Americans worked together to plan the first Thanksgiving feast.

As we work on this theme, many of our activities will cover other curriculum areas, including reading, writing, science, math, art, and cooking projects. Here are some of the many learning activities we are planning:

1. writing our own recipes for how to make Thanksgiving dinner
2. making a book of facts about the first Thanksgiving
3. making a shopping list of what we would need to buy for dinner and figuring out the cost of our dinner using ads from grocery stores
4. reading many fiction and nonfiction books about Thanksgiving

At the end of our theme, we will be having a sharing feast. In the same spirit of cooperation and sharing that marked the first Thanksgiving, our class will be baking together and serving the food at our feast. If you would like to send other healthful snack food for our feast, please send it with your child on_____. I have included a list of nutritious snacks to choose from.

We are always thankful for parent participation in our learning!

Sincerely,

_____

- -

List of possible snacks: popcorn (already popped), pretzels, fresh fruit, bread, crackers, celery or carrot sticks, vegetables and dip, fruit snacks

(I am always happy to hear your ideas for other nutritious snack food!)

Name _____

I would like to send _____ for the sharing feast.

Please return this slip by _____ if you plan to participate.

Daily Journal Topics: Thanksgiving

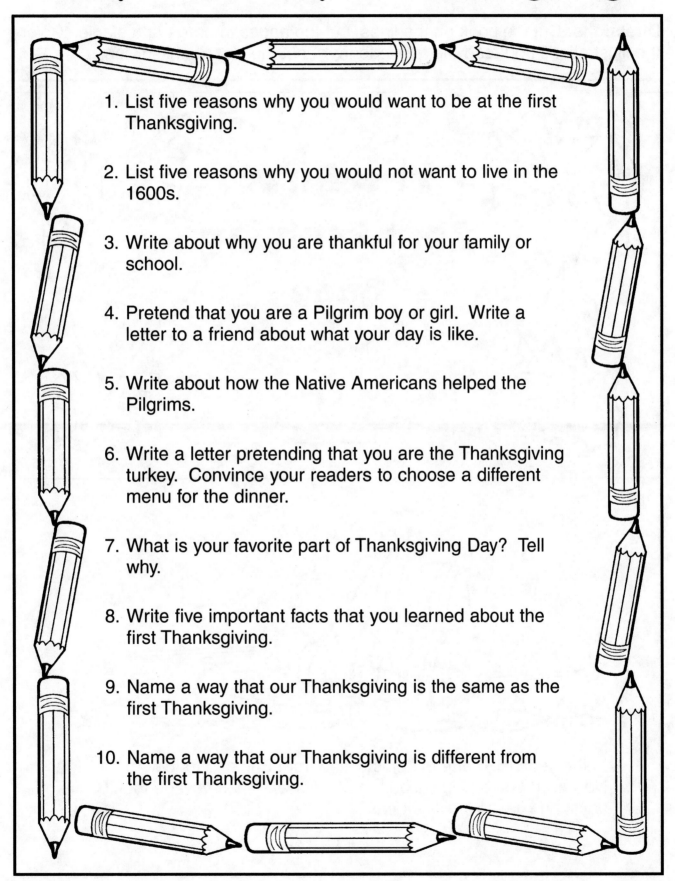

1. List five reasons why you would want to be at the first Thanksgiving.

2. List five reasons why you would not want to live in the 1600s.

3. Write about why you are thankful for your family or school.

4. Pretend that you are a Pilgrim boy or girl. Write a letter to a friend about what your day is like.

5. Write about how the Native Americans helped the Pilgrims.

6. Write a letter pretending that you are the Thanksgiving turkey. Convince your readers to choose a different menu for the dinner.

7. What is your favorite part of Thanksgiving Day? Tell why.

8. Write five important facts that you learned about the first Thanksgiving.

9. Name a way that our Thanksgiving is the same as the first Thanksgiving.

10. Name a way that our Thanksgiving is different from the first Thanksgiving.

The First Thanksgiving Book

Directions: Cut the book on the lines, put the pages in order, and staple. Color the illustrations and read the text to learn about the first Thanksgiving.

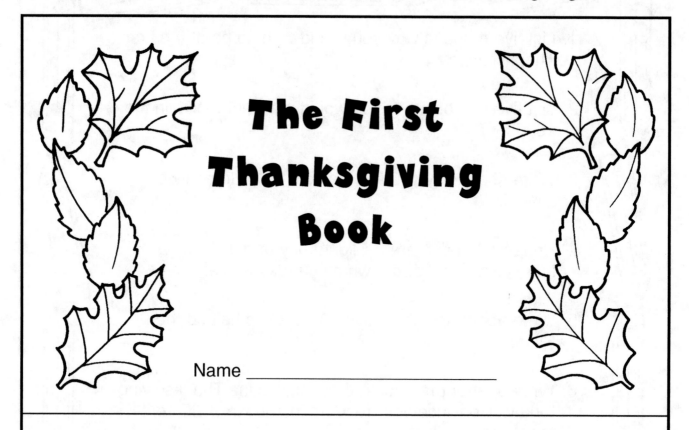

The First Thanksgiving Book

Name _____

In the year 1620, the Pilgrims sailed from England to look for the New World on a ship called the *Mayflower*. Their voyage took 65 days, and it was a difficult trip.

1

The First Thanksgiving Book *(cont.)*

The Pilgrims landed near Plymouth Rock and started to build homes. The first winter many people died because there wasn't enough food to eat.

2

In the spring of 1621, the Pilgrims became friends with the Wampanoag tribe of Native Americans.

3

The First Thanksgiving Book *(cont.)*

The Wampanoag helped the Pilgrims learn how to hunt better and how to plant crops, including corn.

4

The fall harvest was so good in 1621 and the Pilgrims were so thankful that they invited their Native American friends to a feast.

5

The First Thanksgiving Book *(cont.)*

The first Thanksgiving feast lasted for three days. Today we remember the Pilgrims when we celebrate Thanksgiving on the fourth Thursday of November, which became a national holiday in 1863.

6

Thanksgiving today is still a day to be thankful for family, friends, and good food.

7

Thanksgiving Problem Solving

Making an organized list is one type of problem solving used in math. Use this sample to help yourself get started.

Christopher's mother said that he could buy one book about Pilgrims and one book about Native Americans. He liked the Pilgrim books called *The Mayflower* and *Thanksgiving.* He liked the Native American books *Legends and Lore* and *Native American Tribes.* How many possible choices did he have?

He can choose these:

1. *The Mayflower* and *Legends and Lore*
2. *The Mayflower* and *Native American Tribes*
3. *Thanksgiving* and *Legends and Lore*
4. *Thanksgiving* and *Native American Tribes*

Christopher has **four** different choices.

Here are more Thanksgiving problems to solve by using an organized list. Make your list on another sheet of blank paper.

1. Isabel's family is trying to plan a menu for Thanksgiving dinner. The choices for the main course are turkey or chicken. The choices for a side dish are stuffing or potatoes. How many different menus can be planned?

2. Debbie is planning on having pies with different toppings for dessert. The pie choices are pumpkin, apple, and cherry. The topping choices are whipped cream or ice cream. How many different desserts can be served?

3. The first grade class is having a Thanksgiving feast. For their snack, they may choose popcorn, pretzels, or crackers. The choices of drinks are apple juice, fruit punch, or milk. How many different snacks can be chosen?

4. Mr. Lowrey's fourth grade class is performing at the Thanksgiving day assembly. They can perform one song and one poem. Their poem choices are "Leftovers" and "The Thanksgiving Parade," both by Jack Prelutsky. Their possible songs are "Run, Turkey, Run" and "What's for Dinner?" How many choices will they have?

5. Carol is making a Thanksgiving art project. She can make her turkey out of a paper plate or a paper bag. She can choose one of the following materials to decorate her turkey: glitter, feathers, or sequins. How many choices will she have?

Headband Pattern

Color and cut out the patterns below. To make the headband attach two or three of the end strips to the center strip.

center strip

end strips

Holiday Word Cards

Directions: Cut out the word cards and laminate them. The cards may be used in a pocket chart for discussion, reading, writing and spelling practice, and work with definitions.

Mayflower
Thanksgiving
Pilgrims
Native Americans
feast

Holiday Word Cards *(cont.)*

England
Squanto
Plymouth Rock
thankful
harvest

Shopping for Thanksgiving Math

Look through food ads from your local grocery store. Make a list of the foods that you would buy for your Thanksgiving dinner and their prices. Figure out the total amount you would have to spend on dinner for your family. Check your math with a calculator.

My Shopping List

Food Items	**Prices**
_____	_____
_____	_____
_____	_____
_____	_____
_____	_____
_____	_____
_____	_____
_____	_____
_____	_____
_____	_____
_____	_____

The total for my Thanksgiving dinner would be _____.

Holiday Shape

Directions: Enlarge this shape on tagboard and color with markers. Cut out and laminate for durability. The shape may be written on with an erasable transparency pen and can be used for brainstorming a list of vocabulary words or writing and reviewing what has been learned about Thanksgiving.

Weekly Theme: Traditional Christmas   Week _____

	Monday	Tuesday	Wednesday	Thursday	Friday
Date					
Theme Activities	Discuss Christmas traditions: what Christmas means to me.	Make lists of holiday food.	Discuss traditions of the Christmas tree.	Discuss traditions of Santa Claus.	Share family holiday memories.
Literature Time	Read *Christmas Time* by Gail Gibbons.	Read *The Gingerbread Man* by Eric A. Kimmel.	Read *The Year of the Perfect Christmas Tree* by Gloria Houston and *Mr. Willowby's Christmas Tree* by Robert Barry.	Read *The Polar Express* by Chris Van Allsburg.	Read *Christmas Tree Memories* by Aliki.
Language Arts	Summarize important holiday facts.	Create a story map for the gingerbread man.	Make a class book of "Our Perfect Christmas Trees."	Create "help wanted" ads for Santa's workshop.	Write a class book about favorite Christmas memories.
Curriculum Connections	Create a family Christmas card.	Make some "classy" cookies.	Conduct Christmas tree research.	Make a Christmas wish list from ads.	Measure the class tree.
Creative Arts	Sing traditional Christmas songs.	Create a gingerbread character.	Choose a theme for your classroom tree.	Create Polar Express paintings.	Make tin punch ornaments.

Overview: Traditional Christmas

Monday

Theme Activities: Ask the children to share what Christmas means to them. Share some of the traditions that you enjoy in your family and ask the children to discuss any special holiday activities their families enjoy. Be sure to discuss the fact that some families may celebrate other holidays instead of Christmas.

Literature Time: Today's selection is *Christmas Time* by Gail Gibbons (Holiday House, 1982). This book gives a historical perspective for Christmas customs, past and present.

Language Arts: Have students use today's literature to note five important facts about Christmas. They can summarize the importance of the holiday in a short paragraph.

Curriculum Connections: One of the holiday traditions of Christmas is to send cards to friends and family. Cards may be created using a variety of materials such as construction paper, markers, glitter, and cutouts from old cards. To link with technology, cards may also be created using a graphics program such as *The Print Shop* or *Kid Pix Studio.*

Creative Arts: Introduce a traditional Christmas carol each day during this theme. Try some old favorites such as "Jingle Bells," "Deck the Halls," "We Wish You a Merry Christmas," "Up on the Housetop," and "The Twelve Days of Christmas" (see bibliography).

Tuesday

Theme Activities: Many families celebrate the holiday with a special meal. Divide the class into small groups and have them list some foods that families share together on Christmas. Discuss the kinds of cookies that might be served and ask if anyone bakes gingerbread men. Today's activities have to do with the story of the gingerbread man.

Literature Time: There are many versions of the gingerbread man. Collect several to read and compare. A particularly delightful version is *The Gingerbread Man* by Eric Kummel (Holiday House, 1993).

Language Arts: Create a story map to summarize the main parts of the story. You can work with the whole class or have small groups work on different parts of the story. In your map be sure to include characters, setting, problem, resolution (how the problem was solved), plot (beginning, middle, and end of the story), and theme (main idea).

Curriculum Connections: Try some creative writing and have students create their own "classy" cookie using their favorite ingredients.

Creative Arts: Enlarge and reproduce the gingerbread shape on page 197 on brown construction paper. Have students cut out the shape and then decide on a gingerbread character they want to create. Possible ideas include a gingerbread angel, reindeer, elf, or Santa. Provide a variety of materials, including scraps of material and trim, lace, sequins, feathers, and pompon balls.

Overview: Traditional Christmas *(cont.)*

Wednesday

Theme Activities: Discuss the tradition of the Christmas tree. Tally how many students use a real tree, an artificial tree, or no tree. For more on the origins of the Christmas tree, look in *The Family Christmas Tree Book* by Tomie dePaola (see bibliography).

Literature Time: Both of today's selections have to do with Christmas trees. *The Year of the Perfect Christmas Tree* by Gloria Houston (Dial Books, 1988) is set in the early 1900s. *Mr. Willowby's Christmas Tree* by Robert Barry (Dell, 1963) offers many opportunities to talk about story sequence.

Language Arts: After reading about Gloria Houston's perfect tree, let the children decide what decorations would make their tree "perfect." Have each student make a page for the class book Our Perfect Christmas Trees. A book cover and format appear on pages 199 and 200.

Curriculum Connections: Do science research on evergreen trees. Ask students to bring in samples of branches and cones from different types of evergreens or collect them on the school grounds. Put nonfiction books about evergreens in the science center or display them on a table with the tree samples. Students can label the cones and branches after their research. Have the class complete the evergreen research page on page 201, using a reference such as *A New True Book—Christmas Trees* (see bibliography). They may do their research individually or in small cooperative groups.

Creative Arts: Put up an artificial tree in your classroom. Brainstorm a list of themes for decorating the tree (such as a gingerbread tree or an all Santa tree). Vote for which theme is the class favorite. Have students make all the decorations, using whatever art supplies are available.

Thursday

Theme Activities: Today's Christmas topic is Santa Claus. Refer to the Gibbons book read earlier in the week for how the customs of Santa Claus and gifts originated. Ask the children if they know different names for Santa, such as Saint Nick. Emphasize the fact that Santa represents the spirit of giving seen at Christmas time.

Literature Time: Take a trip to the North Pole on *The Polar Express* by Chris Van Allsburg (Houghton Mifflin, 1985). Ask the class what they would choose as the first gift of Christmas. More activities related to *The Polar Express* can be found in *Connecting Holidays and Literature* by Deborah Cerbus and Cheryl Rice (Teacher Created Materials, 1992).

Overview: Traditional Christmas *(cont.)*

Thursday *(cont.)*

Language Arts: Have the class create some want ads for Santa's workshop. Write descriptions for different jobs to be found at the North Pole. Use the ad form on page 202.

Curriculum Connections: Gather some ads from newspapers, fliers, and Christmas catalogs. Have the class go "shopping" with a Christmas wish list (see page 203). List the price of each item and have the students total the cost.

Creative Arts: Using tempera paint in Christmas colors, have students each paint their own engines for the Polar Express. At the bottom of the painting or on a separate piece of paper, have them write a story which tells where they would go on their Polar Express trip and what they would see and do. Older students can type the story on the computer.

Friday

Theme Activities: Share memories of favorite Christmas celebrations. Students may want to show some family photographs from past holidays.

Literature Time: In today's book, *Christmas Tree Memories* by Aliki (HarperCollins, 1991), a family reminisces about special times represented by the ornaments on their tree.

Language Arts: Ask the class to write about a favorite Christmas memory. When the story is complete, enlarge one of the shapes found on pages 204 and 205 and place the story on the holiday shape. They can then be displayed on a bulletin board.

Curriculum Connections: Use the class Christmas tree to practice measuring skills. Students can estimate the height and circumference of the tree and then take measurements in inches or centimeters. Prior to decorating the tree, have them estimate how long a paper chain would need to be to wrap around the tree three or four times.

Creative Arts: Create some ornaments to take home for special memories of this school year. Tin-punch ornaments are fairly easy to make and will be treasured for years. Foil is available in rolls or sheets at craft stores. The patterns can be laid on the tin and traced with a ballpoint pen (the tin is soft, and you will see where the pen pressed down). Holes are punched with a nail. You may need to tap the nail with a small hammer, and you will need to place a piece of flat wood underneath before you punch the design. Cut around the ornament shape with sharp scissors. Patterns for ornaments can be found on pages 204 and 205. Solid lines are for cutting the ornaments out. The dotted line is for the tin-punch design. If you don't want to cut out the ornaments, the tin-punch design alone can be punched on the metal part of the lid of a canning jar.

This Week's Theme

Traditional Christmas

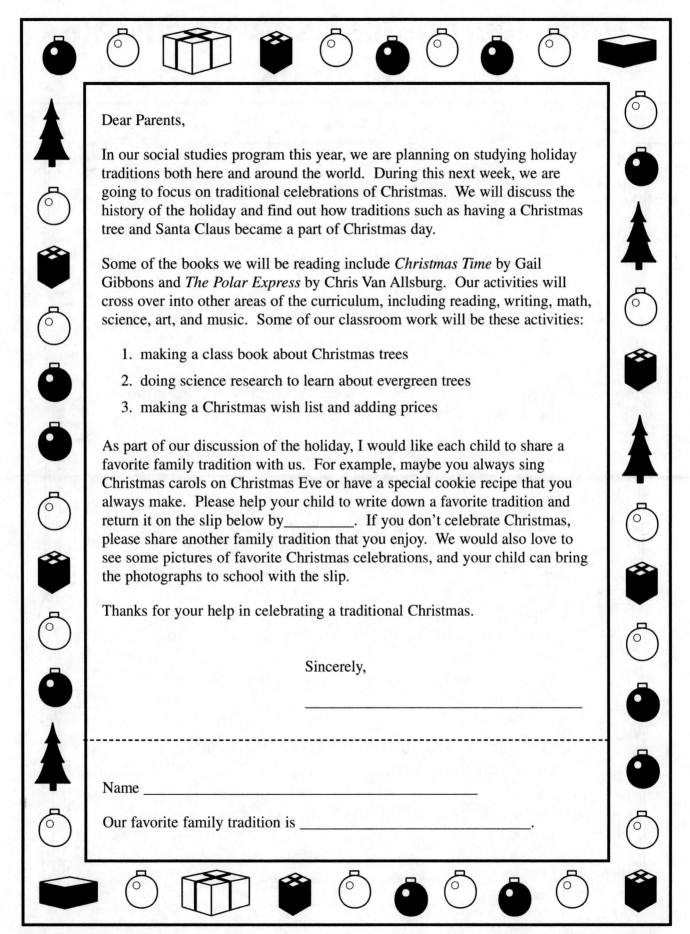

Dear Parents,

In our social studies program this year, we are planning on studying holiday traditions both here and around the world. During this next week, we are going to focus on traditional celebrations of Christmas. We will discuss the history of the holiday and find out how traditions such as having a Christmas tree and Santa Claus became a part of Christmas day.

Some of the books we will be reading include *Christmas Time* by Gail Gibbons and *The Polar Express* by Chris Van Allsburg. Our activities will cross over into other areas of the curriculum, including reading, writing, math, science, art, and music. Some of our classroom work will be these activities:

1. making a class book about Christmas trees

2. doing science research to learn about evergreen trees

3. making a Christmas wish list and adding prices

As part of our discussion of the holiday, I would like each child to share a favorite family tradition with us. For example, maybe you always sing Christmas carols on Christmas Eve or have a special cookie recipe that you always make. Please help your child to write down a favorite tradition and return it on the slip below by_____. If you don't celebrate Christmas, please share another family tradition that you enjoy. We would also love to see some pictures of favorite Christmas celebrations, and your child can bring the photographs to school with the slip.

Thanks for your help in celebrating a traditional Christmas.

Sincerely,

_____

- -

Name _____

Our favorite family tradition is _____.

Daily Journal Topics: A Traditional Christmas

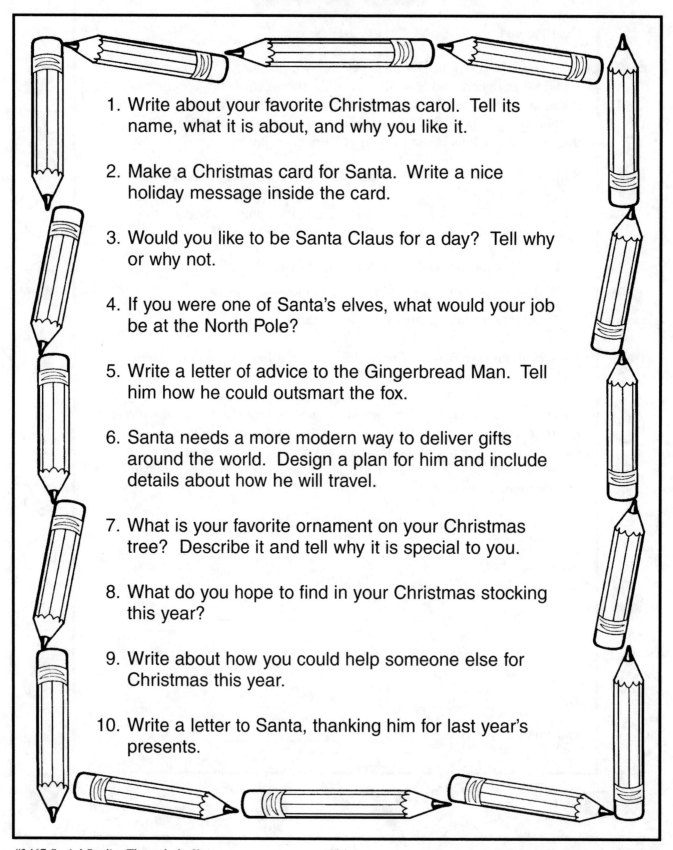

1. Write about your favorite Christmas carol. Tell its name, what it is about, and why you like it.

2. Make a Christmas card for Santa. Write a nice holiday message inside the card.

3. Would you like to be Santa Claus for a day? Tell why or why not.

4. If you were one of Santa's elves, what would your job be at the North Pole?

5. Write a letter of advice to the Gingerbread Man. Tell him how he could outsmart the fox.

6. Santa needs a more modern way to deliver gifts around the world. Design a plan for him and include details about how he will travel.

7. What is your favorite ornament on your Christmas tree? Describe it and tell why it is special to you.

8. What do you hope to find in your Christmas stocking this year?

9. Write about how you could help someone else for Christmas this year.

10. Write a letter to Santa, thanking him for last year's presents.

Gingerbread Characters

Enlarge the gingerbread shape and trace it onto brown construction paper. Cut out the shape and create a gingerbread character such as a gingerbread reindeer, elf, or angel. Decorate the character with construction paper, glitter, sequins, feathers, lace, trim, ribbon, yarn, scraps of material, and pompon balls. Add a loop of ribbon at the top and use the character as an ornament for the class tree.

Our Perfect Christmas Trees

Purpose: Children will each create a page for a class book titled Our Perfect Christmas Trees, based on *The Year of the Perfect Christmas Tree* by Gloria Houston. The pages will describe each student's idea of the perfect Christmas tree.

Materials

- Our Perfect Christmas Trees Book Cover (page 199)
- Our Perfect Christmas Trees Paper (page 200)
- pencils, markers, crayons, construction paper

Preparation: Reproduce a shape paper for each student to write on (additional pages if you plan on doing a first draft and a final copy). Reproduce one front cover for the class book and color with markers. Mount the cover on green tagboard and cut a back cover for the class book the same color and the same size. Laminate for durability.

Instructions: Ask the children how they would decorate their tree to make it "perfect." The children will write about their trees on the lined paper. The space at the bottom can be used for an illustration, or children may cut a construction paper tree to paste on the page and then decorate with markers, crayons, and paper scraps cut into ornament shapes.

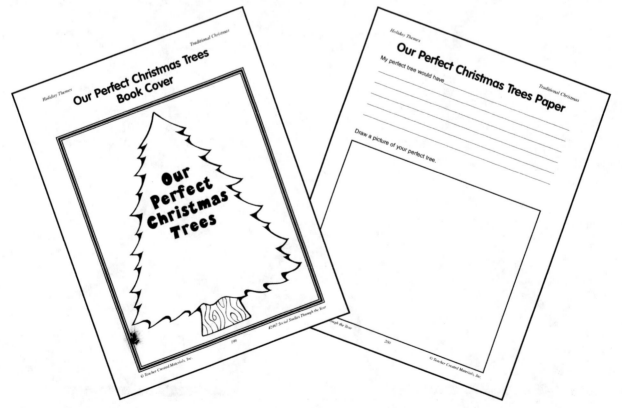

Our Perfect Christmas Trees
Book Cover

Our Perfect Christmas Trees Paper

My perfect tree would have_____

_____

_____

_____

_____

_____

Draw a picture of your perfect tree.

Research Detective _____

Be a Christmas Tree Detective

Use resource books to research the answers to these questions.

1. Who had the first Christmas tree?

    _____

2. Why are pine trees called evergreens?

    _____

3. What are the seeds of Christmas or pine trees called?

    _____

4. What are the baby trees called?

    _____

5. How many Christmas trees are sold each year in the United States?

    _____

6. What did the first Christmas trees have instead of lights?

    _____

7. How long does it take Christmas trees to grow to the right size?

    _____

8. How does a Christmas tree farm help the environment?

    _____

Name _____ Date _____

 # Help Wanted!

Jolly Old St. Nick is in need of helpers for the following job:

_____.

If you are interested, please apply at the North Pole, Santa's Workshop.

Job Description:

_____

_____

_____

_____

_____

_____

_____

_____

_____

_____

_____

_____

Special Skills or Talents Needed for the Job:

_____

_____

_____

_____

_____

_____

_____

_____

_____

_____

_____

_____

Name _____ Date _____

Make a list of what you would like for Christmas. Use ads and catalogs to find the prices. Add your total to see what your shopping trip will cost.

My Christmas Wish List

What I Would Like	Price
_____	_____
_____	_____
_____	_____
_____	_____
_____	_____
_____	_____
_____	_____
_____	_____
_____	_____
_____	_____
_____	_____

Ornament Shapes

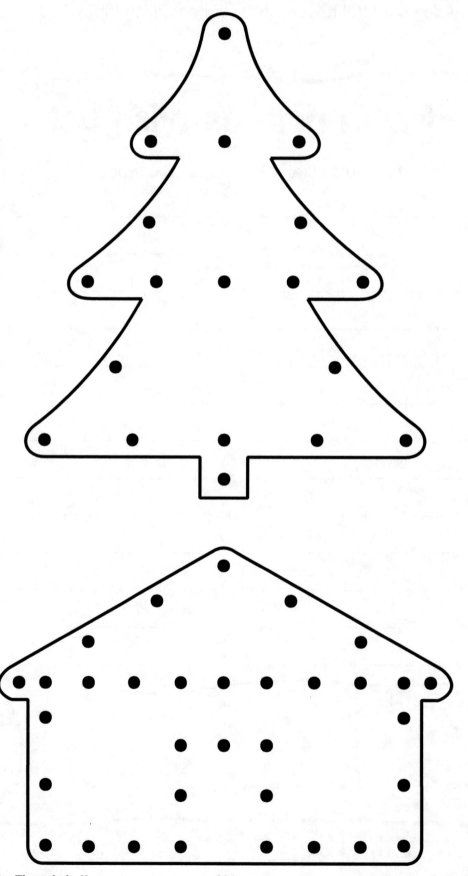

Ornament Shapes *(cont.)*

Special note for snowman: After making the tin snowman, add twig arms with a hot glue gun. A felt hat may also be added.

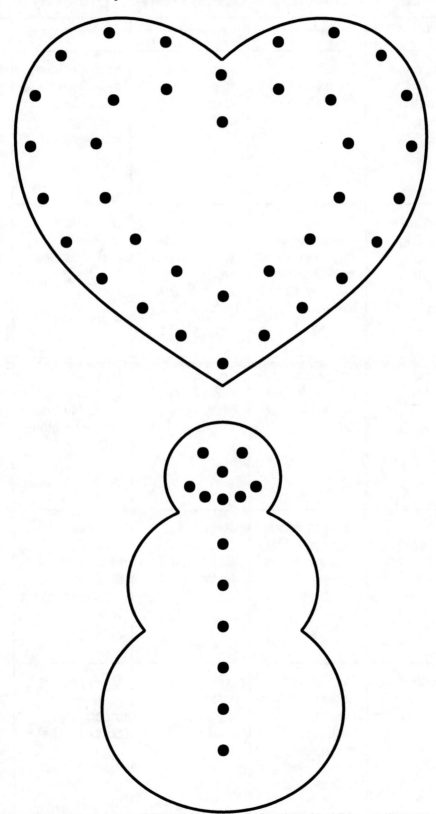

Weekly Theme: A Trip to Washington, D.C.   Week _____

	Monday	Tuesday	Wednesday	Thursday	Friday
Date					
Theme Activities	Introduce the city of Washington, D.C.	Discuss the importance of Washington, D.C.	Introduce a map of Washington, D.C.	Show famous monuments, memorials, and buildings in Washington, D.C.	List "must" things to do and to see in Washington, D.C.
Literature Time	Begin chapter book, *Look Out, Washington, D.C.!* by Patricia Reilly Giff.	Continue chapter book and read *A Visit to Washington, D.C.,* by Jill Krementz.	Continue chapter book and read *The Story of the White House* by Kate Waters.	Continue chapter book and read *City! Washington, D.C.*	Finish the chapter book *Look Out, Washington, D.C.!*
Language Arts	List items needed for a trip to Washington, D.C.	List places of interest to visit in Washington, D.C.	Complete White House Facts.	Read and complete mini-book, My Book of Washington, D.C.	Write a diary of experiences on an imaginary trip to Washington, D.C.
Curriculum Connections	Study the map of the United States.	Determine how many miles your location is from Washington, D.C.	Complete Calculate Your Way Through the White House.	Use the Internet to learn more about Washington, D.C.	Make a walking tour map of Washington, D.C.
Creative Arts	Sing patriotic songs.	Create paintings of the various historical monuments, memorials, and buildings.	Create postcards of the White House.	Make posters or travel brochures advertising a trip to Washington, D.C.	Create a three-dimensional model of the city of Washington, D.C.

Overview: A Trip to Washington, D.C.

Monday

Theme Activities: Introduce the city of Washington, D.C., to your students by helping them locate it on a map of the United States. Guide them in noticing that a star denotes where the city is. Discuss the significance of the star.

Literature Time: Begin reading the realistic chapter book *Look Out, Washington, D.C.!* by Patricia Reilly Giff to your students. Plan to read a section of this book each day during this theme.

Language Arts: Instruct students to think about the things they would need to take on a trip to Washington, D.C. Have students work in pairs to make a list of these items.

Curriculum Connections: Duplicate a map of the United States (page 377) for each student. Children will locate and label Washington, D.C., as well as their own city.

Creative Arts: Help students learn a variety of patriotic songs, such as "America," "The Star-Spangled Banner," and "America the Beautiful." *The Magic of Music* (Cherry Lane Music, 1998) is a good source of songs.

Tuesday

Theme Activities: Discuss the importance of Washington, D.C., as the capital city of the United States of America, where the president, members of Congress, and government officials work and make the laws for our country.

Literature Time: Read the picture book *A Trip to Washington, D.C.,* by Jill Krementz to your class, as well as continuing to read the chapter book *Look Out, Washington, D.C.!*

Language Arts: As a follow-up to the picture book, have each student make a list of places of interest to visit in Washington, D.C. Have students prioritize their lists, and write to explain why they selected their first choice.

Curriculum Connections: Use a map of the United States that has a scale of miles to determine how many miles you live from Washington, D.C. Discuss the possible ways to travel there. Determine which mode of transportation would be the fastest and which would be most economical.

Creative Arts: Encourage your students to create paintings of the various historical monuments, memorials, government buildings, and historical locations in Washington, D.C. Use a long strip of paper as a background and add the title "A Trip to Washington, D.C." Display the paintings on the background as a colorful mural during your thematic unit.

Overview: A Trip to Washington, D.C. *(cont.)*

Wednesday

Theme Activities: Introduce a map of the city of Washington, D.C. (page 214), pointing out the various historical buildings and locations noted on the map.

Literature Time: Read *The Story of the White House* by Kate Waters to your class, as well as continuing to read the chapter book *Look Out, Washington, D.C.!*

Language Arts: Duplicate White House Facts (page 213) for each of your students. Have the students use reference materials such as today's literature selection, an encyclopedia, or *The Ladybird Guide to Presidents of the United States* (Ladybird Books, 1997) to complete the fact sheet.

Curriculum Connections: Have students use calculators to determine mathematical information about the White House by completing Calculate Your Way Through the White House (page 216).

Creative Arts: Duplicate the postcard format on page 379 for students to use in creating their own postcards (picture, friendly note, and address) about the White House.

Thursday

Theme Activities: Show your students postcards, photographs, posters, or travel brochures of several sights in Washington, D.C.

Literature Time: Read excerpts from a more challenging book, such as *City! Washington, D.C.* by Shirley Cilmo or *Washington, D.C.* by Catherine Reef. Continue reading the chapter book *Look Out, Washington, D.C.!*

Language Arts: Duplicate the informational mini-book, My Book of Washington, D.C. on pages 217–220.

Curriculum Connections: Guide your students in visiting a Web site on the Internet such as *www.whitehouse.gov/* to learn more about Washington, D.C. (Remember to always visit the site yourself before your students do.)

Creative Arts: Have students make posters or folded travel brochures to advertise taking a trip to Washington, D.C.

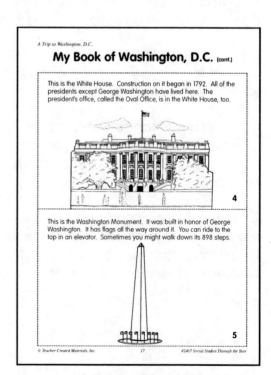

A Trip to Washington, D.C.

My Book of Washington, D.C. (cont.)

This is the White House. Construction on it began in 1792. All of the presidents except George Washington have lived here. The president's office, called the Oval Office, is in the White House, too.

4

This is the Washington Monument. It was built in honor of George Washington. It has flags all the way around it. You can ride to the top in an elevator. Sometimes you might walk down its 898 steps.

5

© *Teacher Created Materials, Inc.*   *17*   *#2467 Social Studies Through the Year*

Overview: A Trip to Washington, D.C. *(cont.)*

━━━━━━━━━━━━━━━━ **Friday** ━━━━━━━━━━━━━━━━

Theme Activities: Make a class list of "must" things to do and places to see if you were taking a trip to Washington, D.C. Have students vote to determine the most popular thing to do or place to visit. Display this list (with tally marks to denote the results of your voting) at your theme area.

"Must See" Places

Capitol Building

White House

Smithsonian Institution

Supreme Court Building

Potomac River

Kennedy Center

Bureau of Engraving and Printing

Literature Time: Finish reading the chapter book *Look Out, Washington, D.C.!* to your class, helping students to notice the last section of the book which lists the characters' favorite places that they visited on their trip.

Language Arts: Have your students imagine that they are taking a trip to Washington, D.C., and have them make a diary of their experiences.

Curriculum Connections: Duplicate a map of Washington, D.C., (page 214) for each student to use in plotting a walking tour, as well as page 215 to practice map reading skills. Keep the pages separate so that students can easily use the map to complete the map skills page and then staple these two pages together when they are finished.

Creative Arts: Encourage students to work at the block center, art center, or construction center to create a three-dimensional model of the city of Washington, D.C. Have students make signs to label each of their creations.

This Week's Theme

A Trip to Washington, D.C.

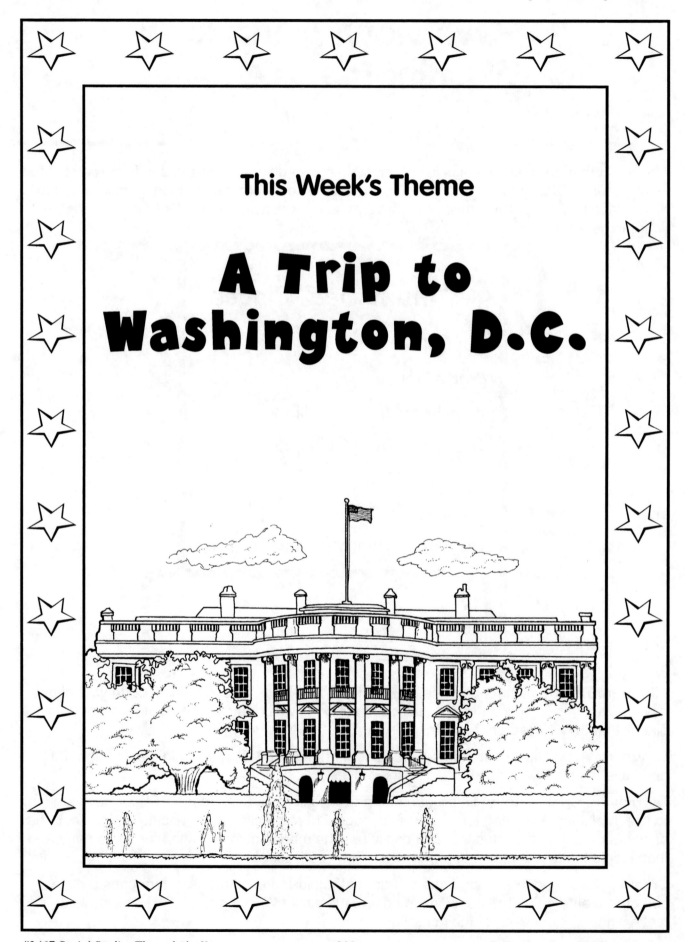

Dear Parents,

Our class is starting a new unit of social studies called "A Trip to Washington, D.C." During our "travels" in the nation's capital, we will be using many important skills, including the use of maps and learning about famous landmarks found in this interesting city. The class will be reading books about Washington, D.C. In addition to social studies, we will be doing activities across the curriculum, including reading, writing, math, art, music, and computers.

As part of our study, your child will be making and bringing home a mini-book about Washington, D.C., to read with you. During our theme we will also participate in the following activities:

1. locating Washington, D.C., on a map of the United States and finding famous landmarks on a map of the city

2. singing patriotic songs such as "The Star-Spangled Banner"

3. using reference books to research facts about the White House

4. visiting the White House Web site on the Internet (Please remember: always visit Web sites yourself before your child does or visit the site with your child. The Web address is *www.whitehouse.gov/*)

You can encourage your child's interest in social studies by visiting the public library to check out more books on this topic. A list is included at the bottom of this letter to get you started.

Thank you for participating in your child's learning.

Sincerely,

_____

- -

Washington, D.C., Book List

Here are some great books to look for at your public library:

The Story of the White House by Kate Waters

A Visit to Washington, D.C. by Jill Krementz

The Star-Spangled Banner by Peter Spier

Look Out, Washington, D.C.! by Patricia Reilly Giff

Stars and Stripes by Leonard Everett Fisher

Daily Journal Topics:
A Trip to Washington, D.C.

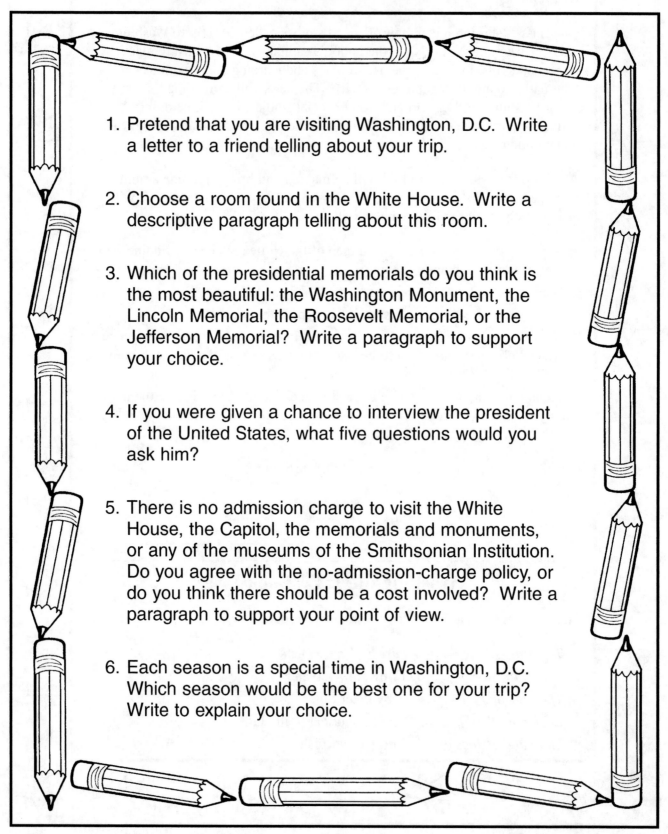

1. Pretend that you are visiting Washington, D.C. Write a letter to a friend telling about your trip.

2. Choose a room found in the White House. Write a descriptive paragraph telling about this room.

3. Which of the presidential memorials do you think is the most beautiful: the Washington Monument, the Lincoln Memorial, the Roosevelt Memorial, or the Jefferson Memorial? Write a paragraph to support your choice.

4. If you were given a chance to interview the president of the United States, what five questions would you ask him?

5. There is no admission charge to visit the White House, the Capitol, the memorials and monuments, or any of the museums of the Smithsonian Institution. Do you agree with the no-admission-charge policy, or do you think there should be a cost involved? Write a paragraph to support your point of view.

6. Each season is a special time in Washington, D.C. Which season would be the best one for your trip? Write to explain your choice.

White House Facts

Name _____ Date _____

Directions:

1. Every president of the United States of America has lived in the White House, except _____.

2. The White House was designed by _____.

3. The president's office is called the _____.

4. The address of te Whiwe House i

_____

____

A Map of Washington, D.C.

Name _____ Date _____

Directions: Use a pencil to draw your route for a possible walking tour. Start and end at the Capitol Building.

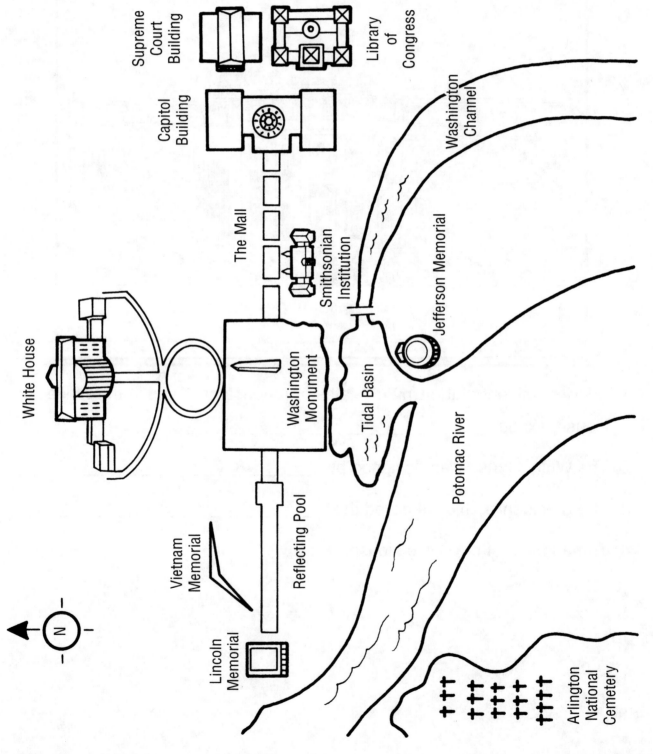

A Map of Washington, D.C. *(cont.)*

Name _____ Date _____

Directions: Use the map on page 214 to answer these questions.

1. The White House is _____ of the Washington Monument.

2. The Capitol Building is _____ of the Smithsonian Institution.

3. The Potomac River is on the _____ side of Washington, D.C.

4. The Reflecting Pool is between the _____ and the _____. This area is also called The Mall.

5. _____ is across the Potomac River from the city of Washington, D.C.

6. The Vietnam Memorial is _____ of the Reflecting Pool, and the Arlington National Cemetery is _____ of it.

7. The _____ Memorial is near the Tidal Basin.

8. The Washington Channel is _____ of the Potomac River.

9. The Lincoln Memorial is on the _____ end of the Mall.

10. The Supreme Court Building is _____ of the Library of Congress.

Calculate Your Way Through the White House

Name _____ Date _____

Directions: Use a calculator to answer the following mathematical questions about the White House.

1. George Washington took the oath of office in 1789. The White House construction began in 1792, but it still was not complete in 1800. How many years after George Washington became president did construction begin?

    _____

2. The president hosts formal dinners in the State Dining Room. This room can seat 140 people. How many more people can sit there than in the seats in your classroom? _____

3. The Rose Garden at the White House was redesigned in 1962. The president uses the Rose Garden for special events. How many years ago was the Rose Garden redesigned? _____

4. Since George Washington was the only president never to live in the White House, how many presidents have lived in the White House?

    _____

5. In 1814 the White House was burned by the British during the War of 1812. How many years ago was the White House burned by the British?

    _____

6. The president's Oval Office was built in 1909. It was moved from the center of the West Wing to the southeast corner in 1934, where it still is. After how many years was the Oval Office moved?_____

7. President John Adams and First Lady Abigail Adams were the first people to live in the White House. They moved there in November 1800. How many years has the White House been the official home of the president?

    _____

My Book of Washington, D.C.

Your teacher will explain the directions for making this book.

My Book of Washington, D.C.

Name_____

Washington, D.C., is the capital of the United States of America. It is between the states of Maryland and Virginia, but it is not a state. The land is called the District of Columbia (D.C.). Find Washington, D.C., on this map.

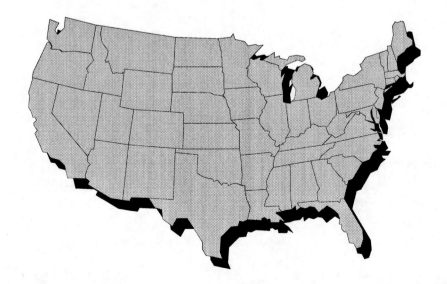

1

My Book of Washington, D.C. *(cont.)*

Washington, D.C., was named in honor of George Washington, the first president of the United States. He chose the location for Washington, D.C. It is across the Potomac River from his home, Mount Vernon.

2

Most of the government offices for the United States are in Washington, D.C. Members of Congress make the laws for the United States. They work in the Capitol Building. This is the Capitol.

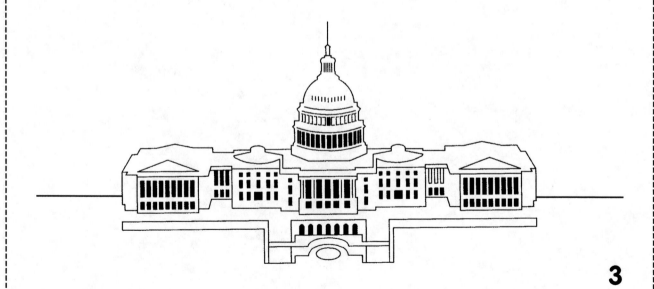

3

My Book of Washington, D.C. *(cont.)*

This is the White House. Construction on it began in 1792. All of the presidents except George Washington have lived here. The president's office, called the Oval Office, is in the White House, too.

4

This is the Washington Monument. It was built in honor of George Washington. It has flags all the way around it. You can ride to the top in an elevator. Sometimes you might walk down its 898 steps.

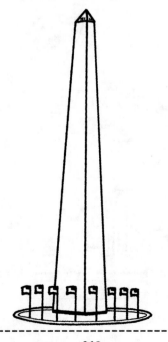

5

My Book of Washington, D.C. *(cont.)*

This is the Lincoln Memorial. It was built in honor of Abraham Lincoln. A huge statue of Abraham Lincoln sitting in a chair is inside the memorial.

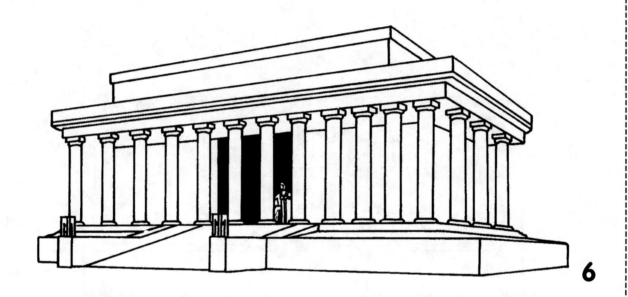

6

The Smithsonian Institution is the world's largest group of museums and art galleries. Most of its buildings are in Washington, D.C.

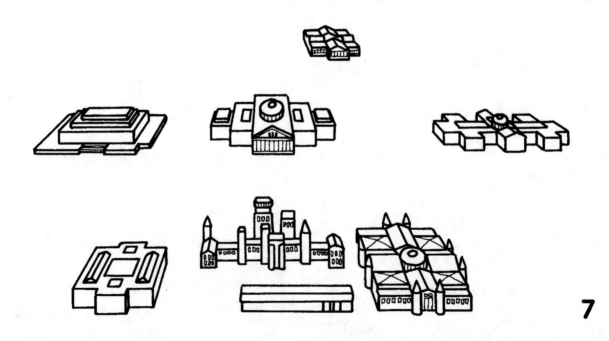

7

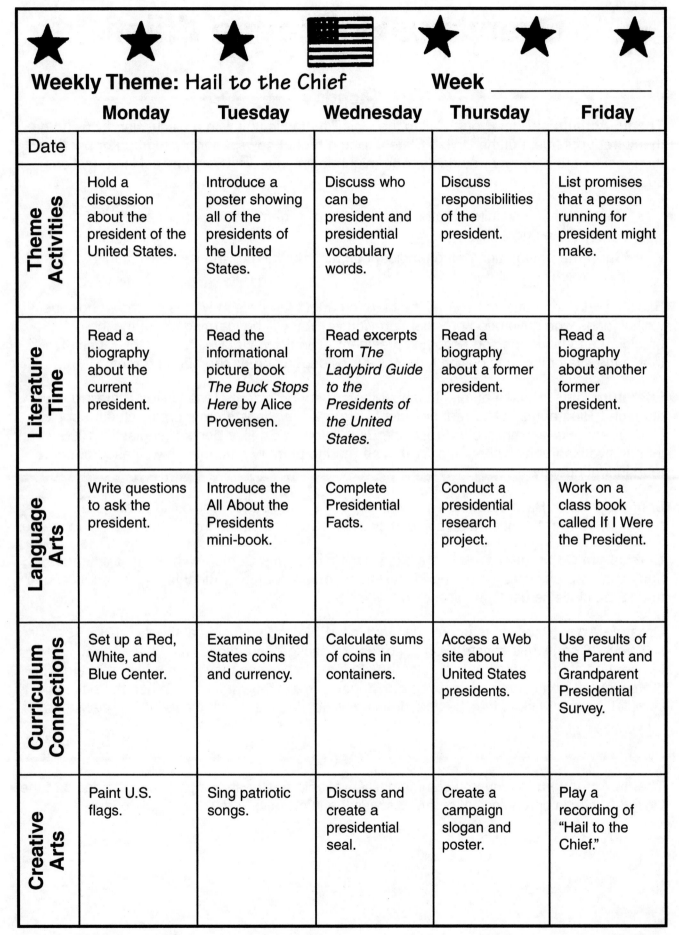

Weekly Theme: Hail *to the* Chief   Week _____

	Monday	Tuesday	Wednesday	Thursday	Friday
Date					
Theme Activities	Hold a discussion about the president of the United States.	Introduce a poster showing all of the presidents of the United States.	Discuss who can be president and presidential vocabulary words.	Discuss responsibilities of the president.	List promises that a person running for president might make.
Literature Time	Read a biography about the current president.	Read the informational picture book *The Buck Stops Here* by Alice Provensen.	Read excerpts from *The Ladybird Guide to the Presidents of the United States.*	Read a biography about a former president.	Read a biography about another former president.
Language Arts	Write questions to ask the president.	Introduce the All About the Presidents mini-book.	Complete Presidential Facts.	Conduct a presidential research project.	Work on a class book called If I Were the President.
Curriculum Connections	Set up a Red, White, and Blue Center.	Examine United States coins and currency.	Calculate sums of coins in containers.	Access a Web site about United States presidents.	Use results of the Parent and Grandparent Presidential Survey.
Creative Arts	Paint U.S. flags.	Sing patriotic songs.	Discuss and create a presidential seal.	Create a campaign slogan and poster.	Play a recording of "Hail to the Chief."

Overview: Hail to the Chief

Monday

Theme Activities: Begin your "Hail to the Chief" thematic unit with a discussion focusing on the current president of the United States. Use a recent newspaper photograph or poster of the president to show your students. You might begin your discussion by asking questions such as these:

- The leader of the United States is called the president. Who is the president of the United States right now?
- (Show the photograph of the president.) Can you tell me who is shown in this photograph? What does he do?

Explain that during this unit you will be learning about the person who is president now, as well as ones who have been president previously. You will be learning about the job of president and how a person becomes president. The theme is "Hail to the Chief" because that is the title of the tune played to honor a president as he or she enters a room.

Literature Time: Read a biography about the current president of the United States to your students. Biographies of current presidents are often available from monthly student book club orders. For example, *Our President: Bill Clinton* by Shelley Bedik (Scholastic, 1993) is an informative biography written at a level to be read to primary students as well as for them to read independently.

Language Arts: Have students each write three questions they would like to ask the president. Use reference materials to answer these questions during the course of the theme.

Curriculum Connections: Set up a "Red, White, and Blue Center" with an assortment of books about presidents for independent reading and research. Students may visit this center during the class center time or reading workshop.

Creative Arts: Have your students paint a United States flag, using a sheet of 12" x 18" (30 cm x 46 cm) white construction paper as the background, along with blue and red tempera paint. Have a sample flag for the students to view as they paint a blue rectangle in the upper left-hand corner and seven red stripes across the white field. When the paint is completely dry, 50 stars may be added, using white chalk. Display these in your classroom.

Tuesday

Theme Activities: Introduce a commercially available poster showing all the presidents of the United States in chronological order. Discuss the information provided on the chart.

Overview: Hail to the Chief *(cont.)*

━━━━━━━━━━━━━━━━━━━ **Tuesday** *(cont.)* ━━━━━━━━━━━━━━━━━━━

Literature Time: Read the informational picture book *The Buck Stops Here: The Presidents of the United States* by Alice Provensen (HarperCollins, 1990) to your class. Challenge them to explain why the most recent president is not included. The notes about the presidents at the back of the book may be useful for students to use for further research.

Language Arts: Prior to today's lesson, duplicate the mini-book All About the Presidents (pages 228–230). Have your students read the book to learn more about selected presidents.

Curriculum Connections: For a math connection, have your students closely examine real United States coins and currency to discover which presidents are shown on each, plus learn the monetary values.

Creative Arts: Teach your students a variety of patriotic songs, such as "America" and "The Star-Spangled Banner." *The Magic of Music* (Cherry Lane Music, 1998) is a good resource for such songs. The words for these songs can be printed on chart paper or prepared as an overhead transparency for the class to read.

━━━━━━━━━━━━━━━━━━━━━ **Wednesday** ━━━━━━━━━━━━━━━━━━━━━

Theme Activities: Discuss who can be president, introduce vocabulary words related to the presidency, and discuss their meanings. (The president must be a "natural-born" citizen of the United States, must have lived in the United States for at least 14 years, and must be at least 35 years old.) Include words such as "natural-born," "citizen," "election," "White House," "Washington, D.C.," "oath of office," "term of office," "veto," "government," "executive branch of government," and "vice president."

Literature Time: Read excerpts from *The Ladybird Guide to the Presidents of the United States* (Ladybird Books, 1997) to your students.

Language Arts: Duplicate Presidential Facts about the lives of selected presidents (page 231). Have students complete the page, using reference materials as needed.

Curriculum Connections: Prepare a set of containers with real coins in each at your math center. Have students calculate the total worth of the coins in each container.

Creative Arts: Display the presidential seal for your students and discuss what is shown. Have students create their own presidential seals, using crayons, markers, or colored pencils.

Overview: Hail to the Chief *(cont.)*

Thursday

Theme Activities: Lead a discussion about the responsibilities of the president's job.

Literature Time: Read a biography about a former president, such as *A Picture Book of Thomas Jefferson* by David A. Adler (Holiday House, 1990) to compare his life with the life of the current president.

Language Arts: Students may work in pairs or independently to conduct their own independent presidential research (page 232) about presidents of their choosing. You may wish to guide students to conduct their research on a president different from those they have already read about in the mini-book, All About the Presidents. Findings may be presented in written or oral form.

Curriculum Connections: Use your school's computer lab or a classroom computer that has access to the Internet to visit a Web site about United States presidents, such as *www.whitehouse.gov/WH/kids/html/pets.html* or *www.whitehouse.gov/* (Remember to always visit the site yourself before your students do.)

Creative Arts: Have students create a campaign slogan about themselves and then use the slogan as the basis for making campaign posters.

Friday

Theme Activities: Brainstorm a list of promises that a person running for president might make.

Literature Time: Read a biography about another former president, such as *A Picture Book of John F. Kennedy* by David A. Adler (Holiday House, 1991).

Language Arts: Have students each complete a page for a class book called If I Were the President (pages 233–235).

Curriculum Connections: Use the information from the student's Parent and Grandparent Presidential Survey to work with students to make a time line, a chart with tally marks, and then a bar graph.

Creative Arts: Play a recording (or sing) "Hail to the Chief" while students play rhythm instruments and march. This may work better outside or in your school music room or gymnasium.

This Week's Theme

Hail to the Chief

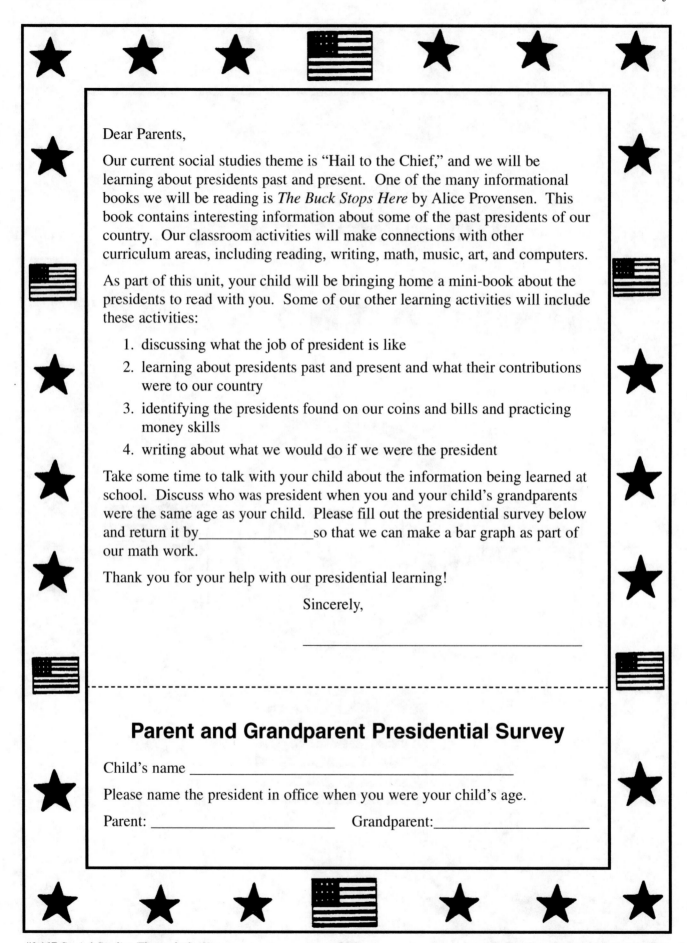

Dear Parents,

Our current social studies theme is "Hail to the Chief," and we will be learning about presidents past and present. One of the many informational books we will be reading is *The Buck Stops Here* by Alice Provensen. This book contains interesting information about some of the past presidents of our country. Our classroom activities will make connections with other curriculum areas, including reading, writing, math, music, art, and computers.

As part of this unit, your child will be bringing home a mini-book about the presidents to read with you. Some of our other learning activities will include these activities:

1. discussing what the job of president is like
2. learning about presidents past and present and what their contributions were to our country
3. identifying the presidents found on our coins and bills and practicing money skills
4. writing about what we would do if we were the president

Take some time to talk with your child about the information being learned at school. Discuss who was president when you and your child's grandparents were the same age as your child. Please fill out the presidential survey below and return it by_____so that we can make a bar graph as part of our math work.

Thank you for your help with our presidential learning!

Sincerely,

_____

Parent and Grandparent Presidential Survey

Child's name _____

Please name the president in office when you were your child's age.

Parent: _____   Grandparent:_____

Daily Journal Topics: Hail to the Chief

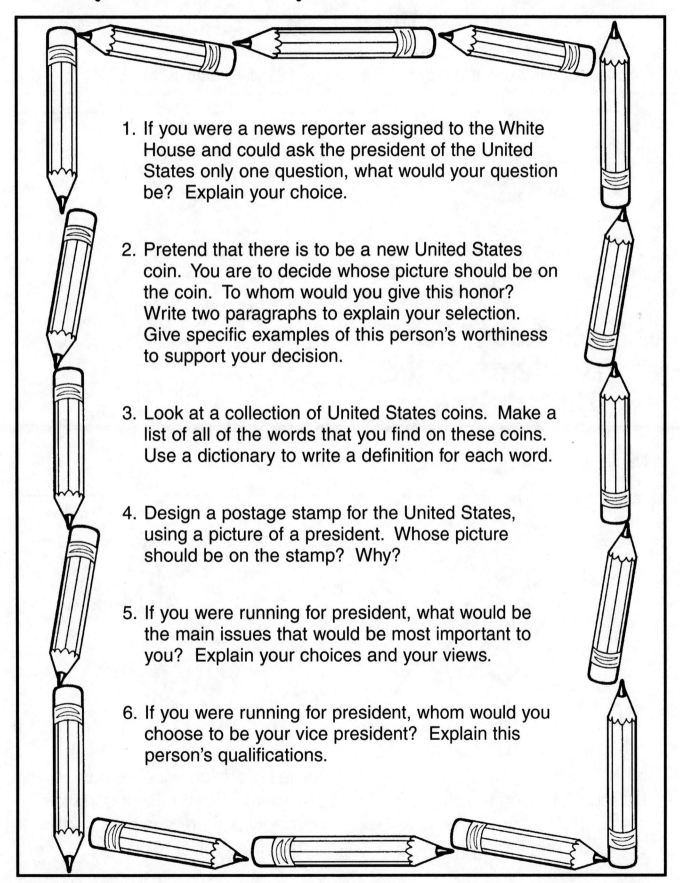

1. If you were a news reporter assigned to the White House and could ask the president of the United States only one question, what would your question be? Explain your choice.

2. Pretend that there is to be a new United States coin. You are to decide whose picture should be on the coin. To whom would you give this honor? Write two paragraphs to explain your selection. Give specific examples of this person's worthiness to support your decision.

3. Look at a collection of United States coins. Make a list of all of the words that you find on these coins. Use a dictionary to write a definition for each word.

4. Design a postage stamp for the United States, using a picture of a president. Whose picture should be on the stamp? Why?

5. If you were running for president, what would be the main issues that would be most important to you? Explain your choices and your views.

6. If you were running for president, whom would you choose to be your vice president? Explain this person's qualifications.

All About the Presidents
Mini-Book

Your teacher will explain the directions for the following activity.

All About the Presidents of the United States

Name _____

George Washington was the first president of the United States.

1

Thomas Jefferson was the third president. He wrote the Declaration of Independence.

2

James Madison was the fourth president. The White House was burned while he was president during the War of 1812.

3

All About the Presidents
Mini-Book *(cont.)*

Abraham Lincoln was the 16th president. He wrote the Emancipation Proclamation to free the slaves and worked to keep the country together during the Civil War.

4

Theodore Roosevelt was the 26th president. The teddy bear was named after him because he refused to shoot a small bear on a hunting trip.

5

Herbert Hoover was the 31st president. He was president during the Great Depression, a sad time during U.S. history.

6

Franklin Delano Roosevelt was the only president elected to four terms of office.

7

All About the Presidents Mini-Book *(cont.)*

Dwight D. Eisenhower was the 34th president. He was president when Alaska and Hawaii became the 49th and 50th states.   **8**

John F. Kennedy was the 35th president. He started the Peace Corps and encouraged the U.S. space program.   **9**

Ronald Reagan was the 40th president. He appointed the first woman Supreme Court justice, Sandra Day O'Connor.   **10**

This is _____, who is president of the United States right now.   **11**

Presidential Facts

Name: _____ Date: _____

Directions: Read the descriptions for each of the following presidents. Use the presidents' names from the word bank to fill in the missing names. You may use reference materials.

Franklin Roosevelt   Abraham Lincoln

James Buchanan   George Washington

Bill Clinton   Grover Cleveland

George Bush   William Taft

John Kennedy

1. _____ was the only president to serve two nonconsecutive terms of office.

2. _____ had a cat named Socks and a dog named Buddy.

3. _____ was the youngest person elected president of the United States.

4. _____ was the only president elected to four terms of office.

5. _____ was the only president who was never married.

6. _____ was the leader of the colonial armies during the American War of Independence.

7. _____ was the president of the United States when the *Titanic* sank.

8. _____ wrote the Emancipation Proclamation.

9. _____ was the president of the United States when the Berlin Wall came down.

Presidential Research

Name: _____ Date: _____

Directions: Use reference materials to conduct your own independent research about a president of your choosing. Use this sheet for recording the information.

- My president's name is _____.

- My president was born on _____.

- My president was from the state of_____.

- My president became the_____president of the United States.

- My president became president of the United States in the year _____ and was president until the year _____.

- My president was a _____ by trade. (What job did he or she have before becoming president?)

- The vice president who served with my president was _____.

I also found these three interesting facts about my president:

1. _____

   _____

2. _____

   _____

3. _____

   _____

If I Were the President

Purpose: For a class book titled If I Were the President of the United States, each child will create a page telling what he or she would do if he or she were the president.

Materials

- If I Were the President Book Cover (page 234)
- If I Were the President Paper (page 235)
- pencils, markers, crayons

Preparation: Reproduce the shape paper for the children to write on. (If you would like children to do a first draft and a final copy, then make enough sheets for this purpose.) Reproduce one front cover for the class book and color it appropriately. Mount the cover on a piece of red tagboard and cut a back cover for your class book the same color and the same size.

Instructions: Ask children what they would do if they were the president of the United States. You might want to record their responses on a chalkboard or chart for children to refer to during their writing. Then the children will write their own responses with details and examples on the presidential paper. Children may use the space at the bottom of the paper for an illustration.

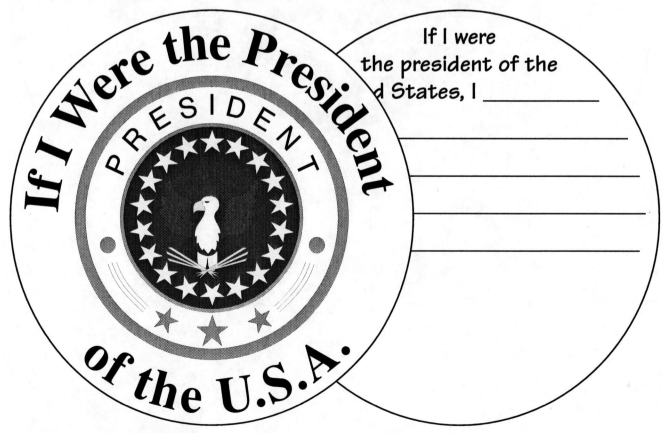

If I Were the President Book Cover

If I Were the President Paper

If I were
the president of the
United States, I _____

_____

_____

_____

_____

★ ★ ★ ★ ★ ★ ★ ★ ★ ★ ★ ★

Weekly Theme: *Hooray for the U.S.A.!*   Week _____

	Monday	Tuesday	Wednesday	Thursday	Friday
Date					
Theme Activities	Discuss What is the United States of America?	Identify regions of the United States.	Introduce the concept of patriotism.	Introduce the concept of national symbols.	Discuss what citizenship means.
Literature Time	Discuss The Declaration of Independence and The Preamble to the U.S. Constitution.	Read and discuss *A Picture Book of the U.S.A.* by Beth Goodman.	Read *Paul Revere's Ride* by Henry Wadsworth Longfellow.	Read *The Flag of the United States* by Dennis B. Fradin.	Read from *The Children's Book of America* edited by William J. Bennett.
Language Arts	Brainstorm a class list of why the United States is special.	Read and share My Book of the United States.	Write essays titled "Why I'm Proud to Be an American."	Complete the National Symbols Riddles.	List ways to be a good citizen.
Curriculum Connections	Use a calculator for U.S.A. Math.	Complete a graph of states in regions.	Discuss and read *The Star-Spangled Banner* by Peter Spier.	Make a mini-book of the Flags of the U.S.A. and an estimating jar.	Discuss how we can protect the earth
Creative Arts	Paint flags of the United States.	Sing "America the Beautiful."	Sing patriotic songs.	Sing "You're a Grand Old Flag."	Create "How to Be a Good Citizen" posters.

Overview: Hooray for the U.S.A.!

================================= **Monday** =================================

Theme Activities: Lead a discussion based upon the question "What is the United States of America?" Emphasize that the United States is the name of our country, that it is located on the continent of North America, that it has 50 states that are "united," and that it represents the pride that citizens of the United States feel for their country.

Literature Time: Explain to your class that the United States was once a part of Great Britain until the settlers in the "colonies" decided that they wanted to have their own separate nation and wrote The Declaration of Independence. Read a copy of The Declaration of Independence to your students and discuss what it means. Explain that the colonists thought more information needed to be written down for our country, and they wrote The Constitution. Locate a copy of The Preamble to the United States Constitution and read it to your students. Discuss what it means.

Language Arts: Work with your students to brainstorm a list of reasons why they think the United States is special. Display the list and add to it throughout this unit.

Curriculum Connections: Duplicate U.S.A. Math on page 243 for your students. They may use a calculator for answers to the mathematical problems that involve our country.

Creative Arts: Discuss the United States flag, with its 13 stripes (to help us remember the original 13 colonies) and 50 stars (one for each state). Students may work at an easel to paint United States flags. Provide a piece of 18" x 24" (46 cm x 61 cm) white construction paper for each student. Guide the students to paint seven red stripes and a field of blue in the upper left-hand corner. Fifty stars may be added, using white chalk after all the paint is dry. Display all of the flags in your classroom during this unit.

================================= **Tuesday** =================================

Theme Activities: Look at a map of the United States and explain that since the United States is so large, it has great diversity. Therefore, it is better to learn about it region by region. Show your students the different regions that you will be learning about: the New England states, the Middle Atlantic states, the Southern states, the Midwestern states, the Rocky Mountain states, the Southwestern states, the Pacific Coast states, Alaska, and Hawaii.

Literature Time: Read and discuss *A Picture Book of the U.S.A.* by Beth Goodman (Scholastic, 1991). The photographs provide a realistic look at each region.

Overview: Hooray for the U.S.A.! *(cont.)*

Tuesday *(cont.)*

Language Arts: Duplicate pages 244–248 for each student to use in making a booklet called My Book of the United States. Students will read the booklet at school and then take it home to share with their parents.

Curriculum Connections: Count the number of states in each region. Make a graph to determine which region of the United States has the most states. You may wish to use an overhead transparency to make a class graph.

Creative Arts: Sing "America, the Beautiful" (*The Magic of Music*, Cherry Lane Music, 1998) with your students. Pick out words that describe the regions of the United States, such as "amber waves of grain," "fruited plain," "sea to shining sea," etc.

Wednesday

Theme Activities: Introduce the concept of "patriotism" to your students so that they will understand that it means to love and honor one's country.

Literature Time: Explain that today's literature selection is about a famous patriot in American history, Paul Revere. Read *Paul Revere's Ride* by Henry Wadsworth Longfellow (Dutton Children's Book, 1990) to your students. (The author's note at the back of the book might be read first to provide your students with background information needed to better enjoy the book.)

Language Arts: Have your students work on essays titled "Why I'm Proud to Be an American." Work through the editing process to publish these essays and have students illustrate them. These will be bound together to make a class book.

Curriculum Connections: Discuss the writing of our national anthem, "The Star-Spangled Banner," by Francis Scott Key during the War of 1812. Then read *The Star-Spangled Banner* by Peter Spier (Doubleday, 1973) to your class to make a connection between history and music. Discuss the proper way for people to stand when they hear the national anthem.

Creative Arts: Choose a variety of patriotic songs to have students learn and sing, such as "Yankee Doodle," "The Star-Spangled Banner," and "America." *The Magic of Music* (Cherry Lane Music, 1998) is a good source of appropriate music.

Thursday

Theme Activities: Introduce the concept of "national symbols," and work with students to compile a list of these symbols. Students will later need to refer to this Glossary of National Symbols.

Overview: Hooray for the U.S.A.! *(cont.)*

Thursday *(cont.)*

Literature Time: Read *The Flag of the United States* by Dennis B. Fradin to your students. This book summarizes many concepts already discussed in this theme, as well as explaining what our flag represents.

Language Arts: Write the words of The Pledge of Allegiance on a large chart or overhead transparency for your students and explain that it is a way to promise to be loyal to the flag and the United States. Discuss the pledge phrase by phrase, as well as the proper way for people to stand when saying it. Duplicate page 249 for your students to complete the National Symbols Riddles.

Curriculum Connections: Reproduce page 250 for your students to make a Flags of the U.S.A. Mini-Book. You might also place small U.S. flag erasers (available from the Oriental Trading catalog, phone number 1-800-228-2269) in your estimating jar at your math area.

Creative Arts: Teach students the song "You're a Grand Old Flag" from *The Magic of Music* (Cherry Lane Music, 1998). Students may wave small U.S. flags while they are singing.

Friday

Theme Activities: Discuss what "citizenship" means, as well as what it means to be a good citizen. Explain how a person is a citizen by birth and how a person may become a citizen of the United States.

Literature Time: Read excerpts from *The Children's Book of America,* edited by William J. Bennett (Simon & Schuster, 1998) to your class. This beautiful book is a good way to conclude your thematic unit on the United States.

Language Arts: Work with your students to compile a list of ways that we can be good citizens of the United States.

Curriculum Connections: One way that we can be good citizens (it may be on your class list) is to take good care of the earth. Have students elaborate on this idea and give specific suggestions we can use to help take care of the earth, such as recycling, reducing, and reusing. Get multiple copies of *Let's Take Care of the Earth* by Rozanne Lanczak Williams (Creative Teaching Press, 1994) for students to read independently.

Creative Arts: Have your students refer to the list of ways to be a good citizen to create their own posters that will tell in words and illustrations "How to Be a Good Citizen."

This Week's Theme

Hooray for the U.S.A.!

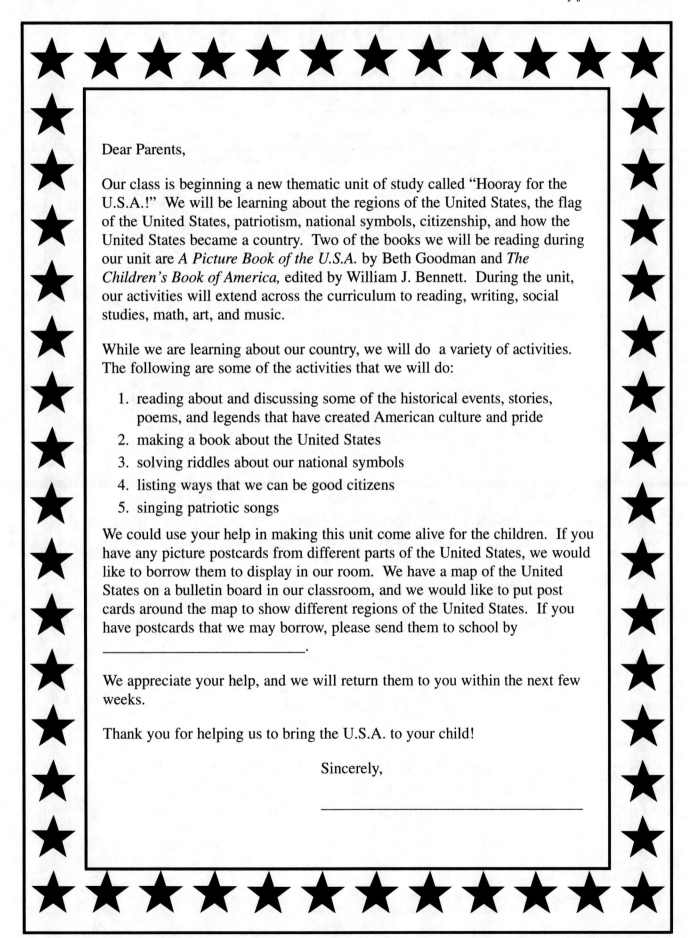

Dear Parents,

Our class is beginning a new thematic unit of study called "Hooray for the U.S.A.!" We will be learning about the regions of the United States, the flag of the United States, patriotism, national symbols, citizenship, and how the United States became a country. Two of the books we will be reading during our unit are *A Picture Book of the U.S.A.* by Beth Goodman and *The Children's Book of America,* edited by William J. Bennett. During the unit, our activities will extend across the curriculum to reading, writing, social studies, math, art, and music.

While we are learning about our country, we will do a variety of activities. The following are some of the activities that we will do:

1. reading about and discussing some of the historical events, stories, poems, and legends that have created American culture and pride
2. making a book about the United States
3. solving riddles about our national symbols
4. listing ways that we can be good citizens
5. singing patriotic songs

We could use your help in making this unit come alive for the children. If you have any picture postcards from different parts of the United States, we would like to borrow them to display in our room. We have a map of the United States on a bulletin board in our classroom, and we would like to put post cards around the map to show different regions of the United States. If you have postcards that we may borrow, please send them to school by

_____.

We appreciate your help, and we will return them to you within the next few weeks.

Thank you for helping us to bring the U.S.A. to your child!

                              Sincerely,

                              _____

Daily Journal Topics:
Hooray for the U.S.A.!

1. Write about the region of the United States where you live. Add specific details to describe your region.

2. Choose your favorite region of the United States. Tell why this is your favorite region.

3. Choose one of the United States of America coins. List the words found on that coin. Tell why you think each word is included on the coin.

4. Write a poem about the United States of America. Try to include information about what you can see in the U.S.A. Write your poem in red, white, and blue.

5. Write a cheer or chant about the United States. Give it the title "Hooray for the U.S.A.!"

6. Use resource materials to write an informational article about one of the national symbols.

7. Write an essay about why you think the United States is a special place to live. Give supporting details to convince your readers to agree with you.

U.S.A. Math

Name _____ Date _____

Directions: If your teacher wishes, you may use a calculator to find the answers to the following mathematical problems.

1. The flag of the United States has five rows with six stars each and four rows with five stars each. How many stars are on the flag of the United States?

2. The Declaration of Independence was approved on July 4, 1776. It said that the United States was not any longer a part of Britain. How many years ago did the United States become free of Britain?

3. The United States made a law that the U.S. flag was to have 13 stars and 13 stripes for the 13 states. This law passed on June 14, 1777. Now June 14 is called Flag Day. How many years ago was the first Flag Day?

4. The first United States flag had 13 stars that stood for the original 13 colonies. How many more stars are on the United States flag now?

5. The Pledge of Allegiance was written by a man named Francis Bellamy in 1892. Congress made it a promise of loyalty to the United States in 1942. How long ago was it written?

6. The words for "The Star-Spangled Banner" were written as a poem by Francis Scott Key in 1814. He was happy because, even though the British were bombing Fort McHenry, in the morning the United States flag was still there. "The Star-Spangled Banner" became the national anthem in 1931 by an act of Congress. How many years after it was written did it become our national anthem?

My Book of the United States

Directions: Read the information about the regions of the United States. Cut on the lines, put the pages in order, and staple. You may color the illustrations.

My Book of the United States

Name _____

The Pacific States

The Pacific states are next to the Pacific Ocean.
There are mountains, tall forests, and beautiful beaches.
The Pacific states are Washington, Oregon, and California.

1

My Book of the United States *(cont.)*

The Rocky Mountain States

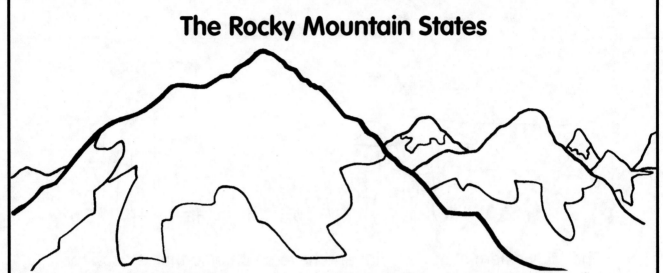

The Rocky Mountains run through this region. Montana, Idaho, Wyoming, Nevada, Utah, and Colorado are in this region. Yellowstone National Park is here.

2

The Southwestern States

The Southwestern states are sunny, hot, and dry.
Arizona, New Mexico, Texas, and Oklahoma are in this region.
The Grand Canyon is here.

3

My Book of the United States *(cont.)*

The Midwestern States

The Midwestern states are flat and have much land that is used for farms. North Dakota, South Dakota, Nebraska, Kansas, Minnesota, Iowa, Missouri, Wisconsin, Illinois, Indiana, Ohio, and Michigan are in this region.

4

The Southern States

The Southern states are flat, but some areas have hills and mountains, too. Arkansas, Louisiana, Mississippi, Virginia, Maryland, Delaware, North Carolina, South Carolina, and Florida are here. You will also find Georgia, Alabama, Tenessee, Kentucky, and West Virginia.

5

My Book of the United States *(cont.)*

The Middle Atlantic States

The Middle Atlantic states have big cities and lots of people. New York, Pennsylvania, and New Jersey are here.

6

The New England States

The New England states are where the early settlers first came after they left England. This explains why we call the area New England. Maine, Vermont, New Hampshire, Massachusetts, Rhode Island, and Connecticut are here.

7

My Book of the United States *(cont.)*

The District of Columbia, Alaska, and Hawaii

  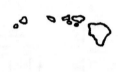

The District of Columbia is not in a state. It is set aside as the capital of the United States. That is what "D.C." means in Washington, D.C.

Alaska is the largest state. It is far north of the other states. Parts of Alaska are very cold all the time.

Hawaii is a state. It is a group of 20 islands in the Pacific Ocean. The weather is always warm. It has a tropical climate.

8

The United States of America

Together all of these regions make the U.S.A! Hooray!

9

National Symbols Riddles

Name _____ Date _____

Directions: Use words from the glossary to answer the following National Symbol Riddles.

Glossary of National Symbols

1. I am the promise that Americans make to be loyal to our country.
   What am I? _____

2. I was carved on the side of a mountain in South Dakota.
   What am I? _____

3. I was presented to the United States by France. I stand in New York Harbor.
   What am I? _____

4. I am the national anthem. What am I? _____

5. I am called "Old Glory." What am I? _____

6. I am seen as a symbol of freedom. What am I?_____

Flags of the U.S.A. Mini-Book

Directions: Look at the different flags that have been official flags of the United States. Color the flag in each box. Cut out the boxes, place them in the correct order, and staple them to make a mini-book.

U.S. Flags Mini-Book

Name_____

1

The Continental Colors (1776)

2

The first Stars and Stripes (1777)

3

The 26-star flag (1795)

4

The 30-star flag (1848)

5

The 36-star flag (1864)

6

The 48-star flag (1912)

7

The 50-star flag (1959)

Weekly Theme: Exceptional Explorers   Week_____

	Monday	Tuesday	Wednesday	Thursday	Friday
Date					
Theme Activities	Discuss what explorers are and their importance.	Begin to brainstorm a list of explorers.	Create a time line of explorers.	Discus exploring the "new frontier."	Examine a list of explorers and explain the research project.
Literature Time	Read *A Picture Book of Christopher Columbus* by David A. Adler.	Read "Meriwether Lewis and William Clark" from *One-Minute Stories of Great Americans.*	Read *Young Amelia Earhart: A Dream to Fly* by Sarah Alcott.	Read *Sally Ride* by Marcia S. Gresko.	Read *Five Brave Explorers* by Wade Hudson.
Language Arts	Read *In 1492* by Jean Marzollo.	Write about the importance of Lewis and Clark.	Write letters about dreams for the future.	Assemble and read My Book of Space Exploration.	Begin creative writing—"If I Were an Explorer."
Curriculum Connections	Trace the voyages of Christopher Columbus.	Trace the expedition of Lewis and Clark.	Trace the route of Amelia Earhart's final flight.	Learn about space exploration.	Conduct an explorer research project.
Creative Arts	Design and create a mural of explorers' ships.	Create watercolor paintings of the wilderness.	Create paper airplanes.	Create a mural of our solar system and beyond.	Paint or draw portraits of explorers.

Overview: Exceptional Explorers

Monday

Theme Activities: Introduce the concept of "explorer" to your students as being one who searches or travels to discover more information. Discuss why explorers are important and how they have contributed to the history of the world.

Literature Time: Read *A Picture Book of Christopher Columbus* by David A. Adler (Holiday House, 1991) to your students. Discuss the importance of the explorations of Christopher Columbus to our history.

Language Arts: Share the rhyme of Columbus' 1492 expedition by reading *In 1492* by Jean Marzollo (Scholastic, 1991) to your students. Encourage them to copy the famous beginning sentence on a piece of white construction paper and then illustrate it.

Curriculum Connections: Discuss the belief at the time of Columbus that the world was flat and why Columbus believed that it was round. How did this influence his explorations? Look at a globe and trace the voyages of Columbus.

Creative Arts: Students may use tempera paints to create a mural of explorers' ships on the ocean. Use resource books and posters as models for the students' paintings.

Tuesday

Theme Activities: Explain that explorers do not always travel across oceans. Guide students to make a list of explorers and add to this list each day during your unit. Provide informational books and materials for students to examine so that they will be able to contribute to this list. (See the bibliography on pages 369–374.)

Literature Time: Read the article called "Meriwether Lewis and William Clark" from *One-Minute Stories of Great Americans* adapted by Shari Lewis (Doubleday, 1990).

Language Arts: Have your students write a paragraph summarizing how the explorations of Lewis and Clark were important to the history of the United States.

Curriculum Connections: Use a map of the United States to trace the route of the expedition of Lewis and Clark.

Creative Arts: Have students use watercolor paints to create pictures of the wilderness that they believe Lewis and Clark saw on their explorations in the northwestern United States. Encourage students to include plant and animal life.

Overview: Exceptional Explorers *(cont.)*

Wednesday

Theme Activities: Use a long strip of adding machine tape to create a time line of explorers you study. Begin by writing the year "1492" on your time line with the name "Christopher Columbus" directly below it. Add "1804–1806" with the names "Lewis and Clark." Add other explorers as you learn about them. Display your time line along your classroom wall at a level where students will be able to see it easily.

1492

Christopher Columbus

1804–1806

Lewis and Clark

Literature Time: Read *Young Amelia Earhart: A Dream to Fly* by Sarah Alcott (Troll, 1992) to your students. Discuss with your students the dream that Amelia had and how she followed that dream.

Language Arts: Lead your students to discuss dreams of what they would like to do during their lives. Have each student put the date at the top of a sheet of paper and write a letter to himself or herself describing the dreams they have. Seal the letter in an envelope and send it home with the student with a note on the outside of the envelope saying "Do Not Open Until _____" (today's date, but 20 years later). The parent letter on page 256 explains this letter to parents so they will be aware of the letter and save it for their child.

Curriculum Connections: Use a globe to trace the route of Amelia Earhart's final expedition.

Creative Arts: Duplicate page 258 for students to use in creating their own paper airplanes. Have them follow directions to decorate, cut, and fold their own airplanes.

Thursday

Theme Activities: Introduce the concept that space exploration is the "new frontier" and that astronauts are the present-day explorers.

Literature Time: Read *Sally Ride* by Marcia S. Gresko (Teacher Created Materials, 1997) and discuss the possibility of your students traveling in space.

Language Arts: Duplicate pages 259–262 for your students to read My Book of Space Exploration. After assembling the pages into a book and reading the book, students will answer the questions at the end of the book by locating the needed information in the book's text.

Overview: Exceptional Explorers (cont.)

════════════════ **Thursday** (cont.) ════════════════

Curriculum Connections: Discuss space exploration with your students. Share your memories of the space program with your students, perhaps beginning with John Glenn's first trip into space, progressing to Neil Armstrong's walk on the moon, and most recently, John Glenn's trip on the space shuttle. Have a variety of materials at your Science Center about space exploration, such as those suggested in the bibliography on pages 369–374.

Creative Arts: Use a large strip of blue bulletin board paper as the background for your students' mural of our solar system, our galaxy, and beyond. Label the mural "The New Frontier for Exploration."

════════════════ **Friday** ════════════════

Theme Activities: Guide your students in examining the list of explorers they have made during your unit. Explain to them that they will each choose an explorer from this list and conduct a research project to learn more about that person and his or her importance in history.

Literature Time: Read *Five Brave Explorers* by Wade Hudson (Scholastic, 1995). This book tells about five African American explorers and their contributions to the history of our country. Add these names to your class list of explorers if they are not already listed.

Language Arts: Have your students write an essay entitled "If I Were an Explorer," in which the students describe what they would explore and why they would choose to explore that area, as well as what they might expect to see there.

Curriculum Connections: Duplicate page 263 for each student to conduct his or her own Explorer Research Project. Each student will use reference materials to complete the project, following the information outline. Explorers may be from the curricular areas of science or social studies. Possible subjects for study include Neil A. Armstrong, Vasco Nuñez de Balboa, Vitus Bering, John Cabot, James Cook, Francisco de Coronado, Jacques-Yves Cousteau, Hernando DeSoto, Sir Francis Drake, Leif Ericson, John H. Glenn, Jr., Henry Hudson, Louis Joliet, Sieur de La Salle, David Livingstone, Ferdinand Magellan, Jacques Marquette, Robert E. Peary, Zebulon Pike, Marco Polo, Juan Ponce de León, and Amerigo Vespucci.

Creative Arts: Students will paint portraits of the explorers they studied during their research projects. Display these portraits in your classroom or hallway, along with the completed research projects.

This Week's Theme

Exceptional Explorers

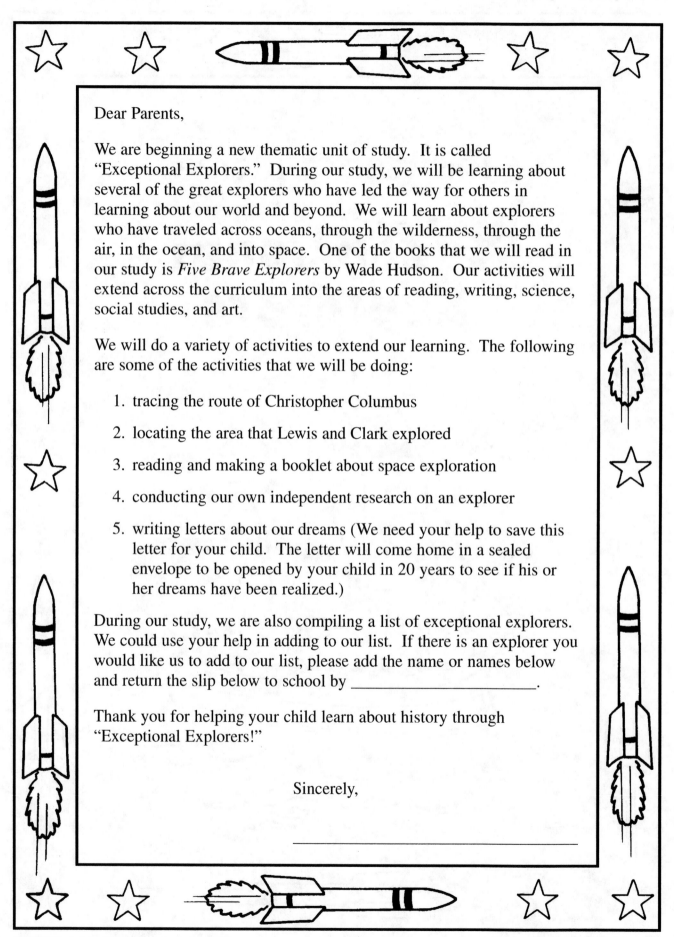

Dear Parents,

We are beginning a new thematic unit of study. It is called "Exceptional Explorers." During our study, we will be learning about several of the great explorers who have led the way for others in learning about our world and beyond. We will learn about explorers who have traveled across oceans, through the wilderness, through the air, in the ocean, and into space. One of the books that we will read in our study is *Five Brave Explorers* by Wade Hudson. Our activities will extend across the curriculum into the areas of reading, writing, science, social studies, and art.

We will do a variety of activities to extend our learning. The following are some of the activities that we will be doing:

1. tracing the route of Christopher Columbus

2. locating the area that Lewis and Clark explored

3. reading and making a booklet about space exploration

4. conducting our own independent research on an explorer

5. writing letters about our dreams (We need your help to save this letter for your child. The letter will come home in a sealed envelope to be opened by your child in 20 years to see if his or her dreams have been realized.)

During our study, we are also compiling a list of exceptional explorers. We could use your help in adding to our list. If there is an explorer you would like us to add to our list, please add the name or names below and return the slip below to school by _____.

Thank you for helping your child learn about history through "Exceptional Explorers!"

Sincerely,

_____

Daily Journal Topics: Exceptional Explorers

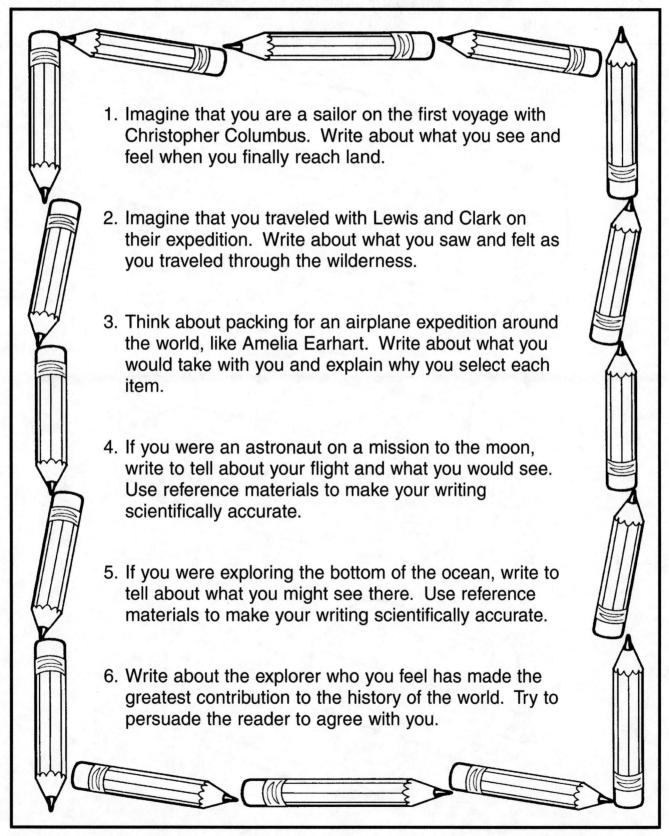

1. Imagine that you are a sailor on the first voyage with Christopher Columbus. Write about what you see and feel when you finally reach land.

2. Imagine that you traveled with Lewis and Clark on their expedition. Write about what you saw and felt as you traveled through the wilderness.

3. Think about packing for an airplane expedition around the world, like Amelia Earhart. Write about what you would take with you and explain why you select each item.

4. If you were an astronaut on a mission to the moon, write to tell about your flight and what you would see. Use reference materials to make your writing scientifically accurate.

5. If you were exploring the bottom of the ocean, write to tell about what you might see there. Use reference materials to make your writing scientifically accurate.

6. Write about the explorer who you feel has made the greatest contribution to the history of the world. Try to persuade the reader to agree with you.

Create Your Own Paper Airplane

Use the paper airplane shapes below to create your own paper airplane. Use markers or crayons to decorate your airplane (and give it a name on its nose, too). Try flying it!

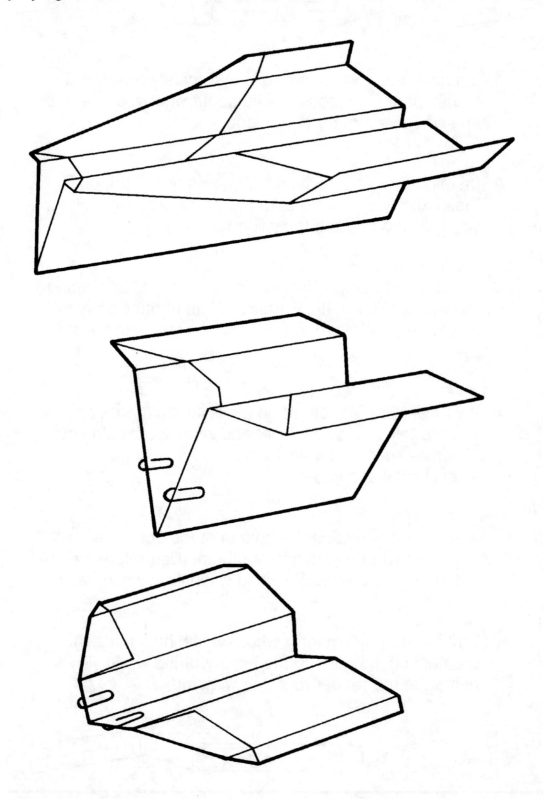

My Book of Space Exploration

Directions: Read the information about space exploration. Cut on the lines, put the pages in the correct order, and staple to make your book. You may color the pictures.

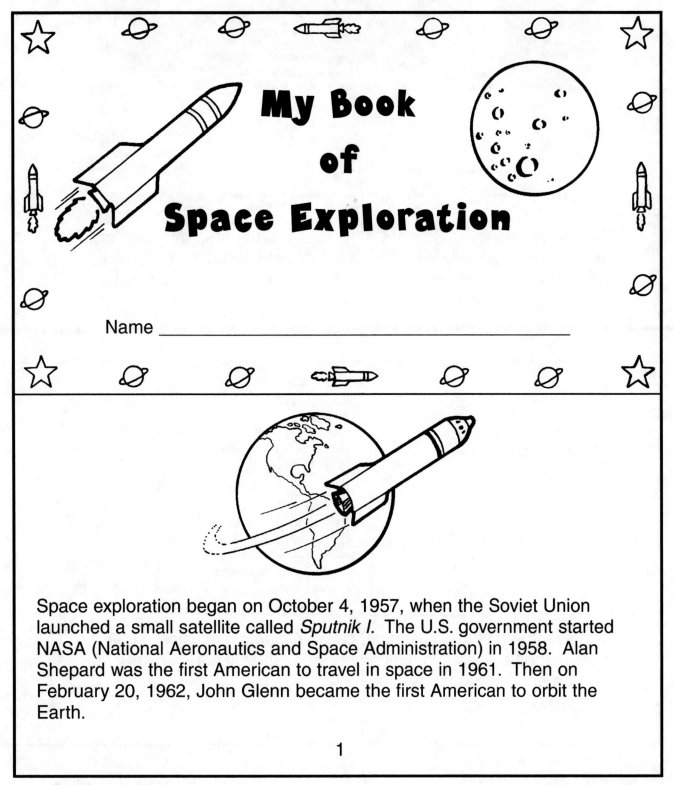

My Book of Space Exploration

Name _____

Space exploration began on October 4, 1957, when the Soviet Union launched a small satellite called *Sputnik I.* The U.S. government started NASA (National Aeronautics and Space Administration) in 1958. Alan Shepard was the first American to travel in space in 1961. Then on February 20, 1962, John Glenn became the first American to orbit the Earth.

1

My Book of Space Exploration *(cont.)*

Neil Armstrong and Edwin Aldrin, Jr., were the first people to walk on the moon on July 20, 1969. Neil Armstrong said, "That's one small step for man and one giant leap for mankind." They put a U.S. flag on the moon.

2

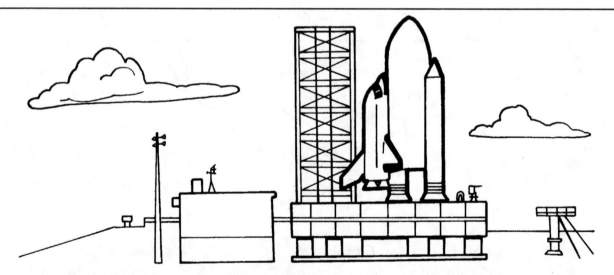

In 1981, the first space shuttle, called *Columbia*, blasted off. A space shuttle goes into space and then lands like an airplane. It can be used over and over again.

3

My Book of Space Exploration *(cont.)*

Sally Ride became the first American woman to travel in space in June 1983. Guion S. Bluford, Jr., was the first African American to travel in space. Franklin R. Chang-Diaz was the first Hispanic American to travel in space.

4

John Glenn made another trip into space at the age of 77 in 1998. This time he was aboard the space shuttle.

5

My Book of Space Exploration *(cont.)*

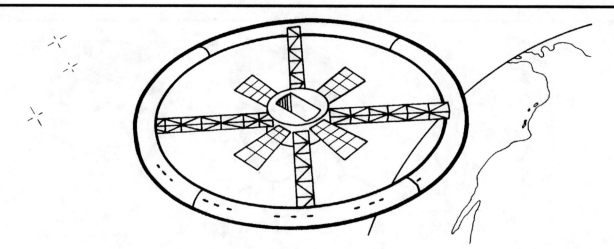

The United States and 15 other nations have begun to build an international space station 220 miles above the Earth. The space shuttle *Endeavor* took one part there in December 1998. Here is a picture of a space station.

6

Answer the following questions:

1. Who was the first American to orbit the Earth? _____

2. When did Neil Armstrong and Edwin Aldrin, Jr., walk on
   the moon?_____

3. What was the first space shuttle named?_____

4. Who was the first American woman to travel
   in space? _____

5. Would you like to explore space? Why or why not? _____

   _____

7

Explorer Research Project

Name _____ Date _____

Directions: Use reference materials to learn more about an explorer of your choice. Write the name of the explorer as the title of your report. Then add your information to the following research framework to complete your report.

I did research to learn more about _____.

This explorer was born in the year _____

in the country of _____.

This explorer is remembered for exploring _____

in the year _____. This exploration was important to the world,

because _____.

This is a picture of the explorer _____.

Weekly Theme: Ingenious Inventors   Week_____

	Monday	Tuesday	Wednesday	Thursday	Friday
Date					
Theme Activities	Lead a class discussion about inventors.	Compile a list of inventors.	Compile a list of the most important inventions.	Classify inventions.	Hold a class discussion about future inventions.
Literature Time	Read "Leonardo da Vinci" from *My First Book of Biographies* by Jean Marzollo and *Leonardo da Vinci* by Ibi Lepscky.	Read *A Picture Book of Benjamin Franklin* by David A. Adler and also in *My First Book of Biographies* by Jean Marzollo.	Read "Marie and Pierre Curie" in *My First Book of Biographies* by Jean Marzollo and *Marie Curie* by Ibi Lepscky.	Read *Thomas Edison* by Shelley Bedik and the entry in *My First Book of Biographies* by Jean Marzollo.	Read "George Washington Carver" from *My First Book of Biographies* by Jean Marzollo.
Language Arts	Compile a list of da Vinci's interests.	Assemble and read My Book of Ingenious Inventors.	Conduct a class survey and graph the "Most Important Invention."	Hold a class discussion of quotations from Thomas Edison.	Write an essay—"If I Were an Inventor."
Curriculum Connections	Learn about da Vinci's famous works of art.	List and discuss Franklin's contributions to the world.	Introduce materials and rules found in a scientific laboratory.	Show students how an electric light bulb works.	Learn how peanuts grow.
Creative Arts	Create personal "Mysterious Smile" paintings.	Develop posters of Franklin's famous sayings.	Make scientist drawings.	Make posters advertising Edison's inventions.	Share *Mistakes That Worked* by Charlotte Foltz Jones. Design an invention.

Overview: Ingenious Inventors

Monday

Theme Activities: Introduce the concept of "inventors" by explaining that inventors use knowledge and imagination to create something that was never made before. Discuss why inventors are important to the world.

Literature Time: Read the article about Leonardo da Vinci in *My First Book of Biographies* by Jean Marzollo (Scholastic, 1994). For additional information, read the book *Leonardo da Vinci* by Ibi Lepscky (Barron's Educational Series, 1993).

Language Arts: After having read the books and the article, have your students work in pairs or as a whole group with the teacher to make a list of the many interests of Leonardo da Vinci, since he is remembered as a talented painter, a scientist, and an inventor.

Curriculum Connections: Guide your students to learn about da Vinci's famous paintings, in particular the *Mona Lisa* and *The Last Supper.* Visit your school or public library or art museum to locate information about photographs of these paintings to share with your students. Mention the "mysterious smile" of the *Mona Lisa* because that will be the theme of the following art project.

Creative Arts: Provide tempera paints and a piece of white construction paper for your young artists to use in painting portraits of themselves with their own "mysterious smiles."

Tuesday

Theme Activities: Work with your students today to begin compiling a list of inventors that the children know. Add to this list throughout the unit.

Literature Time: Read *A Picture Book of Benjamin Franklin* by David A. Adler (Holiday House, 1990). You might also want to read the entry about Benjamin Franklin in *My First Book of Biographies* by Jean Marzollo (Scholastic, 1994).

Language Arts: Duplicate pages 271–274 for your students to read My Book of Ingenious Inventors. After assembling the pages into a book and reading the book, students will answer the questions at the end of the book by locating the needed information in the book's text.

Curriculum Connections: Discuss the many contributions that Benjamin Franklin made to the world. List these contributions.

Overview: Ingenious Inventors *(cont.)*

Tuesday *(cont.)*

Creative Arts: Read through several of Benjamin Franklin's famous sayings with your students. Students will choose one of the sayings to write at the top of a sheet of white construction paper (12" x 18" or 30 cm x 46 cm) and then illustrate the saying, using crayons or colored pencils. Possible sayings would include "Early to bed and early to rise, makes a man healthy, wealthy, and wise," "A penny saved is a penny earned," "God helps them that help themselves," and "Little strokes fell mighty oaks."

Wednesday

Theme Activities: Work with students today to list the most important inventions in the world. Compare this list with your list of inventors.

Literature Time: Read the entry called "Marie and Pierre Curie" from *My First Book of Biographies* by Jean Marzollo (Scholastic, 1994). For more information about the childhood of Marie Curie, read *Marie Curie* by Ibi Lepscky (Barron's Educational Series, 1990).

Language Arts: Have your students participate in a class survey to determine which invention they feel is the most important. Make a graph to show the results of your survey.

Curriculum Connections: If possible, wear a white lab coat today as you introduce your students to some basic materials and safety rules that would be found in a laboratory. Materials should include beakers, test tubes, eyedroppers, Bunsen burners, and chemicals. Rules might include listening to and following all directions, wearing goggles, and reporting spills immediately to the teacher.

Creative Arts: Have your students make drawings of scientists, and then display these in your science area.

Thursday

Theme Activities: Look at your list of inventions and have students classify them according to categories, such as transportation, communication, science, making life easier or more enjoyable, promoting safety or health, plus others determined by your students.

Literature Time: Read *Thomas Edison: Great American Inventor* by Shelley Bedik (Scholastic, 1995). You may read the entry on Thomas Edison in *My First Book of Biographies* by Jean Marzollo (Scholastic, 1994) for more information.

Language Arts: Explain that Thomas Edison liked to work with a team of people on an invention. A famous quotation often attributed to Edison is that "Genius is one percent inspiration and 99 percent perspiration." Let students talk in pairs or in small groups to determine what he meant by this.

Overview: Ingenious Inventors *(cont.)*

Thursday *(cont.)*

Curriculum Connections: Duplicate page 275 for each of your students. Guide students to read through the text and the diagram to learn how an electric light bulb works.

Creative Arts: Many people consider Thomas Edison to be the greatest inventor of the 20th century. Students will make posters advertising the many inventions of Thomas Edison. These may be displayed with the title "Thomas Edison: The Wizard of Menlo Park."

Friday

Theme Activities: Discuss what inventions might possibly be created in the future. What needs do we have for new forms of transportation? communication? safety? health? science? technology? ways to make life easier or more enjoyable? others? Make a semantic map of these possible future inventions.

Literature Time: Read the entry "George Washington Carver" from *My First Book of Biographies* by Jean Marzollo (Scholastic, 1994).

Language Arts: Have your students write an essay called "If I Were an Inventor," in which they will explain what they would do if they were inventors. What would they invent and why? Would they work alone? with a partner? with a team?

Curriculum Connections: Duplicate page 276 for each of your students. Since George Washington Carver discovered hundreds of different products that could be made from peanuts, guide your students to read through the text and the diagram to learn how peanuts grow.

Creative Arts: Share the book *Mistakes That Worked: 40 Familiar Inventions and How They Came to Be* by Charlotte Foltz Jones (Doubleday, 1991). Then have your students design their own inventions by drawing a diagram, labeling the parts, and writing a brief explanation to describe what their inventions would do and how they would work.

This Week's Theme

Ingenious Inventors

Dear Parents,

We are beginning a new thematic unit about "Ingenious Inventors." We will be learning about the many people who have used their ingenuity and genius to create inventions that have made our world the place that it is today. We will learn about early inventors such as Leonardo da Vinci and Benjamin Franklin and many of the inventions of Thomas Edison, as well as the inventions of several other inventors. We will read about several inventors whose biographies are found in a book called *My First Book of Biographies* by Jean Marzollo. During our unit, we will do activities that will extend across the curriculum into reading, writing, science, history, math, and art.

The following are some activities that we will be doing:

1. reading and making a book about famous inventors
2. conducting a class survey and graphing the results to determine what we think is the most important invention
3. learning how an electric light bulb works
4. reading about Benjamin Franklin's contributions to the world, in addition to his inventions
5. designing our own inventions

You may help your child to learn more about "Ingenious Inventors" by taking a trip to your public library and reading more about inventors and inventions. The strip at the bottom of this page may be cut off and taken with you to the library to help you get a start on your search for information.

Thank you for helping your child learn more about the many "Ingenious Inventors" who have shaped our world!

Sincerely,

_____

Good Books About Inventors and Their Inventions

Mistakes That Worked: 40 Familiar Inventions and How They Came to Be by Charlotte Foltz Jones (Doubleday, 1991)

Thomas Edison: Great American Inventor by Shelley Bedik (Scholastic, 1995)

Five Notable Inventors (Great Black Heroes) by Wade Hudson (Scholastic, 1995)

Daily Journal Topics:
Ingenious Inventors

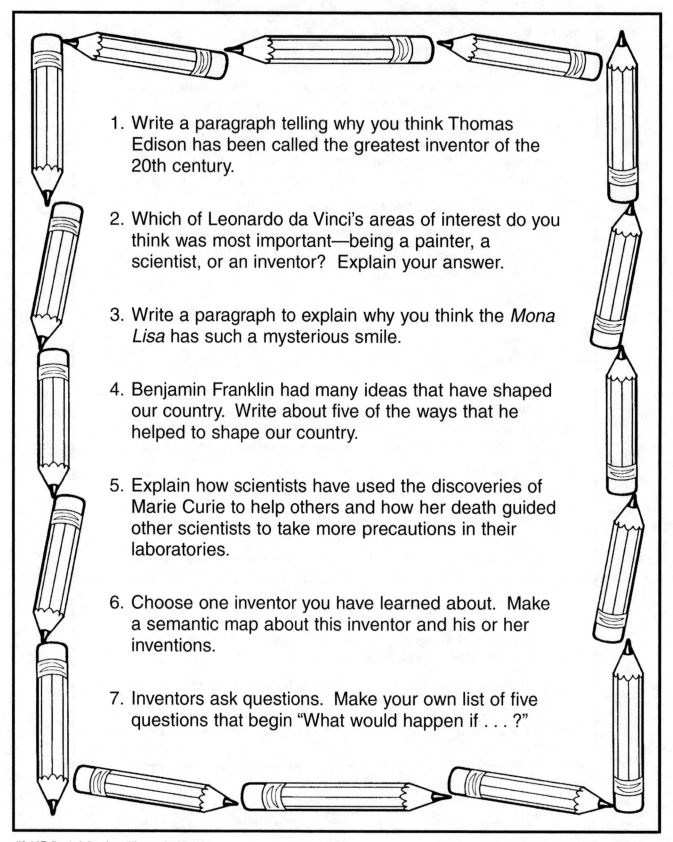

1. Write a paragraph telling why you think Thomas Edison has been called the greatest inventor of the 20th century.

2. Which of Leonardo da Vinci's areas of interest do you think was most important—being a painter, a scientist, or an inventor? Explain your answer.

3. Write a paragraph to explain why you think the *Mona Lisa* has such a mysterious smile.

4. Benjamin Franklin had many ideas that have shaped our country. Write about five of the ways that he helped to shape our country.

5. Explain how scientists have used the discoveries of Marie Curie to help others and how her death guided other scientists to take more precautions in their laboratories.

6. Choose one inventor you have learned about. Make a semantic map about this inventor and his or her inventions.

7. Inventors ask questions. Make your own list of five questions that begin "What would happen if . . . ?"

My Book of Ingenious Inventors

Directions: Read the information about inventors. Cut on the lines. Put pages in the correct order and staple to make your own book. You may color the illustrations.

My Book
of
Ingenious Inventors

Name_____

Thomas Alva Edison was one of the greatest inventors in history. He invented the electric light bulb that turned electricity into light on October 19, 1879. He also invented the phonograph (record player) and a machine to show movies.

1

My Book of Ingenious Inventors *(cont.)*

Alexander Graham Bell invented the telephone in 1876.

2

Many inventors worked to make the automobile in the late 1800s and early 1900s. Charles and Frank Duryea, Henry Ford, Ransom Olds, Charles King, and Alexander Winton were among these inventors.

3

My Book of Ingenious Inventors *(cont.)*

Orville Wright made the first flight in a flying machine on December 17, 1903. Orville and Wilbur Wright had invented the airplane.

4

Vannevar Bush invented the analog computer in 1930. It was very big.

5

My Book of Ingenious Inventors *(cont.)*

Jonas Salk invented a vaccine to protect against polio in 1955. Polio was a disease that had made many children very sick.

6

Complete the following sentences.

1. The electric light bulb was invented by _____.

2. The telephone was invented by_____.

3. The first airplane was invented by _____

   and_____.

4. The analog computer was invented by _____.

5. The polio vaccine was invented by Dr. _____.

7

How an Electric Light Bulb Works

Name _____ Date _____

Directions: Read the information below to learn how an electric light bulb works. The diagram will also help you understand how an electric bulb works.

Thomas Edison and His Incandescent Lamp

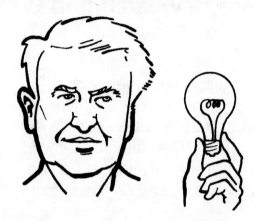

The electric light bulb was invented by Thomas Alva Edison in 1879. He called it an "incandescent lamp." It was his most famous invention.

Electricity flows through the filament of an incandescent bulb. The filament gets hot. The heat makes the filament give off energy. This energy is light.

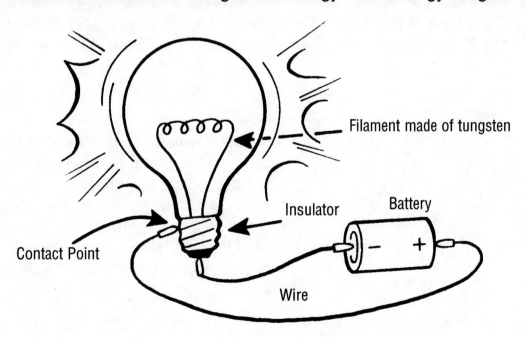

Filament made of tungsten

Insulator

Battery

Contact Point

Wire

Edison's invention of the electric light bulb helped the world, because

_____

_____.

How Peanuts Grow

Name _____ Date _____

Directions: Read the information below to learn how peanuts grow. The diagram will also help you understand how peanuts grow. You may color the illustrations.

George Washington Carver's Work with Peanuts

George Washington Carver was a scientist. He studied peanuts. He discovered more than 300 uses for peanuts in 1921. Cereal, ink, peanut butter, and a milk substitute are some of the products that can be made from peanuts.

The peanut is a type of plant called a *legume*. That means that it makes its fruit in pods or shells that have one or more seeds inside. These seeds are the peanuts.

Peanuts themselves grow under the ground. The stems and leaves of the plant are above the ground. A flower opens on the stem. When the flower falls off, the part where the flower was grows and is called a *peg*. The peg goes into the ground and grows into the peanut pod.

George Washington Carver's work with peanuts was important to the world

because _____

_____.

Weekly Theme: Famous Figures in History   Week _____

	Monday	Tuesday	Wednesday	Thursday	Friday
Date					
Theme Activities	What makes a person famous? What is history?	Make a list of famous people in history.	Categorize famous people.	Guide discussion of present-day famous people and heroes.	How might we become famous people in history?
Literature Time	Read *A Picture Book of Harriet Tubman* by David A. Adler and *The Story of Ruby Bridges* by Robert Coles.	Read *A Picture Book of Helen Keller* and *A Picture Book of Eleanor Roosevelt* by David A. Adler.	Read "Mohandas Gandhi" (*My First Book of Biographies*) and "Susan B. Anthony" (*One-Minute Stories of Great Americans*).	Read *Albert Einstein* by Ibi Lepscky and the entry in *My First Book of Biographies* by Jean Marzollo.	Read "Neil Armstrong and Edwin Aldrin, Jr." from *My First Book of Biographies* by Jean Marzollo.
Language Arts	Practice independent reading of biographies.	Create a Venn diagram to compare the lives of Helen Keller and Eleanor Roosevelt.	Discuss how to peacefully solve the world's problems.	Assemble and read My Book of Famous Figures in History.	Write an essay—"How I Will Become a Famous Figure in History."
Curriculum Connections	Organize and read My Mini-Book of Famous African Americans.	Consider physical challenges.	Develop a Who's Who of American Coins.	Learn about a compass and magnetic fields.	Read about the moon and the moon landing.
Creative Arts	Sing an African American spiritual.	Use musical instruments to feel vibrations.	Sing "Let There Be Peace on Earth."	Listen to some classical violin music.	Make drawings of the moon landing.

Overview: Famous Figures in History

Monday

Theme Activities: Introduce the concept of "fame" to your students as being the condition of someone who is well-known, usually for doing something exceptional. Discuss with your students what might make a person famous. Depending upon the age and prior knowledge of your students, you may need to discuss what "history" means.

Literature Time: Plan to read books about two famous African Americans. First read *A Picture Book of Harriet Tubman* by David A. Adler (Holiday House, 1992) to learn about an early African American. Then read *The Story of Ruby Bridges* by Robert Coles (Scholastic, 1995) to learn about a more recent African American. Help your students to note the differences in periods in history.

Language Arts: Encourage your students to go to your classroom collection of biographies to read related books independently. See the bibliography on pages 369–374.

Curriculum Connections: Duplicate pages 284–286 for each student to make and read the booklet called My Mini-Book of Famous African Americans.

Creative Arts: Sing an African American spiritual with your students, such as "Swing Low, Sweet Chariot" from *The Magic of Music* (Cherry Lane Music, 1998).

Tuesday

Theme Activities: Begin to make a list of famous people in history that your students know. Add to the list each day during your thematic study.

Literature Time: Plan to read books about these famous American women. First read *A Picture Book of Helen Keller* by David A. Adler (Holiday House, 1990). Then read *A Picture Book of Eleanor Roosevelt* by David A. Adler (Holiday House, 1991). Help your students to notice that both women lived at about the same time in history.

Language Arts: Work with your students to summarize the information they learned about Helen Keller and Eleanor Roosevelt by making a Venn diagram (page 380) to compare their lives.

Overview: Famous Figures in History *(cont.)*

===== **Tuesday** *(cont.)* =====

Curriculum Connections: Work with your students to imagine what their lives would be like if they could not see. Have student volunteers wear blindfolds for a few minutes. Have other students press their ears closed so they cannot hear for a few minutes. (Be sure that students are safe during this simulation time.) Show students a sample of Braille writing and sign language, both of which were used by Helen Keller.

Creative Arts: Explain that people who are deaf can "hear" music by feeling vibrations of musical instruments. Use a variety of drums to have students experience the vibrations.

===== **Wednesday** =====

Theme Activities: Add to your list of famous people and then begin to categorize people on your list according to how they became famous. Categories might include inventors, scientists, politicians, explorers, world leaders, sports figures, musicians, artists, authors, and people who work to help others.

Literature Time: Plan to read about two people who worked to make the world a better place. Read "Mohandas Gandhi" from *My First Book of Biographies* by Jean Marzollo (Scholastic, 1994). Then read "Susan B. Anthony" from *One-Minute Stories of Great Americans* by Shari Lewis (Doubleday, 1990).

Language Arts: Work with students to list ways that world problems could be solved peacefully and how they would make the world a better place.

Curriculum Connections: Begin by explaining that Susan B. Anthony is the only woman yet shown on a United States coin. (A new coin featuring Sacajawea is being considered but has not been minted as of this printing.) Bring in samples of each United States coin, and discuss who is on each coin. Duplicate page 287 for each of your students to complete.

Creative Arts: Since Gandhi was known for his contributions to world peace, sing "Let There Be Peace on Earth" by Sy Miller and Jill Jackson (*World Famous Popular Songs*, Charles Hansen Music and Books, 1971) with your students.

===== **Thursday** =====

Theme Activities: Guide children in thinking of present-day famous people and heroes. Current athletes, musicians, authors, and actors may enter your list of famous figures today.

Overview: Famous Figures in History *(cont.)*

Thursday *(cont.)*

Literature Time: Read *Albert Einstein* by Ibi Lepscky (Barron's Educational Series, 1982) to help students learn about the difficult childhood of Albert Einstein. Then read "Albert Einstein" from *My First Book of Biographies* by Jean Marzollo (Scholastic, 1994) to learn about the accomplishments of Einstein.

Language Arts: Duplicate pages 288–291 for your students to read My Book of Famous Figures in History. After assembling the pages into a book and reading it, students will answer the questions at the end by locating the needed information in the book's text.

Curriculum Connections: Since Einstein was curious about a compass and magnetic fields when he was a child, provide your students with hands-on experiences using a compass and using magnets. Duplicate page 292 for your students to record what they learn in their investigations.

Creative Arts: Play a recording of some classical violin music (or have an older student come into your classroom to demonstrate how to play the violin). Emphasize that Einstein was an accomplished violinist.

Friday

Theme Activities: Lead your students in a discussion to think of ways in which they might become famous. The possibilities are endless!

Literature Time: Read "Neil Armstrong and Edwin Aldrin, Jr." from *My First Book of Biographies* by Jean Marzollo (Scholastic, 1994) to enable your students to learn about the first two people to walk on the surface of the moon.

Language Arts: Guide your students in writing an essay entitled "How I Will Become a Famous Figure in History." Encourage students to think of their interests to guide them in their writing.

Curriculum Connections: Duplicate page 293 for your students to read about the moon and the moon landing. Read *The Moon Book* by Gail Gibbons to your class for additional information.

Creative Arts: Provide pencils and white construction paper for students to draw the moon's surface, as well as their interpretations of astronauts landing on the moon.

This Week's Theme

Famous Figures in History

Dear Parents,

Our class is beginning a new thematic study called "Famous Figures in History." We will be learning about a variety of people who have become famous for the contributions that they have made to the world. We will learn about people who have worked to assure that everyone has freedom (Harriet Tubman), people who worked to help others (Helen Keller), people who were scientists (Albert Einstein), and people who were the "first" ever to do something (Neil Armstrong). Several of these famous people are included in an anthology called *My First Book of Biographies* by Jean Marzollo. We will extend our learning in this theme across the curriculum into reading, writing, history, science, music, and art.

Here are some of the activities that we plan on doing:

1. making a mini-book about famous African Americans
2. enjoying various styles of music (a spiritual, classical violin, modern)
3. learning what famous people are depicted on American coins
4. reading biographies of other famous people independently
5. learning about the moon and the astronauts who have been there

You may help your child learn more about famous people by taking a trip to your public library and locating the section on biographies that are written at a suitable level for your child. A list of selected biographies is given below to get you started in your search at the library.

Thank you for your help in encouraging your child to read about real people who have made our world a better place!

Sincerely,

_____

Good Biographies for Children

A Picture Book of Florence Nightingale by David A. Adler (Holiday House, 1992)

Young Orville and Wilbur Wright: First to Fly by Andrew Woods (Troll, 1992)

Pablo Picasso by Ibi Lepscky (Barron's Educational Series, 1992)

The Children's Book of Heroes edited by William J. Bennett (Simon & Schuster, 1997)

Harriet Tubman by Marcia S. Gresko (Teacher Created Materials, 1997)

Daily Journal Topics: Famous Figures in History

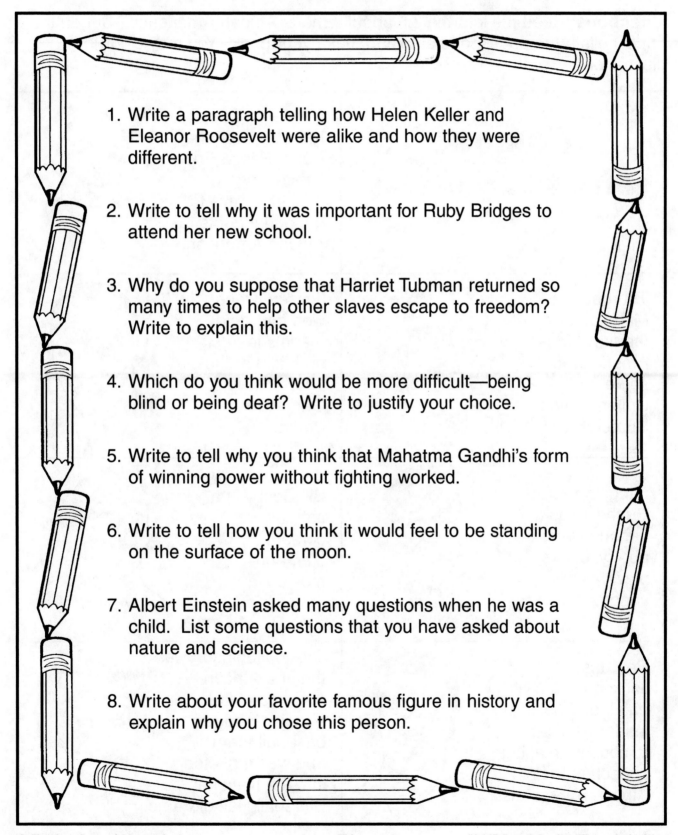

1. Write a paragraph telling how Helen Keller and Eleanor Roosevelt were alike and how they were different.

2. Write to tell why it was important for Ruby Bridges to attend her new school.

3. Why do you suppose that Harriet Tubman returned so many times to help other slaves escape to freedom? Write to explain this.

4. Which do you think would be more difficult—being blind or being deaf? Write to justify your choice.

5. Write to tell why you think that Mahatma Gandhi's form of winning power without fighting worked.

6. Write to tell how you think it would feel to be standing on the surface of the moon.

7. Albert Einstein asked many questions when he was a child. List some questions that you have asked about nature and science.

8. Write about your favorite famous figure in history and explain why you chose this person.

My Mini-Book of Famous African Americans

Directions: Read the information about famous African Americans. Cut on the lines, collate the pages, and staple to make your book. You may color the illustrations.

Famous African Americans

Name _____

Dr. Martin Luther King, Jr., won the Nobel Peace Prize for working in peaceful ways to get equal rights for African Americans.

Thurgood Marshall was the first African American to serve on the United States Supreme Court.

Jesse Owens won four gold medals in track and field at the 1936 Olympic Games in Berlin.

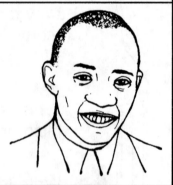

Langston Hughes was a famous writer of poetry, books, plays, and songs.

Bill Cosby is a famous comedian, TV star, and movie star.

Rev. Jesse Jackson is a civil rights and political leader who is famous for making speeches to help African Americans.

Jackie Robinson was the first African American to play on a major-league baseball team and was inducted into the National Baseball Hall of Fame.

My Mini-Book of Famous African Americans *(cont.)*

Mary McLeod Bethune helped educate African Americans and worked with four presidents to further expand educational opportunities.

George Washington Carver was a scientist famous for agricultural research and for discovering the many uses of peanuts.

Harriet Tubman led hundreds of slaves to freedom in the north on the Underground Railroad.

Louis Armstrong was a famous jazz trumpet player and band leader.

Sojourner Truth was the first African American woman to travel through the country making speeches against slavery.

Ralph Bunche worked at the United Nations and was the first African American to win the Nobel Peace Prize.

Wilma Rudolph was the first African American woman to win three gold medals for track at the Olympics.

Benjamin Banneker was an astronomer, mathematician, inventor, surveyor, and the first African American to receive a presidential appointment.

My Mini-Book of Famous African Americans *(cont.)*

Patricia Roberts Harris was the first African American woman to serve as a United States Ambassador in another country.

Booker T. Washington was a teacher who founded the Tuskegee Institute to train African Americans to become carpenters, farmers, mechanics, and teachers.

Shirley Chisholm was the first African American woman to become a member of the United States Congress.

In 1983, Guion Bluford was the first African American to go into space.

Marian Anderson became the first African American soloist to sing with the Metropolitan Opera in New York City.

Phillis Wheatley had a book of poems published in 1773 and became the first major African American poet.

Rosa Parks refused to give up her bus seat to a white passenger in Montgomery, Alabama. This helped to start the civil rights movement.

Matthew Henson, an African American explorer, discovered the North Pole with Robert Peary.

Who's Who of American Coins

Name _____　Date _____

Directions: Look at the picture on each of the coins. Read the description about the person. Look in the word box for that person's name and write the name on the line next to the coin.

Word Box

Susan B. Anthony　　　　John F. Kennedy　　　　Franklin Roosevelt
Abraham Lincoln　　　　George Washington　　　Thomas Jefferson

---

1. This person was the third president of the United States. The coin is worth five cents. _____

2. This person was the president who encouraged the United States space program. The coin is worth 50 cents. _____

3. This person was the first president of the United States. The coin is worth 25 cents. _____

4. This person is the only woman shown on a United States coin. The coin is worth one dollar. _____

5. This person was elected as president for four terms of office. The coin is worth 10 cents. _____

6. This person was called Honest Abe. The coin is worth one cent. _____

My Book of Famous Figures in History

Directions: Read the information about famous figures in history. Cut on the lines, collate the pages in order, and staple to make your book. You may color the illustrations.

My Book of Famous Figures in History

Name _____

Frederick Douglass had been a slave in the South. He escaped to the North, became an educated man, and with powerful speeches persuaded many people to work to abolish slavery in our country.

1

My Book of Famous Figures
in History *(cont.)*

Helen Keller rose above her physical disabilities and helped other disabled people live better lives. Helen was blind and deaf, but she earned great achievements.

2

Eleanor Roosevelt worked to help children and poor people. She believed that all people should be free and equal. She was married to President Franklin Delano Roosevelt. She was called "First Lady of the World."

3

My Book of Famous Figures in History *(cont.)*

Mohandas Gandhi lived in India. He helped people learn how to become more powerful without fighting.

4

Susan B. Anthony worked to change the law that said women in the United States could not vote. She believed women should be able to vote.

5

My Book of Famous Figures in History *(cont.)*

Albert Einstein was a scientist who explained energy by his "theory of relativity." He created ideas to explain light, time, and space.

6

Answer the questions below.

1. Who persuaded others to work for abolishing slavery?

   _____

2. Who was "First Lady of the World"?

   _____

3. Who explained energy, light, time, and space?

   _____

4. Who worked to give women the right to vote?

   _____

5. Who had peaceful ways to gain power?

   _____

7

My Compass and Magnet Observations

Name _____ Date _____

Directions: When Albert Einstein was a child, he was fascinated by a compass and magnetic fields. Work with a real compass and read magnets to answer the following questions.

1. The needle on a compass always points

   _____.

2. The four directions shown on a compass

   are _____, _____,

   _____, and _____.

3. The ends of a magnet have the

   most _____.

   The ends are called *poles*.

4. The north pole of one magnet

   _____

   the north pole of the other magnet.

5. The north pole of one magnet

   _____

   the south pole of the other magnet.

6. The south pole of one magnet

   _____

   the south pole of the other magnet.

The Moon

Name _____ Date _____

Directions: Read the article below about the moon. Refer to the article to answer the questions which follow.

The moon is made of rock and dust. The moon has no air, no water, and no life. The surface of the moon has depressions called craters. The moon is the earth's nearest neighbor. It is only about 238,900 miles (384,000 km) away.

The moon does not make its own light. It reflects the sun's light.

The moon goes around the Earth. It takes about one month for the moon to go all the way around the earth one time.

The moon appears to look different at different times of the month, but it never really changes. The different shapes that we see are called the phases of the moon. We see the different amounts of the sun's light that are being reflected on the moon.

New Moon   Crescent   First Quarter   Gibbous   Full Moon   Gibbous   Last Quarter   Crescent

Neil Armstrong and Edwin Aldrin were the first people to walk on the moon. They walked on the moon on July 20, 1969.

1. How is the moon different from Earth? _____

_____

2. Where does the moon get its light?_____

_____

3. What do we call the moon's different shapes? _____

_____

4. Who were the first people to walk on the moon? _____

_____

Weekly Theme: The Father of Our Country   Week _____

	Monday	Tuesday	Wednesday	Thursday	Friday
Date					
Theme Activities	Play the Who Is It? guessing game to introduce George Washington.	Chart important events in the life of George Washington.	Discuss the Washington Monument.	Why do we honor George Washington? Discuss.	Write words to describe George Washington.
Literature Time	Read *A Picture Book of George Washington* by David A. Adler and *George Washington: A Picture Biography*.	Read *George Washington* (Easy Theme Readers: Famous Americans) by Marcia S. Gresko.	Read *A Visit to Washington, D.C.* by Jill Krementz.	Read *My First Presidents' Day Book* by Aileen Fisher.	Read *George Washington's Breakfast* by Jean Fritz.
Language Arts	Read "George and the Cherry Tree" from *George Washington: A Picture Biography* by James Cross Giblin.	Provide multiple copies of *George Washington* by Marcia S. Gresko.	Complete The Washington Monument questions.	Read and complete My Book About George Washington.	Compare what you eat for breakfast with Washington's meals.
Curriculum Connections	Locate Washington's birthplace and relevant places on a U.S. map.	Do map study of The United States in 1789.	Examine a U.S. quarter and a U.S. one-dollar bill.	How many quarters are in the estimating jar?	Practice using coins and one-dollar bills.
Creative Arts	Cut out George Washington silhouettes.	Make posters for "George Washington's Rules of Good Behavior."	Do quarter rubbings.	Read about and sing "Yankee Doodle."	Make your own three-cornered hat.

Overview: The Father of Our Country

Monday

Theme Activities: To introduce George Washington to your students, play a game of Who Is It? using clues such as these:

1. *He lived in Virginia.*
2. *His picture is on the quarter.*
3. *His home was called Mount Vernon.*
4. *He was the first president of the United States.*

Literature Time: Read *A Picture Book of George Washington* by David A. Adler (Holiday House, 1989) to your students. You might also read *George Washington: A Picture Biography* by James Cross Giblin (Scholastic, 1992).

Language Arts: Read the story "George and the Cherry Tree" on pages 44 and 45 in *George Washington: A Picture Biography* by James Cross Giblin (Scholastic, 1992). Challenge students to choose whether they believe this story is true. Direct them to write an explanation with their reasons.

Curriculum Connections: Use a map of the United States to locate the birthplace of George Washington in Virginia. Also locate New York City, Philadelphia, and Washington, D.C., as the capitals of the United States.

Creative Arts: Use the George Washington Silhouette pattern on page 301 for students to use in tracing on black construction paper and cutting out their own silhouettes of Washington. Glue the silhouette on blue or red construction paper and glue white stars around it to make a banner.

Tuesday

Theme Activities: Work with students to retell the important events in the life of George Washington. Write them on a chart to serve as a time line of his life.

Literature Time: Read *George Washington* (Easy Theme Readers: Famous Americans) by Marcia S. Gresko (Teacher Created Materials, 1997), discussing each page as you read.

Language Arts: Provide multiple copies of *George Washington* by Marcia S. Gresko for your students to read independently. The readable text will enable your beginning readers to be successful as they read.

Curriculum Connections: Look at a map of the United States, and locate the 50 states. Explain that at the time that George Washington was first elected president of the United States, there were only 13 states: New York, Massachusetts, Connecticut, Rhode Island, New Hampshire, New Jersey, Pennsylvania, Delaware, Maryland, Virginia, North Carolina, South Carolina, and Georgia. Locate these states on the U.S. map to see how the U.S. has grown.

Overview: The Father of Our Country *(cont.)*

═══════════════ **Tuesday** *(cont.)* ═══════════════

Creative Arts: Refer to "George Washington's Rules of Good Behavior" that are included in *George Washington: A Picture Biography* by James Cross Giblin. Students will choose a rule and use crayons or colored pencils to make a poster for the rule by writing the rule in their best printing and then illustrating it.

═══════════════ **Wednesday** ═══════════════

Theme Activities: Show a picture of the Washington Monument to begin your discussion of the monuments that we now have to honor George Washington. Include Washington state, Washington, D.C., the quarter, the one-dollar bill, Mount Rushmore, and a university in your discussion.

Literature Time: Read *A Visit to Washington, D.C.,* by Jill Krementz (Scholastic, 1987) to introduce your students to the city named after George Washington, as well as the Washington Monument.

Language Arts: Duplicate page 302 for each of your students to read independently about the Washington Monument and complete the comprehension questions.

Curriculum Connections: Provide each pair of your students with a U.S. quarter and a U.S. one-dollar bill since George Washington's picture is on both. Direct students to examine each closely, looking at the pictures and words included on both. Make a list of what students see on each.

Creative Arts: Provide students with pieces of white paper or newsprint. Students place the paper on top of a quarter and use the side of a pencil point or crayons to color over the quarter, thus making quarter rubbings.

═══════════════ **Thursday** ═══════════════

Theme Activities: Lead your students in a discussion to determine why we honor George Washington and why there are so many things named after him.

Literature Time: Read the first half of *My First Presidents' Day Book* by Aileen Fisher (Childrens Press, 1987), which tells about some of the highlights of Abraham Lincoln's life (the book is about both presidents that we honor on Presidents' Day).

Language Arts: Duplicate pages 303–307 for students to read the informative text My Book About George Washington and complete the comprehension exercise that accompanies the book.

Overview: The Father of Our Country *(cont.)*

════ Thursday *(cont.)* ════

Curriculum Connections: At your math area, put 10 quarters into a jar as a reference for your students. Set up an identical jar as your estimating jar with more than 10 quarters in it. Students may write their estimates on a sheet of paper with the title "How Many Quarters?" next to the estimating jar. Count the quarters after all students have made their estimates; then put the quarters into piles of four to determine how many dollars the quarters make.

Creative Arts: Read the article "Yankee Doodle" in *The Children's Book of America,* edited by William J. Bennett, to explain how the song fit into the time period and life of George Washington. Then sing the song with your students.

════ Friday ════

Theme Activities: Enlarge the silhouette of George Washington found on page 301 on a large sheet of chart paper. Have students suggest words to tell about George Washington and write them on the enlarged silhouette.

Literature Time: Read *George Washington's Breakfast* by Jean Fritz (Trumpet Club, 1969) to your class and encourage them to be historians along with the main character as he searches to find out what George Washington really ate for breakfast.

Language Arts: Use a large sheet of chart paper to compile a list of what your students ate for breakfast. Ask students to notice if anyone ate the same foods for breakfast that George Washington ate for breakfast.

Curriculum Connections: Provide one-dollar bills, quarters, dimes, nickels, and pennies for students to use in practicing their money skills.

Creative Arts: Provide materials for your students to make their own three-cornered hats, called tricorn hats. Duplicate pages 308 and 309 on blue construction paper for the three sides of the hat. An adult should staple the three sides together to fit each child's head. Add a gold seal to the front of the hat.

This Week's Theme

The Father of Our Country

Dear Parents,

Our class is beginning a new thematic study about George Washington called "The Father of Our Country." We will be learning about the life of George Washington and why he is called "The Father of Our Country." We will also learn about several of the ways that he is still honored and remembered. One of the books that we will read during the course of our study is *George Washington: A Picture Biography* by James Cross Giblin. In addition to history, our study will extend across the curriculum into literature, reading, writing, math, art, and music.

One of our projects will be to make and read an informational book called My Book About George Washington that will be brought home to read with you. During our unit, we will also be doing the following activities:

1. learning about the Washington Monument
2. examining a U.S. quarter and a U.S. one-dollar bill
3. singing "Yankee Doodle" and relating it to George Washington
4. making posters for "George Washington's Rules of Good Behavior"
5. learning what George Washington ate for breakfast

You can help your child learn more about George Washington by visiting your public library and looking for additional books about him. A suggested list of suitable books is provided below. You can also help your child look for ways that George Washington is remembered, such as having his picture on money and his likeness as a part of Mount Rushmore.

Thank you for helping your child learn more about George Washington, the "Father of Our Country."

                      Sincerely,

                      _____

Suggested Books About George Washington

A Picture Book of George Washington by David A. Adler

George Washington by Marcia S. Gresko

A Visit to Washington, D.C. by Jill Krementz

George Washington's Breakfast by Jean Fritz

My First Presidents' Day Book by Aileen Fisher

Daily Journal Topics:
The Father of Our Country

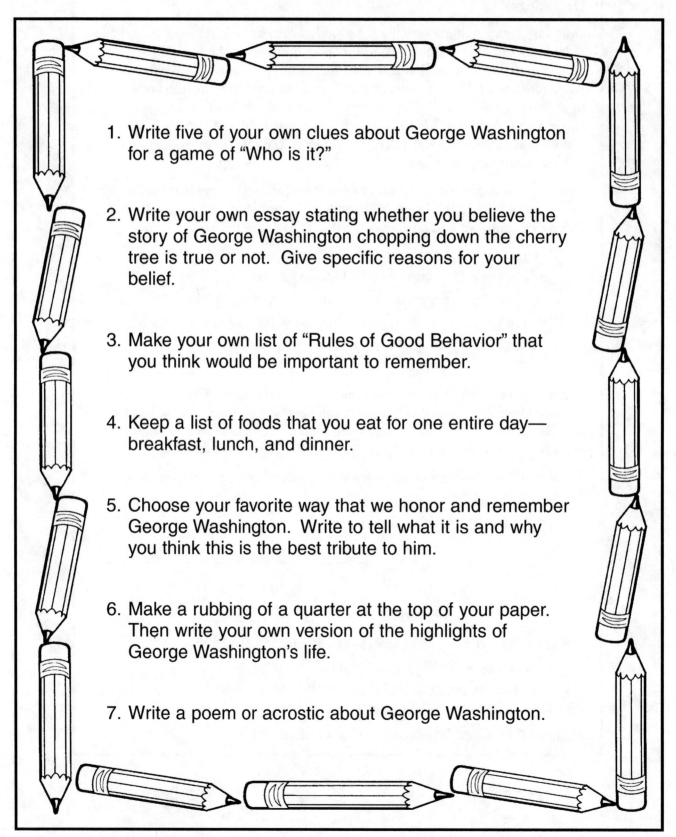

1. Write five of your own clues about George Washington for a game of "Who is it?"

2. Write your own essay stating whether you believe the story of George Washington chopping down the cherry tree is true or not. Give specific reasons for your belief.

3. Make your own list of "Rules of Good Behavior" that you think would be important to remember.

4. Keep a list of foods that you eat for one entire day—breakfast, lunch, and dinner.

5. Choose your favorite way that we honor and remember George Washington. Write to tell what it is and why you think this is the best tribute to him.

6. Make a rubbing of a quarter at the top of your paper. Then write your own version of the highlights of George Washington's life.

7. Write a poem or acrostic about George Washington.

George Washington Silhouette

Directions: Trace and cut out this silhouette of George Washington on black construction paper. Mount the silhouette on blue or red construction paper and cut out the white stars to glue around the silhouette.

The Washington Monument

Name _____ Date _____

Directions: Read the information about the Washington Monument. Then answer the questions below using complete sentences.

The Washington Monument was built to honor George Washington, the first president of the United States. The Washington Monument was built in Washington, D.C. It was begun in 1848. It was completed in 1884.

The shape of the monument is called an *obelisk*. That means it is a four-sided pillar that forms a pyramid at the top. It is made of marble.

The Washington Monument is 555 feet high. That makes it the tallest building in Washington, D.C. There is a stairway with 898 steps to the top, but visitors take an elevator to get to the top.

1. Where was the Washington Monument built?

   _____

2. How many years did it take for the Washington Monument to be completed?

   _____

3. What shape is the Washington Monument?

   _____

4. What is the tallest building in Washington, D.C.?

   _____

5. Would you like to visit the Washington Monument? Why or why not?

   _____

   _____

   _____

   _____

My Book About George Washington

Read the information about George Washington. Cut on the lines, put the pages in correct order, and staple. You may color the illustrations.

My Book
About
George Washington

Name _____

George Washington was born on February 22, 1732, in Virginia. America was still a colony of England then.

1

My Book About
George Washington *(cont.)*

George Washington learned to be a surveyor. He traveled into the wilderness to measure the land and make maps.

2

George Washington's home was a farm called Mount Vernon.

3

My Book About
George Washington *(cont.)*

George Washington married Martha Custis. She had two children.

4

George Washington was the general of the American army during the Revolutionary War. He wanted America to be a separate country, not part of England.

5

My Book About
George Washington *(cont.)*

America gained its independence. Now it was the United States of America. George Washington was elected as the first president of the United States in 1789. Then New York was the capital of the United States.

6

George Washington was president for eight years. The new capital of the United States, Washington, D.C., was named in honor of him.

7

My Book About
George Washington *(cont.)*

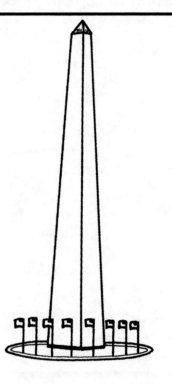

George Washington was called the
"Father of our Country." The Washington
Monument was built to help us remember
him.

8

Complete the following sentences.

1. George Washington's home was called _____.

2. George Washington was the general of the _____
   army during the Revolutionary War.

3. George Washington was elected the _____
   president of the United States.

4. The capital of the United States is_____,
   D.C. It was named for him.

5. George Washington is called the_____.

9

Make a Three-Cornered Hat

Directions: Cut out the three pieces of the three-cornered hat. Staple the three sides together to fit, using the tabs.

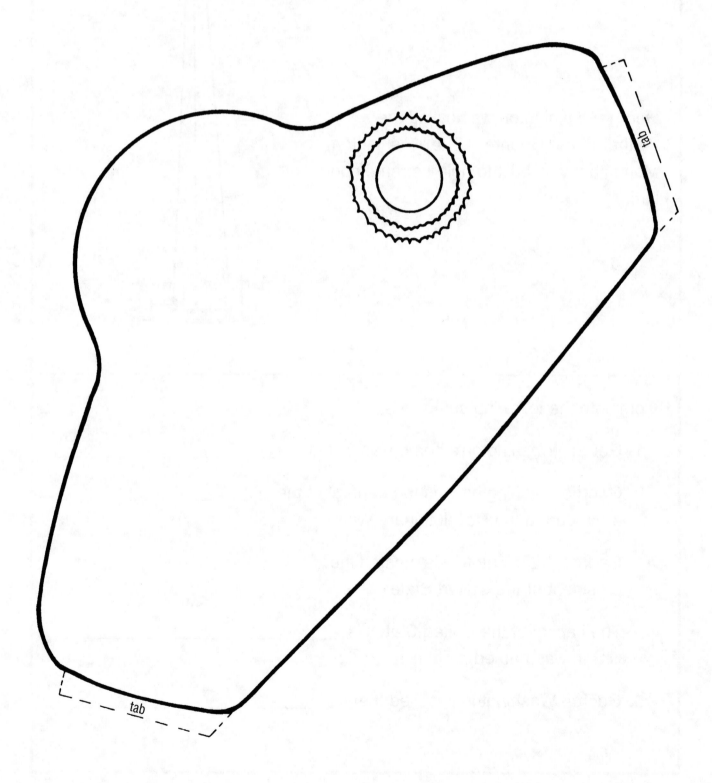

Make a Three-Cornered Hat *(cont.)*

See directions on page 308.

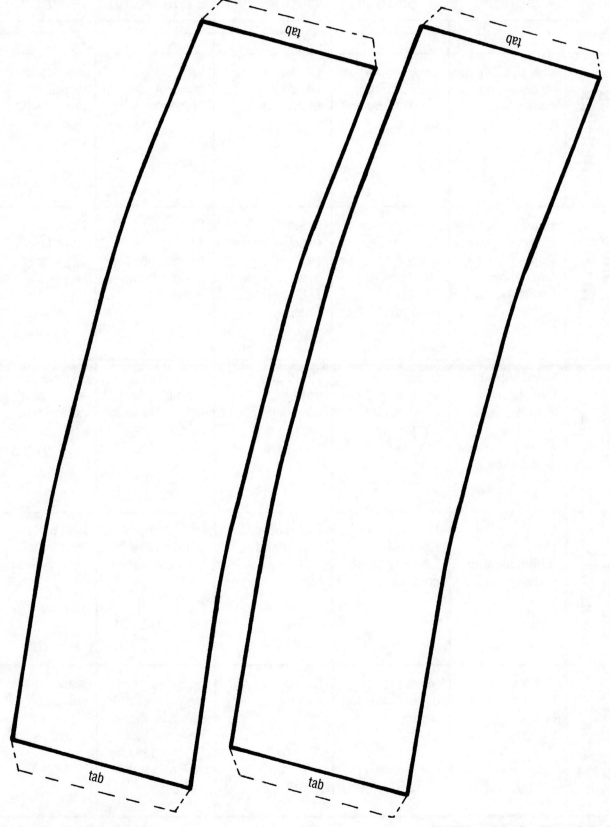

Weekly Theme: *Honest Abe* Week _____

	Monday	Tuesday	Wednesday	Thursday	Friday
Date					
Theme Activities	Play the Who Is It? guessing game.	Chart important events in the life of Abraham Lincoln.	Discuss the Lincoln Memorial.	Why do we honor Abraham Lincoln?	Brainstorm words to describe Abraham Lincoln.
Literature Time	Read *A Picture Book of Abraham Lincoln* by David A. Adler.	Read *Abraham Lincoln* (Easy Theme Readers— Famous Americans) by Marcia S. Gresko.	Read *The Inside-Outside Book of Washington, D.C.* by Roxie Munro.	Read part 2 of *My First Presidents' Day Book* by Aileen Fisher.	Read *Just Like Abraham Lincoln* by Bernard Waber.
Language Arts	Read "Abraham Lincoln's School Day's" from *The Children's Book of America.*	Provide multiple copies of *Abraham Lincoln* by Marcia S. Gresko.	Read and answer questions about the Lincoln Memorial.	Assemble and read My Book About Abraham Lincoln.	Extend the above story to create a new ending.
Curriculum Connections	Locate Lincoln's birthplace and relevant places on a U.S. map.	How tall was Abraham Lincoln? Make comparisons.	Examine a U.S. penny and a U.S. five-dollar bill.	How many pennies are in the estimating jar?	Complete Heads or Tails: Penny Math.
Creative Arts	Cut out the Abraham Lincoln Silhouette.	Make three-dimensional log cabins.	Do penny rubbings.	Listen to or sing "The Battle Hymn of the Republic" and "The Battle Cry of Freedom."	Make your own stovepipe hat.

Overview: Honest Abe

Monday

Theme Activities: To introduce Abraham Lincoln to your students, play a game of Who Is It? using clues such as these:

1. *He was born in Kentucky.*
2. *He was born in a log cabin.*
3. *He wore a stovepipe hat.*
4. *He was president during the Civil War.*

Literature Time: Read *A Picture Book of Abraham Lincoln* by David A. Adler (Holiday House, 1989) to help your students become acquainted with the life of Abraham Lincoln.

Language Arts: Read "Abraham Lincoln's School Days" from *The Children's Book of America* edited by William J. Bennett (Simon & Schuster, 1998) so that your students will learn about the childhood of Lincoln. Then have students think about their own lives and their school. Lead your students in a discussion comparing their school days with the school days of Abraham Lincoln. How are they alike? How are they different? How did Abraham Lincoln's early years determine the kind of adult he grew up to be?

Curriculum Connections: Use a map of the United States to locate the birthplace of Abraham Lincoln. Trace the path he took during his lifetime from Kentucky to Indiana; to Illinois; down the Mississippi River to New Orleans; to New Salem, Illinois; to Springfield, Illinois; to Washington, D.C.; and to his final resting place in Springfield, Illinois.

Creative Arts: Use the Abraham Lincoln Silhouette pattern on page 317 for students to use in tracing on black construction paper and cutting out their own silhouettes of Abraham Lincoln. Glue the silhouette on blue or red construction paper and glue white stars and white stripes around the silhouette to make a banner.

Tuesday

Theme Activities: Work with students to retell the important events in the life of Abraham Lincoln. Write them on a chart to serve as a time line of his life.

Literature Time: Read *Abraham Lincoln* (Easy Theme Readers: Famous Americans) by Marcia S. Gresko (Teacher Created Materials, 1997), discussing each page as you read. Invite your students to read it with you on the second reading.

Language Arts: Provide multiple copies of *Abraham Lincoln* by Marcia S. Gresko for your students to read independently. The readable text in this book will allow your beginning readers to be successful as they read.

Overview: Honest Abe *(cont.)*

=========================== **Tuesday** *(cont.)* ===========================

Curriculum Connections: Abraham Lincoln is said to have been 6'4" (193 cm) tall. (You may wish to note that George Washington is said to have been 6'2" [188 cm] tall.) Mark each of these heights on the wall in your classroom or hallway. Draw a life-size Lincoln and Washington to correlate with each height. Then measure each of your students (and yourself, too). Have children trace around each other and color the outlines to look like real children. Post these life-size children along the wall next to the two presidents to compare heights.

Creative Arts: In the construction center of your classroom, encourage children to use building materials to make three-dimensional log cabins. If you collect paper towel tubes, your students might use them to make larger log cabins. Build a frontier scene around your log cabin.

=========================== **Wednesday** ===========================

Theme Activities: Show a picture of the Lincoln Memorial to your students to begin discussing the penny, names of cities and streets, the five-dollar bill, and Mount Rushmore.

Literature Time: Provide a quick tour of Washington, D.C., by reading *The Inside-Outside Book of Washington, D.C.* by Roxie Munro (Dutton Children's Books, 1987). Call your students' attention to the final pages of the book that show the outside and inside of the Lincoln Memorial.

Language Arts: Duplicate page 318 for each of your students to read independently about the Lincoln Memorial and complete the comprehension questions.

Curriculum Connections: Provide each pair of students with a penny and show the group a five-dollar bill for them to examine closely. Direct students' attention to the picture of Lincoln on the front of each and the picture of the Lincoln Memorial on the back of each. Make a list of what the students see on each.

Creative Arts: Provide students with pieces of white paper or newsprint. Students place the paper on top of a penny and use the side of a pencil point or crayon to color over the penny, thus making penny rubbings.

=========================== **Thursday** ===========================

Theme Activities: Discuss with your students why we honor Abraham Lincoln and why he is called "Honest Abe."

Overview: Honest Abe *(cont.)*

Thursday *(cont.)*

Literature Time: Read the second half of the book *My First Presidents' Day Book* by Aileen Fisher (Childrens Press, 1987), which tells about some of the highlights of the life of Abraham Lincoln in verse. (The first half of the book is about George Washington since the book is about both presidents that we honor on Presidents' Day.)

Language Arts: Duplicate pages 319–323 for students to read the informative My Book About Abraham Lincoln and complete the comprehension exercise that accompanies the book.

Curriculum Connections: At your math area, put pennies into your estimating jar. Set up an identical jar with 10 pennies in it as a reference for your students. Students may write their estimates on a sheet of paper with the title "How Many Pennies?" next to the estimate jar. Count the pennies after all students have made their estimates and put the pennies into piles of 10 to determine how many cents you have all together by counting tens and ones.

Creative Arts: Listen to recordings of songs or help your students sing songs that are associated with Abraham Lincoln and the time during which he lived, such as "The Battle Hymn of the Republic" and "The Battle Cry of Freedom." Good sources for songs are *Wee Sing America* (Price/Stern/Sloan, 1987) and *The Magic of Music* (Cherry Lane Music, 1998).

Friday

Theme Activities: Enlarge the silhouette of Abraham Lincoln on page 317 on a large sheet of chart paper. Have students suggest words to tell about Abraham Lincoln and write them on the enlarged silhouette.

Literature Time: Read the fiction book *Just Like Abraham Lincoln* by Bernard Waber (Scholastic, 1964) to your students and meet a character named Mr. Potts, who resembled Abraham Lincoln in many ways.

Language Arts: After reading *Just Like Abraham Lincoln* by Bernard Waber, have your students extend the story to create a new ending. At the end of the book, a new neighbor moves in, and this neighbor looks just like George Washington. Students might title their extended story "Just Like George Washington."

Curriculum Connections: Duplicate page 324 for your students to complete Heads or Tails: Penny Math.

Creative Arts: Make your own stovepipe hat, using a sheet of 12" x 18" (30 cm x 46 cm) black construction paper rolled into a cylinder and stapled. Cut slits on one end of the cylinder and flatten these strips onto the black construction paper brim that you cut about 2" (5 cm) wider than the cylinder. Glue the strips onto the brim.

This Week's Theme

Honest Abe

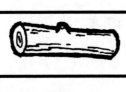

Dear Parents,

We are beginning a new thematic unit of study about Abraham Lincoln. Our unit is called "Honest Abe" since that is one of the names by which he was known. We will be learning about the life of Abraham Lincoln and why he was called "Honest Abe," as well as why he is one of the most respected presidents of the United States. One of the books that we will be reading during our unit is *A Picture Book of Abraham Lincoln* by David A. Adler. In addition to history, our study will extend across the curriculum into literature, reading, writing, math, geography, art, and music.

One project that we will do during our unit will be to make and read an informational book called My Book About Abraham Lincoln. It will be sent home with your child so that your child may share it with you. We will also be doing the following activities during our study of Abraham Lincoln:

1. comparing our heights with the height of Abraham Lincoln
2. learning about Lincoln's school days and comparing them to ours
3. estimating and counting how many pennies are in our estimating jar
4. extending the book *Just Like Abraham Lincoln* by Bernard Waber to create our own new endings
5. learning about the Lincoln Memorial

You can help your child learn more about Abraham Lincoln and about the history of the United States by visiting your public library. A suggested list of books about Abraham Lincoln is given below, as well as an anthology of American history for children.

Thank you for helping your child learn more about Abraham Lincoln and his contributions to the United States.

Sincerely,

_____

- -

Suggested Books About Abraham Lincoln

Abraham Lincoln by Marcia S. Gresko
My First Presidents' Day Book by Aileen Fisher
The Children's Book of America edited by William J. Bennett

Daily Journal Topics:
Honest Abe

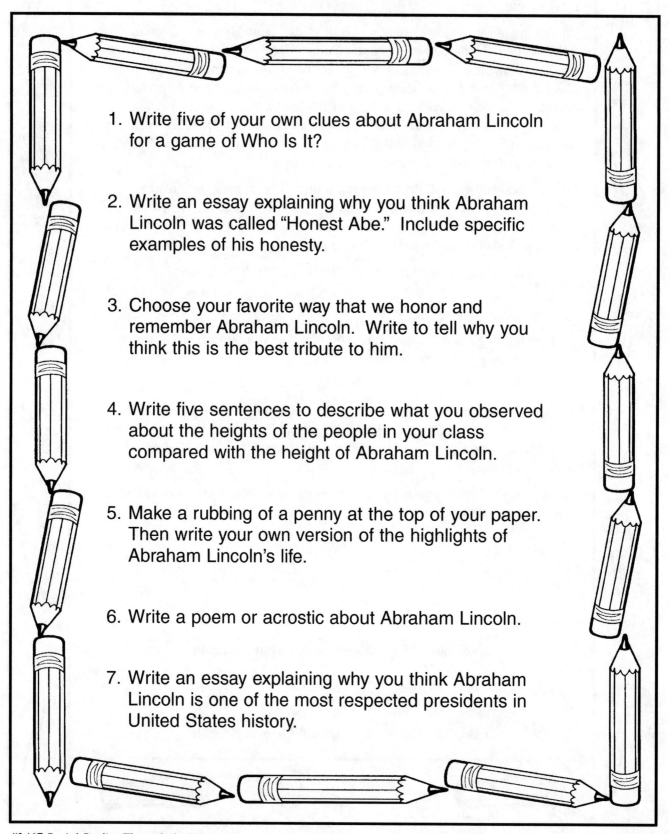

1. Write five of your own clues about Abraham Lincoln for a game of Who Is It?

2. Write an essay explaining why you think Abraham Lincoln was called "Honest Abe." Include specific examples of his honesty.

3. Choose your favorite way that we honor and remember Abraham Lincoln. Write to tell why you think this is the best tribute to him.

4. Write five sentences to describe what you observed about the heights of the people in your class compared with the height of Abraham Lincoln.

5. Make a rubbing of a penny at the top of your paper. Then write your own version of the highlights of Abraham Lincoln's life.

6. Write a poem or acrostic about Abraham Lincoln.

7. Write an essay explaining why you think Abraham Lincoln is one of the most respected presidents in United States history.

Abraham Lincoln Silhouette

Directions: Trace and cut out this silhouette of Abraham Lincoln on black construction paper. Mount the silhouette on blue or red construction paper and cut out the white stars and stripes to glue around the silhouette.

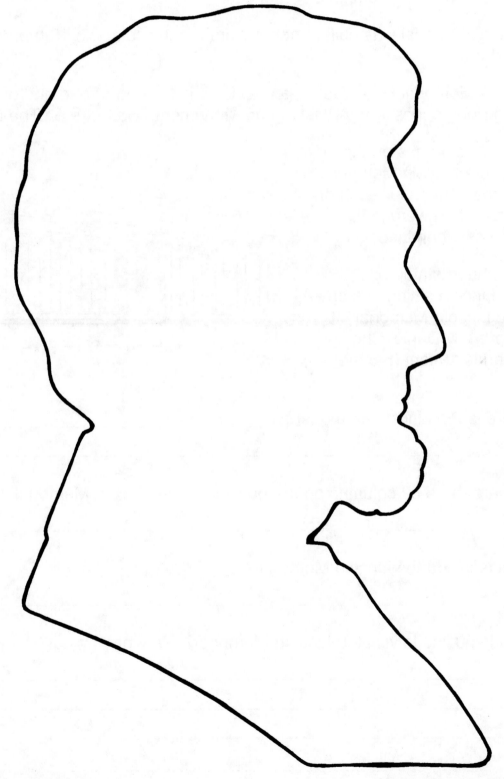

The Lincoln Memorial

Name _____ Date _____

Directions: Read the information about the Lincoln Memorial. Answer the questions below, using complete sentences.

The Lincoln Memorial was built to honor Abraham Lincoln, the 16th president of the United States.

The Lincoln Memorial is in Washington, D.C. It is located at one end of the Reflecting Pool, opposite the Washington Monument. Both are on The Mall.

There are 32 columns on the outside of the Lincoln Memorial. There is one column for each of the 32 states that were in the United States when Lincoln died.

There is a huge statue of Abraham Lincoln sitting in a chair inside the Lincoln Memorial. It was sculpted by Daniel Chester French and is 19 feet (5.8 meters) tall.

1. Where is the Lincoln Memorial? _____

_____

2. Why are there 32 columns on the outside of the Lincoln Memorial?

_____

3. What is inside the Lincoln Memorial? _____

_____

4. Would you like to visit the Lincoln Memorial? Why or why not?

_____

_____

_____

My Book About Abraham Lincoln

Directions: Read the information about Abraham Lincoln. Cut on the lines, put the pages in correct order, and staple. You may color the illustrations.

My Book
About
Abraham Lincoln

Name _____

Abraham Lincoln was born on February 12, 1809. He was born in a log cabin in Kentucky.

1

My Book About Abraham Lincoln *(cont.)*

Abraham and his sister Sarah helped on their farm. Abraham helped chop down trees to build a log cabin when they moved to Indiana.

2

Abraham did not go to school every day because he worked on the farm. But he loved to read books. He read books that he borrowed from other people.

3

My Book About Abraham Lincoln *(cont.)*

Abraham Lincoln had many jobs as an adult. He was a clerk in a general store. He was a mailman, too.

Then he decided to study law, and he became a lawyer. He moved to Springfield, Illinois.

4

He met and married Mary Todd in 1842. They had four children: Robert, Thomas, William, and Edward.

5

My Book About Abraham Lincoln *(cont.)*

Abraham Lincoln was elected president of the United States in 1860. The Civil War began while he was president. He wrote the Emancipation Proclamation that freed the slaves in 1863. He gave a speech called the Gettysburg Address to help keep the United States together. The war lasted for four years.

6

Abraham Lincoln was assassinated five days after the war ended in 1865. The people of the United States were very sad. They had lost their president.

7

My Book About Abraham Lincoln *(cont.)*

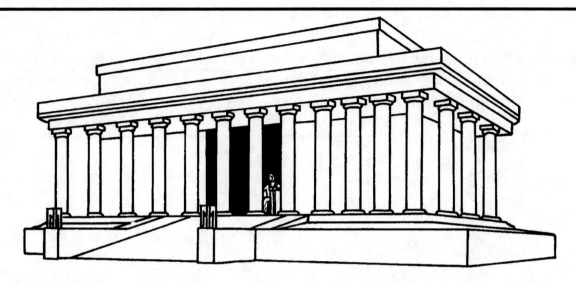

Abraham Lincoln will always be remembered. The Lincoln Memorial honors him. Many people believe that he was one of our greatest presidents.

8

Answer the following questions.

1. Where was Abraham Lincoln born? _____

2. What did Abraham Lincoln borrow from other people?

   _____

3. When was Abraham Lincoln elected president of the United States?

   _____

4. What did the Emancipation Proclamation do?

   _____

5. Why do you think Abraham Lincoln is called one of our greatest
   presidents? _____

   _____

9

Heads or Tails: Penny Math

Name _____ Date _____

Directions: Flip a penny 100 times. In the appropriate boxes below, use tally marks to keep track of each head or tail that comes up. Summarize your results by completing the sentences at the bottom.

Heads

Tally Marks

Tails

Tally Marks

I had _____ heads.

I had _____ tails.

I had more _____ than _____ .

I had fewer _____ than _____ .

I have a dream . . .   I have a dream . . .

This Week's Theme: Martin Luther King, Jr. **Week** _____

	Monday	Tuesday	Wednesday	Thursday	Friday
Date					
Theme Activities	Who was Dr. Martin Luther King, Jr.? Discuss.	Review important dates to remember in King's life.	Discuss the civil rights movement.	Discuss the "I Have a Dream" speech.	Learn about establishing a new holiday.
Literature Time	Read *A Picture Book of Martin Luther King, Jr.* by David A. Adler.	Read *Martin Luther King, Jr.—A Man Who Changed Things* by Carol Greene.	Read *Happy Birthday, Martin Luther King* by Jean Marzollo.	Read *What Is Martin Luther King, Jr., Day?* by Margot Parker.	Read *Martin Luther King Day* by Linda Lowery.
Language Arts	Compile a class fact book of Dr. King.	Write about what you would change in our world.	Write an essay—" Whom Do You Admire?"	Try writing a speech.	Assemble and read a mini-book about Dr. King's life.
Curriculum Connections	Make a chart of important dates.	Make a time line of Martin Luther King's life.	Celebrate January, African American history month.	Research famous words to remember.	Learn about the Nobel peace prize.
Creative Arts	Plan a schoolwide celebration.	Make a peace pledge.	Learn some songs of peace.	Create "We Have a Dream" paintings.	Create peace posters and signs.

Overview: Martin Luther King, Jr.

Monday

Theme Activities: Assess students' prior knowledge by asking what they know about Martin Luther King, Jr. Write the information on chart paper. Also record any questions the students would like to have answered about Dr. King.

Literature Time: Read *A Picture Book of Martin Luther King, Jr.* by David A. Adler (Scholastic, 1989) to learn facts about Dr. King's life. Start a fact chart to summarize information from all nonfiction selections read this week. Each day add any new information from the book read.

Language Arts: After reading today's literature, have students work in small groups to summarize the book. They should write down six to ten important events from his life. After this, have the students work in groups of two to three to write and illustrate one fact. The facts can be compiled into a class fact book about Dr. King.

Curriculum Connections: Many nonfiction books contain a chart of important dates. Ask students to make a list of some of the important dates in today's biography. As books are read this week, add to the list if necessary.

Creative Arts: Plan a schoolwide celebration of Dr. King's birthday as a lead into African American history month, celebrated in January. The school may want to become involved in projects to benefit your community, a perfect way to celebrate Dr. King's dream of people working together.

Tuesday

Theme Activities: Review some of the important dates in Dr. King's life. Circle his birthday, January 15, on the calendar.

Literature Time: Today's book is *Martin Luther King, Jr.—A Man Who Changed Things* by Carol Greene. After reading the book, discuss changes that Dr. King effected in our country.

Language Arts: Dr. King's contributions brought changes to many people's lives. Discuss with the class how they would change the world if they could. Stress the idea that one person can make a big difference. Have students write about the changes that they would make.

Curriculum Connections: Learning how to make a time line is a good strategy for understanding and remembering important historical dates. Using the charts being developed, have students work in small groups to make a time line of Dr. King's life. If the class is unfamiliar with time lines, you may want to show some samples from other books or show a time line of your own life. For younger students, you may want to make the time line as a whole group activity.

Overview: Martin Luther King, Jr. (cont.)

=== **Tuesday** (cont.) ===

Creative Arts: A dove is a sign of peace, and Dr. King believed in peaceful solutions to problems. Show students the dove picture found on page 332 and ask them what the word "peace" means. Discuss how they can contribute to peace in their world, at home, and at school. Ask them to write their own peace pledge to explain their plan to promote peace. For example, "When my best friend won't share a football, I will talk about the problem instead of arguing or yelling."

=== **Wednesday** ===

Theme Activities: Several of the books mention the civil rights movement which may be unfamiliar terms to younger students. Discuss what civil rights are in terms of equal treatment for everyone and how Dr. King and others worked in the "movement" to ensure those rights.

Literature Time: This selection, *Happy Birthday, Martin Luther King* by Jean Marzollo (Scholastic, 1993), is written in an informational picture-book format.

Language Arts: Discuss why Dr. King and other leaders like Abraham Lincoln are studied and admired. Ask the students to name other people whom they admire for making our world a better place. Have them write an essay about the person they admire and tell why this person has earned their respect.

Curriculum Connections: African American history month is celebrated in January and affords a perfect opportunity to study other famous Americans such as Jackie Robinson, Harriet Tubman, and Rosa Parks. More information on these and other well-known African Americans can be found in the mini-book found on pages 284–286.

Creative Arts: Learn some songs with the theme of peace such as "Let There Be Peace on Earth" by Sy Miller and Jill Jackson, *World-Famous Popular Songs* (Charles Hansen Music and Books, 1973); "Peace Like a River" (Traditional), *Kids' Songs and Jubilee* (Klutz Press, 1990); and "One Light, One Sun" by Raffi and "To Everyone in the World" (Traditional), *The Second Raffi Songbook* (Crown, 1986).

=== **Thursday** ===

Theme Activities: Dr. King's "I Have a Dream" speech is one of the most important speeches ever made. The text of the speech can be found in today's literature selection. Discuss the speech—what it means and why the words are still important today.

Literature Time: Read *What Is Martin Luther King, Jr., Day?* by Margot Parker which tells the history of the holiday in story form.

Overview: Martin Luther King, Jr. *(cont.)*

Thursday *(cont.)*

Language Arts: Read some other famous speeches to the class such as the Gettysburg Address by Abraham Lincoln or President John F. Kennedy's famous words from his inaugural address: "Ask not what your country can do for you; ask what you can do for your country." Discuss how a good speech can evoke strong feelings in people and talk about what makes a good speech. If you have older students, you may want to have them try to write a short speech about Dr. King and his contribution to our society.

Curriculum Connections: Have students do some research in biographies of other famous people to find notable quotes. For example, the well-known words spoken by Neil Armstrong as he stepped on the moon: "One small step for man, one giant leap for mankind."

Creative Arts: Provide students with a variety of drawing and painting materials. Ask them to create drawings or paintings which depict their dreams for themselves, their families, their community, their country, or their world.

Friday

Theme Activities: Wrap up this theme by learning about how Dr. King's birthday became a holiday. Discuss what your school is doing in honor of his birthday.

Literature Time: Read *Martin Luther King Day* by Linda Lowery (Scholastic, 1987) for a complete description of how his birthday became a holiday. The book ends with some thoughts on Martin Luther King Day from his wife Coretta Scott King and others.

Language Arts: To summarize all that has been learned this week, make the nonfiction book about Dr. King found on pages 333–338. After assembling, reading, and coloring the pages, the book can be taken home to share with families.

Curriculum Connections: In December 1964, Dr. King was awarded the Nobel peace prize. Talk about what this honor means and how Dr. King gave the money away to help others.

Creative Arts: Promote the idea of peace with some historical posters and signs. Have students create pictures which promote the ideas of peace among all people of the world. Include captions with the posters and display them in your room or in the halls of your school.

I have a dream . . .

This Week's Theme

Martin Luther King, Jr.

I have a dream . . . .   *I have a dream . . .*

I have a dream . . .

I have a dream . . .

Dear Parents,

This week we will be studying about a famous American—Dr. Martin Luther King, Jr. Our class will read about his life, using several biographies, including *A Picture Book of Martin Luther King, Jr.,* by David Adler and *Martin Luther King Day* by Linda Lowery. As we learn about Dr. King's life, we will list information and important dates on several charts which we will add to throughout the week.

We will be discussing how Dr. King's birthday became a holiday, and then we will study other famous African Americans such as Rosa Parks and Jackie Robinson. Our learning will stress the idea of using peaceful means to solve problems.

During the theme study, our activities will cover many areas of our curriculum, including reading, writing, music, and art. Some of our learning will include these activities:

1. making a book about Dr. King's life

2. learning about the Nobel prize and why it was given to Dr. King

3. writing about a person we most admire

4. making a time line of important events in Dr. King's life

Please take a few minutes each day to discuss with your child what is being learned in this social studies theme. Your child will bring home a book about Dr. King to read to you at the end of this unit. We hope that you enjoy the book. Thanks for sharing in your child's learning.

Sincerely,

_____

I have a dream . . .

Daily Journal Topics: Martin Luther King, Jr.

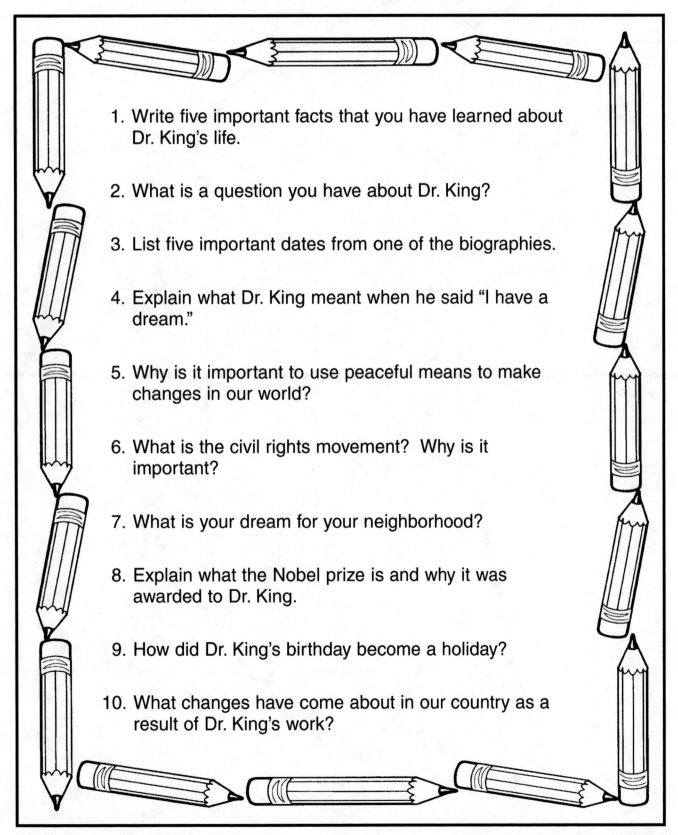

1. Write five important facts that you have learned about Dr. King's life.

2. What is a question you have about Dr. King?

3. List five important dates from one of the biographies.

4. Explain what Dr. King meant when he said "I have a dream."

5. Why is it important to use peaceful means to make changes in our world?

6. What is the civil rights movement? Why is it important?

7. What is your dream for your neighborhood?

8. Explain what the Nobel prize is and why it was awarded to Dr. King.

9. How did Dr. King's birthday become a holiday?

10. What changes have come about in our country as a result of Dr. King's work?

Peace Pledge

Directions for this activity can be found on page 327.

My peace pledge is

My Book About Martin Luther King, Jr.

Directions: Cut the book on the lines, put the pages in order, and staple to make your own booklet. Read the text and color the illustrations.

All About Martin Luther King, Jr.

Name _____

Martin Luther King, Jr., is a famous American leader who promoted peaceful change.

1

My Book About
Martin Luther King, Jr. *(cont.)*

Martin Luther King, Jr. was born in Atlanta, Georgia, on January 15, 1929. His father was a minister, and his mother was a teacher.

2

Martin loved to read books, and he was a good student. He read about famous black Americans like George Washington Carver.

3

My Book About
Martin Luther King, Jr. *(cont.)*

Even as a young boy, Martin noticed that all people were not treated equally. He started to think about how he could help people.

4

Martin graduated from high school when he was only 15. He went to college and became a minister.

5

My Book About
Martin Luther King, Jr. *(cont.)*

Martin met a woman named Coretta Scott while going to school in Boston. They decided to get married on June 18, 1953.

6

After Dr. King moved to Montgomery, Alabama, he began to work to change unjust laws. He gave speeches and led peaceful protests.

7

My Book About
Martin Luther King, Jr. *(cont.)*

Dr. King made his most famous speech at a march in Washington, D.C., in August 1963. His speech began with the words "I have a dream."

8

Dr. King was awarded the Nobel peace prize in December 1964 for his work.

9

My Book About
Martin Luther King, Jr. *(cont.)*

Sadly, Dr. King was killed in April 1968. To honor his memory and his work, Congress voted in 1983 to make a national holiday called Martin Luther King, Jr., Day.

10

We honor Dr. King's life each year with parades and other celebrations to remember his dream.

11

Weekly Theme: Early American Life   Week _____

	Monday	Tuesday	Wednesday	Thursday	Friday
Date					
Theme Activities	Discuss how people lived long ago.	Introduce and discuss immigration to America.	Explain the Westward Movement.	Discuss and describe early American family life.	Brainstorm ideas about early American schools.
Literature Time	Read *Long Ago and Today* by Rozanne Lanczak Williams and *100 Years Ago* by Donna Marriott.	Read *Watch the Stars Come Out* by Riki Levinson.	Read *Going West* by Jean Van Leeuwen and *Next Spring an Oriole* by Gloria Whelan.	Read *Winter Days in the Big Woods* by Laura Ingalls Wilder and *Ox-Cart Man* by Donald Hall.	Read *A One-Room School* by Bobbie Kalman.
Language Arts	Make a Then and Now Mini-Book.	Compile a list of countries of students' origins.	Pack your own covered wagon.	Write an innovation: Summer Days in the Big Woods.	Make a Hornbook and What Was a One-Room Schoolhouse? booklet.
Curriculum Connections	Complete A Shopping Trip: Then and Now.	Locate countries of origin on a world map or globe.	Introduce the *Oregon Trail* CD-ROM.	Visit an early American homestead exhibit.	Visit an early American schoolhouse exhibit.
Creative Arts	Make silhouettes of students.	Make paintings of the Statue of Liberty.	Make models of covered wagons.	Create a mural of an early American homestead.	Try early American schoolhouse singing games.

Overview: Early American Life

Monday

Theme Activities: Discuss with your class how they think people lived long ago. This will allow you to assess their prior knowledge about early American life.

Literature Time: Read two books to the class that are suitable for your young readers: *Long Ago and Today* by Rozanne Lanczak Williams (Creative Teaching Press, 1996) and *100 Years Ago* by Donna Marriott (Creative Teaching Press, 1998). You might want to have multiple copies of these two books available for students to read independently or as a part of your guided reading groups.

Language Arts: Duplicate pages 346 and 347 for each of your students to make their own Then and Now Mini-Books.

Curriculum Connections: Explain to your students that the cost of items now is much different from the cost of those same items many years ago. Duplicate page 348 for your students to complete A Shopping Trip: Then and Now.

Creative Arts: Explain that silhouettes were a treasured art form 100 years ago. Then use an overhead projector (or other light source) to make silhouettes of each of your students to display and send home as a gift for parents.

Tuesday

Theme Activities: Introduce and discuss immigration to America and how it made America the "melting pot" of the world.

Literature Time: Read *Watch the Stars Come Out* by Riki Levinson (E. P. Dutton, 1985) to learn about two children who immigrated to American to join their parents. The children journey to America on a ship alone, see the Statue of Liberty as they travel through New York Harbor, and enter the country through Ellis Island.

Language Arts: Use the information brought by your students from home (or known by your students), telling from which countries their ancestors came. Work with your students to make a class list of the countries from which their ancestors came. Display this list on a bulletin board with the title "Where Did Immigrants Come From?"

Curriculum Connections: Next to your list of countries of students' ancestors' origins, display a world map. Use a length of yarn to connect the name of each country to its location on the map.

Overview: Early American Life *(cont.)*

━━━━━━━━━━━━━━━━━━━━ **Tuesday** *(cont.)* ━━━━━━━━━━━━━━━━━━━━

Creative Arts: Since most of the early immigrants who came to America entered the country through New York Harbor and saw the Statue of Liberty as they entered, students will make paintings of the Statue of Liberty for display.

━━━━━━━━━━━━━━━━━━━━━━━ **Wednesday** ━━━━━━━━━━━━━━━━━━━━━━━

Theme Activities: Explain to your students that after immigrants came to America and settled along the eastern seaboard, many settlers decided to travel west to make new lives for themselves. The United States was expanding to the west, and many settlers decided to travel west to the new land. This was called the Westward Movement.

Literature Time: Read the picture book *Going West* by Jean Van Leeuwen (Dial Books for Young Readers, 1992) to your class. You might also want to read the chapter book *Next Spring an Oriole* by Gloria Whelan (Random House, 1987) to your students, or your students might read the book independently if it is at their reading level (RL: 3.3).

Language Arts: Duplicate page 349 for students to complete— Pack Your Own Covered Wagon.

Curriculum Connections: Introduce the CD-ROM *Oregon Trail II* (MECC, 1994) to your students. This will enable your students to practice their problem solving, math, and history skills while experiencing the trip west.

Creative Arts: Provide cereal boxes, cylinders, and fabric for students to create their own models of covered wagons.

━━━━━━━━━━━━━━━━━━━━━━━ **Thursday** ━━━━━━━━━━━━━━━━━━━━━━━

Theme Activities: Discuss how early American families lived: what their houses looked like, what they ate, what they did for fun, how families earned money to buy what they needed, how they got their food and clothing, etc.

Literature Time: Introduce your students to the series of My First Little House books that are based upon the Little House Books written by Laura Ingalls Wilder. Read *Winter Days in the Big Woods* from this series. You might want to read one of the Little House chapter books to your class or have them available for your readers to read independently. (See the bibliography on pages 369–374 for other titles from this series.) Also read the classic *Ox-Cart Man* by Donald Hall (Penguin Books, 1979) to your class for more information about early American family life.

Overview: Early American Life *(cont.)*

═══════════════════ **Thursday** *(cont.)* ═══════════════════

Language Arts: Have your students refer to *Winter Days in the Big Woods* and have them work with you to create a class writing innovation called Summer Days in the Big Woods. Write each new sentence at the top of a sheet of 18" x 24" (46 cm x 61 cm) white construction paper. Have students work in pairs to illustrate each page in your new class book. Add a cover that includes the title and authors, as well as a page at the back of the book for each of your students to sign as "Contributing Authors and Illustrators."

Curriculum Connections: Check with your local Chamber of Commerce for information about museums in your area that may have an exhibit or an authentic early American homestead which your students may visit. If possible, arrange a field trip for your students to visit a homestead so that they will learn about this era by actually seeing how early American settlers lived.

Creative Arts: After visiting an early American homestead or using the information you have learned by reading about them, have your students work to create a mural of an early American homestead, using crayons, watercolors, or chalk. Encourage students to include the cabin, the barn, the barnyard, the fields, the "outhouse," and an orchard.

═══════════════════ **Friday** ═══════════════════

Theme Activities: Challenge students to brainstorm ideas of what early American schools might have been like. Students may have some ideas or may have read about them in their independent reading.

Literature Time: Read *A One-Room School* by Bobbie Kalman (Crabtree Publishing, 1994) from the Historic Communities series to help your students learn more about the schools that early American children attended.

Language Arts: Duplicate page 350 for each of your students to use in making their own hornbook. The hornbook may be mounted on a piece of brown tagboard or cardboard to make it more sturdy. Duplicate pages 351–353 for students to read their own booklets called What Is a One-Room Schoolhouse?

Curriculum Connections: Check with your local chamber of commerce for information about museums in your area that may have an exhibit or an authentic early American schoolhouse which your students may visit. If possible, arrange a field trip to visit a one-room schoolhouse and/or ask someone who attended one to come talk to the class so they will better understand how early American children learned.

Creative Arts: Sing and play two of the games that American children enjoyed in the past and that are still known today: "Ring Around the Rosy" and "The Farmer in the Dell."

This Week's Theme

Early American Life

Dear Parents,

Our class is beginning a new unit of thematic study. We will be learning about "Early American Life." We will learn how people lived long ago, as well as about the immigration of people to America, the Westward Movement, early American settlers, and the early American one-room schoolhouse. During the unit, we will read several books, including *Watch the Stars Come Out* by Riki Levinson and *Winter Days in the Big Woods* by Laura Ingalls Wilder. Our unit activities will extend across the curriculum into literature, reading, writing, math, history, geography, technology, art, and music.

As one project in our study, your child will be making a Then and Now mini-book to compare how people lived 100 years ago with how we live now. We will also be doing the following activities:

1. making paintings of the Statue of Liberty
2. deciding what items would be essential to pack in a covered wagon
3. creating a mural of an early American homestead
4. making a booklet called What Was a One-Room Schoolhouse?

We could use your help with one aspect of our learning. We will be discussing from which countries our students' ancestors came. Please discuss this with your child and list below the names of the countries from which your child's ancestors came so that we may locate these countries on our world map bulletin board called "Where Did Our Ancestors Come From?" Please send in this information by _____.

Thank you for your help in making "Early American Life" come alive for your child!

                          Sincerely,

                          _____

- -

Where Did My Child's Ancestors Come From?

My child's ancestors came from the following countries:

_____

Signed _____

Daily Journal Topics:
Early American Life

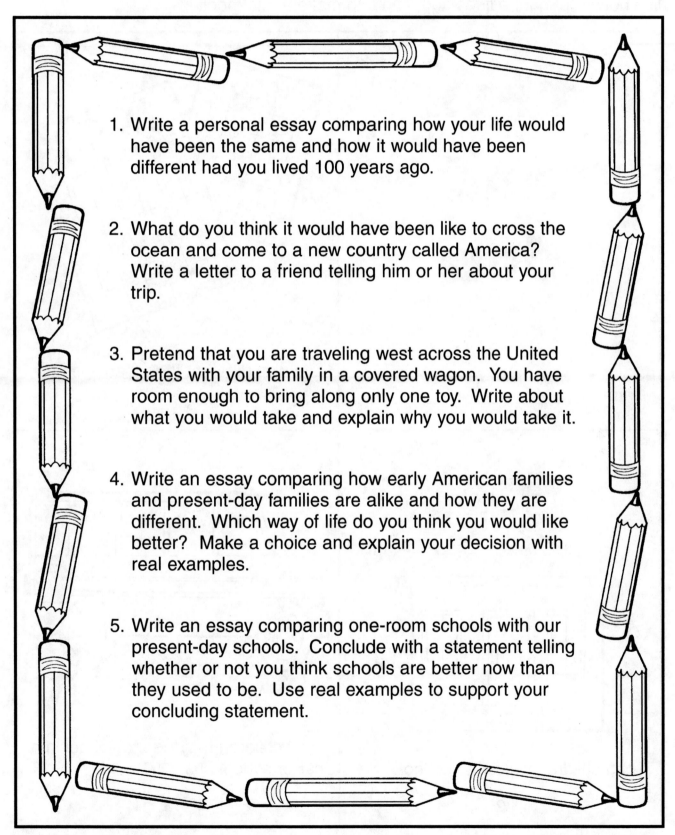

1. Write a personal essay comparing how your life would have been the same and how it would have been different had you lived 100 years ago.

2. What do you think it would have been like to cross the ocean and come to a new country called America? Write a letter to a friend telling him or her about your trip.

3. Pretend that you are traveling west across the United States with your family in a covered wagon. You have room enough to bring along only one toy. Write about what you would take and explain why you would take it.

4. Write an essay comparing how early American families and present-day families are alike and how they are different. Which way of life do you think you would like better? Make a choice and explain your decision with real examples.

5. Write an essay comparing one-room schools with our present-day schools. Conclude with a statement telling whether or not you think schools are better now than they used to be. Use real examples to support your concluding statement.

Then and Now Mini-Book

Directions: Read the information about how people lived then and how people live now. Cut on the lines and staple to make a mini-book.

Then and Now

Name _____

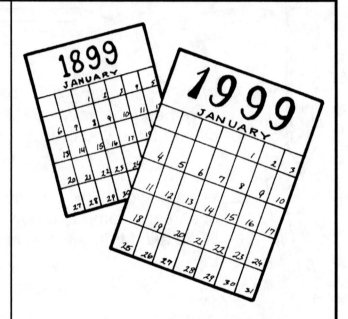

Life was different then than it is now.

1

Then children walked to school.

2

Now children may ride to school in a car or school bus.

3

Then and Now Mini-Book *(cont.)*

Then families grew much of their food on their farms.

4

Now families go to a supermarket to buy their food.

5

Then children dressed in clothes made by their families.

6

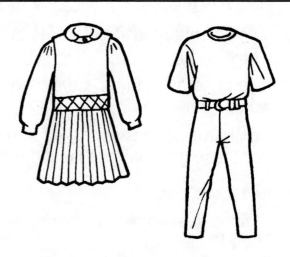

Now children dress in different clothes that families buy. Even though life was different then than it is now, both were just right!

7

A Shopping Trip: Then and Now

Name _____ Date _____

Directions: Prices on basic items have changed over the past 100 years. Use a calculator and the Then and Now Price Lists below to calculate the answers to the following questions.

Then Price List	
box of cereal	$0.15
bar of soap	$0.05
gallon of milk	$0.20
pound of sugar	$0.06
pound of butter	$0.27
toothbrush	$0.04

Now Price List	
box of cereal	$3.89
bar of soap	$0.34
gallon of milk	$2.19
pound of sugar	$0.42
pound of butter	$3.69
toothbrush	$0.89

1. How much more does a box of cereal cost now than it did then?_____

2. How much less did a gallon of milk cost then than it does now? _____

3. If you went to the store now to buy cereal, milk, and sugar, how much would it cost? _____

4. If you had gone to the store then to buy cereal, milk, and sugar, how much would it have cost? _____

5. Compare your answers in #3 and #4. How much more does it cost now to buy these three items than it did then? _____

Bonus Questions:

1. What is total amount of money needed to purchase all the items on the Then Price List? _____

2. What is the total amount of money needed to purchase all the items on the Now Price List? _____

3. What is the difference between the totals on the Then Price List and the Now Price List? _____

Note: Prices from 100 years ago were taken from the section called "1900–1904" in *The Value of a Dollar: Prices and Incomes in the U.S.*, edited by Scott Derks. Current prices were based on a random sampling of items in Midland, Michigan, as of December 1998.

Pack Your Own Covered Wagon

Name _____ Date _____

Directions: Look at the list of items below. Decide which ones you think an early American family would need to have with them to settle in the west. List your selected items below and draw them in the covered wagon.

Possible Items for Your Covered Wagon

ax	pails	piano	seeds	camera	shovel
tools	TV	trunk	flour	bacon	sugar
pizza	water	bowls	radio	cups	freezer

I would take the following items in my covered wagon:

1. _____   5. _____   9. _____

2. _____   6. _____   10. _____

3. _____   7. _____   11. _____

4. _____   8. _____   12. _____

Make a Hornbook

Directions: Color the paddle part of the hornbook brown. Cut out the hornbook. Glue the hornbook on cardboard or brown tagboard that is cut to the same size and shape. Use your best printing to write the alphabet and numerals on the hornbook.

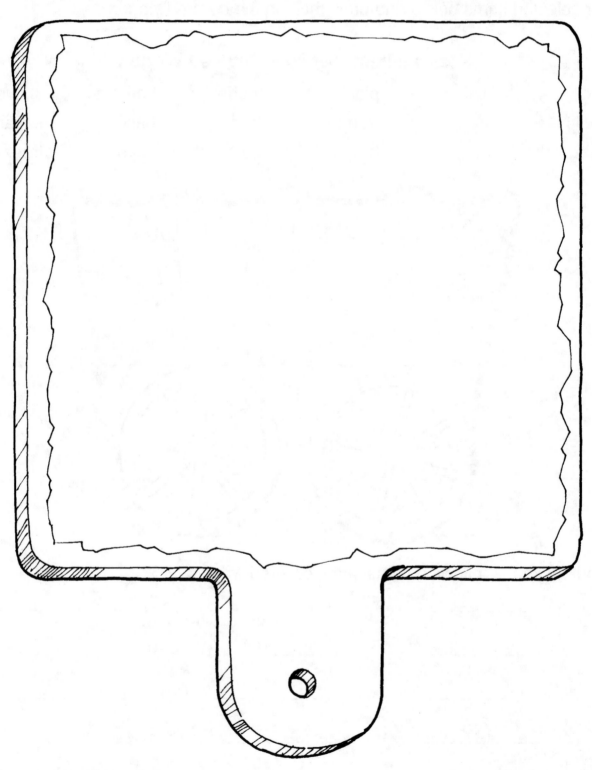

What Was a One-Room Schoolhouse?

Directions: Read the information about the one-room schoolhouse. Cut on the lines, put the pages in the correct order, and staple to make your own booklet. You may color the illustrations.

What Was a One-Room Schoolhouse?

Name _____

Dodge School

A long time ago children went to a school with their neighbors. There was one classroom for all of the students in kindergarten through the eighth grade.

1

What Was a One-Room Schoolhouse? *(cont.)*

The children walked to the schoolhouse. Sometimes they walked a mile or even farther. They walked on cold and snowy days too.

2

There was one teacher in a one-room school. The teacher swept the school, started the wood stove to heat the school, and taught every subject for all grades.

3

What Was a One-Room Schoolhouse? *(cont.)*

The children took turns working with the teacher. They helped each other. They learned to read, to write, to spell, to do arithmetic, and to know about the world.

4

All the children brought their lunches from home. They ate together. Then they had recess together. The children learned together and played together too.

5

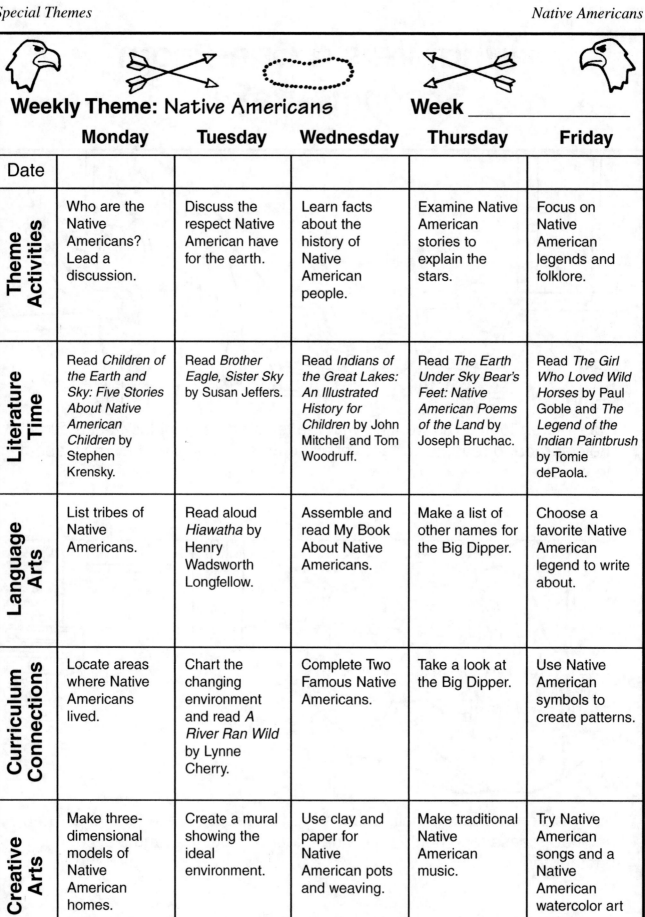

Weekly Theme: Native Americans Week _____

	Monday	Tuesday	Wednesday	Thursday	Friday
Date					
Theme Activities	Who are the Native Americans? Lead a discussion.	Discuss the respect Native American have for the earth.	Learn facts about the history of Native American people.	Examine Native American stories to explain the stars.	Focus on Native American legends and folklore.
Literature Time	Read *Children of the Earth and Sky: Five Stories About Native American Children* by Stephen Krensky.	Read *Brother Eagle, Sister Sky* by Susan Jeffers.	Read *Indians of the Great Lakes: An Illustrated History for Children* by John Mitchell and Tom Woodruff.	Read *The Earth Under Sky Bear's Feet: Native American Poems of the Land* by Joseph Bruchac.	Read *The Girl Who Loved Wild Horses* by Paul Goble and *The Legend of the Indian Paintbrush* by Tomie dePaola.
Language Arts	List tribes of Native Americans.	Read aloud *Hiawatha* by Henry Wadsworth Longfellow.	Assemble and read My Book About Native Americans.	Make a list of other names for the Big Dipper.	Choose a favorite Native American legend to write about.
Curriculum Connections	Locate areas where Native Americans lived.	Chart the changing environment and read *A River Ran Wild* by Lynne Cherry.	Complete Two Famous Native Americans.	Take a look at the Big Dipper.	Use Native American symbols to create patterns.
Creative Arts	Make three-dimensional models of Native American homes.	Create a mural showing the ideal environment.	Use clay and paper for Native American pots and weaving.	Make traditional Native American music.	Try Native American songs and a Native American watercolor art project.

Overview: Native Americans

Monday

Theme Activities: Lead your class in a discussion to determine who is meant by the term "Native Americans." Explain that the term means the inhabitants (and their descendants) of the Americas when Europeans first arrived. They were incorrectly called "Indians" because the early explorers believed that they had arrived in the Indies. Use "Native Americans" during the course of this unit.

Literature Time: Read *Children of the Earth and Sky: Five Stories About Native American Children* by Stephen Krensky (Scholastic, 1991). The introduction, which provides good basic information about Native Americans, is followed by five stories about the experiences of realistic (but imaginary) Native American children. Ask your students to identify how the children's lives from tribe to tribe were alike and how they were different. A chart to organize this information would be helpful.

Language Arts: Begin making a class list of Native American tribes. The tribes mentioned in the above book will give your students a start on this list. Add to this list during your study.

Curriculum Connections: Use a United States map to locate areas where Native American children from Krensky's book lived. Children may use the U.S. map from page 377 to make their own maps. The map key should identify each of the five tribes with a correlated color. Students will then use colored pencils to identify each tribe's area.

Creative Arts: Students may use materials from nature (sand, water, mud, sticks, bark) to create three-dimensional models of Native American homes.

Tuesday

Theme Activities: Explain to your students that Native Americans traditionally have a strong respect and love for nature and the earth. Protecting nature from pollution is the theme of today's work.

Literature Time: Read *Brother Eagle, Sister Sky* by Susan Jeffers (Dial Books for Young Readers, 1991) to your class. (A commercially available cassette tape of nature sounds playing softly in the background may add to the effect of this book.) The beautiful illustrations sensitively portray the beauty of the earth, while the text is Chief Seattle's message about the Native American's love for the earth. Be sure to read the epilogue written by Susan Jeffers, which explains the warning given by Chief Seattle and how it was unheeded. Ask children what they can do to follow the words of Chief Seattle.

Overview: Native Americans (cont.)

Tuesday (cont.)

Language Arts: Read aloud the classic poem *Hiawatha* by Henry Wadsworth Longfellow (Dial Books for Young Readers, 1983) to your students. This book is also available on cassette tape from Scholastic with appropriate sound effects.

Curriculum Connections: Compare our world's environment now with the world as described and illustrated in the previously suggested literature. A chart with the headings "THEN" and "NOW" will help to organize your students' suggestions. The book *A River Ran Wild* by Lynne Cherry (Bantam Doubleday Dell, 1992) provides the history of the Nashua River's environment and the changes it has undergone.

Creative Arts: Guide your students in creating a mural showing the beauty of nature and the earth. Crayons, colorful chalk or pastels, or watercolors should be available for the students' use.

Wednesday

Theme Activities: Begin by discussing how Native Americans first came to be in America. Ask your students about the presence of Native Americans in America today, with questions such as "Are there Native Americans now?" "How do they dress?" "Where do they live?" "Do they go to school?"

Literature Time: Read *Indians of the Great Lakes: An Illustrated History for Children* by John Mitchell and Tom Woodruff (Suttons Bay Publications, 301 St. Joseph, Box 361, Suttons Bay, Michigan 49682). Since this is a lengthy history, you may want to read the book to your class in more than one sitting.

Language Arts: Reproduce the informational text My Book About Native Americans (pages 361–365) for each student to read.

Curriculum Connections: Guide students in learning about two of the many Native Americans who played an important role in the history of our country by completing Two Famous Native Americans (pages 366 and 367).

Creative Arts: Try these two art ideas. First, have your students use clay to form pots like those that Native Americans might have used. The clay may be rolled into a long "snake" and then coiled to form a pot. Second, students may use a 12" x 18" (30 cm x 46 cm) sheet of construction paper to practice the art of weaving, as Native Americans still create beautiful blankets. Cut slits in the paper. Then use the strips that are 1" x 12" (2.5 cm x 30 cm) to go over . . . under . . . over . . . under, etc.

Overview: Native Americans *(cont.)*

Thursday

Theme Activities: Look at a diagram of the Big Dipper constellation. Ask students to identify it. Explain that Native Americans named the grouping of stars with their own names, depending upon what the constellation looked like to them. The Big Dipper was seen as a large bear by Native Americans.

Literature Time: Read *The Earth Under Sky Bear's Feet: Native American Poems of the Land* by Joseph Bruchac (Philomel Books, 1995) to further explain the view of the Big Dipper as a large bear that circles the night sky.

Language Arts: Use a drawing of the grouping of stars that we call the Big Dipper and have students brainstorm a list of other possible names for this constellation. Have students justify their ideas.

Curriculum Connections: Have students complete Take a Look at the Big Dipper (page 368).

Creative Arts: Use rhythm instruments and recorders to have students create their own traditional Native American music. Students may make their own drums from large plastic tubs, five-quart ice cream pails, etc.

Friday

Theme Activities: Introduce to your classroom collection a variety of books that focus on Native American legends and stories, explaining that the Native American culture has a wealth of folklore to explore.

Literature Time: Read two such folklore selections today: *The Girl Who Loved Wild Horses* by Paul Goble (Bradbury Press, 1978) and *The Legend of the Indian Paintbrush* by Tomie dePaola (Aladdin Books, 1988). The books may be read at two different sittings, depending upon the age of your students.

Language Arts: Students may write a response choosing their favorite of the two legends and explain why they made the choice they did.

Curriculum Connections: Students may use Native American symbols to create their own patterns.

Creative Arts: Use a simple drum beat to accompany the children as they chant the "songs" found on the last page of *The Girl Who Loved Wild Horses.* Additionally, the children may use watercolors to create their own Native American paintings.

This Week's Theme

Native Americans

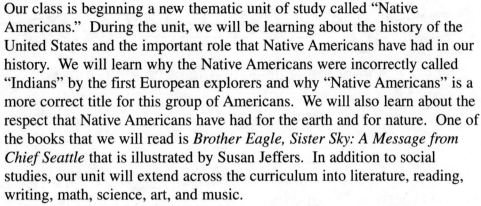

Dear Parents,

Our class is beginning a new thematic unit of study called "Native Americans." During the unit, we will be learning about the history of the United States and the important role that Native Americans have had in our history. We will learn why the Native Americans were incorrectly called "Indians" by the first European explorers and why "Native Americans" is a more correct title for this group of Americans. We will also learn about the respect that Native Americans have had for the earth and for nature. One of the books that we will read is *Brother Eagle, Sister Sky: A Message from Chief Seattle* that is illustrated by Susan Jeffers. In addition to social studies, our unit will extend across the curriculum into literature, reading, writing, math, science, art, and music.

For one project in this study, your child will be making and reading an informational book about Native Americans that will be taken home to be read with you. During the thematic study, we will also be doing the following activities:

1. learning about a few Native American tribes and how they lived
2. learning about two selected famous Native Americans
3. making Native American pottery, weaving, and music
4. reading and writing about favorite Native American legends

You might encourage your child's interest in Native Americans by visiting a museum exhibit of Native American artifacts or by visiting your public library to learn more about Native Americans. A list of related books is given below.

Thank you for helping the history of our Native Americans come alive for your child.

Sincerely,

Native American Book List

Here are a few books to help you learn more about Native Americans:

The Legend of the Bluebonnet and *The Legend of the Indian Paintbrush* by Tomie dePaola

Indians of the Great Lakes: An Illustrated History for Children by John Mitchell and Tom Woodruff

Buffalo Woman by Paul Goble

Children of the Earth and Sky: Five Stories About Native American Children by Stephen Krensky

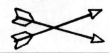

Daily Journal Topics: Native Americans

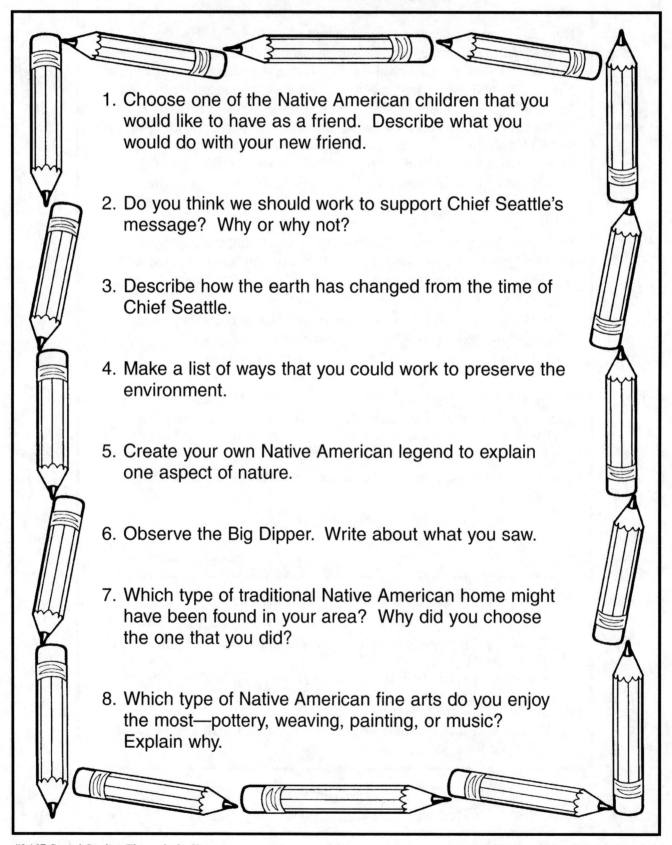

1. Choose one of the Native American children that you would like to have as a friend. Describe what you would do with your new friend.

2. Do you think we should work to support Chief Seattle's message? Why or why not?

3. Describe how the earth has changed from the time of Chief Seattle.

4. Make a list of ways that you could work to preserve the environment.

5. Create your own Native American legend to explain one aspect of nature.

6. Observe the Big Dipper. Write about what you saw.

7. Which type of traditional Native American home might have been found in your area? Why did you choose the one that you did?

8. Which type of Native American fine arts do you enjoy the most—pottery, weaving, painting, or music? Explain why.

My Book About Native Americans

Directions: Read the information about Native Americans. Cut on the lines, put the pages in order, and staple to make your booklet. You may color the illustrations.

My Book About Native Americans

Name _____

Native Americans lived in North America long before explorers came from Europe.

1

My Book About Native Americans *(cont.)*

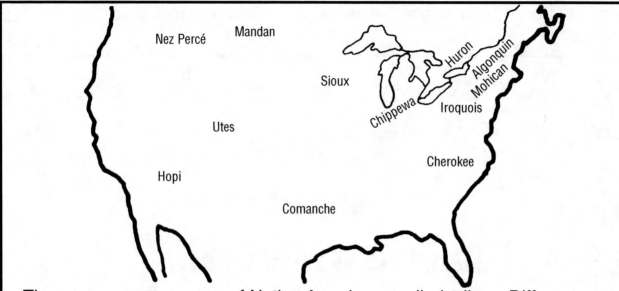

There were many groups of Native Americans called *tribes*. Different tribes lived in different areas of North America.

2

The Hurons traveled the Great Lakes area in birch bark canoes.

3

My Book About Native Americans *(cont.)*

Pueblos were the homes of the Hopis in the Southwest.

4

The Algonquins built wigwams in the Northeast.

5

My Book About Native Americans *(cont.)*

Tribes of the Plains built tipis. They rode horses and hunted buffalo.

6

Native Americans had great respect for the earth and nature.

7

My Book About Native Americans *(cont.)*

Today Native Americans dress, work, learn, and live as they choose.

8

Native Americans may gather together at powwows to celebrate their heritage.

9

Two Famous Native Americans

Name _____ Date _____

Directions: Read about these two famous Native Americans. Then answer the questions on page 367.

Sacajawea

Sacajawea was one of the most important explorers in United States history. She traveled with Meriwether Lewis and William Clark on their expedition to explore the Pacific Northwest.

Sacajawea was a member of the Shoshone tribe. She traveled with Lewis and Clark so that she could talk with Native Americans they met along the way.

They left from Fort Mandan and paddled up the Missouri River in canoes. They rode horses to cross the Rocky Mountains. They reached the Pacific Ocean in 1806. The 8,000-mile trip to the Pacific Ocean and back took a year. When the trip was over, she returned to North Dakota to live.

Sequoya

Sequoya was a member of the Cherokee tribe. He was born in Tennessee in about 1760.

Sequoya became a silversmith when he grew up. He made jewelry from silver that he traded with other Native Americans and the European settlers.

Sequoya could not read, but he was interested in the settlers' newspapers.

Two Famous Native Americans *(cont.)*

Since the Cherokee did not have a way to write their ideas on paper, Sequoya invented an alphabet for writing the Cherokee language. He taught other Native Americans to read his language and wrote articles about Cherokee history for them to read.

Sequoya went to Mexico to study other Native American languages. California's enormous redwood trees in Sequoia National Park are named for him.

Questions

Directions: Find the answers to the following questions in the informational text. Underline your answers in the text. Write your answers below in complete sentences.

1. With whom did Sacajawea travel to the Pacific Ocean?

   _____

2. Why did Sacajawea go on the expedition?

   _____

3. Over which mountain range did Sacajawea travel?_____

   _____

4. To which Native American tribe did Sacajawea belong?_____

   _____

5. What did Sequoya invent? _____

   _____

6. How did Sequoya became interested in written languages?

   _____

7. What is named in honor of Sequoya? _____

   _____

8. To which Native American tribe did Sequoya belong? _____

   _____

Take a Look at the Big Dipper

Name _____ Date _____

Directions: Look at the diagram of the Big Dipper. Answer the questions below.

● **North Celestial Pole**

1. The stars above form a _____
   called the Big Dipper.

2. The Native Americans called the constellation _____.

3. There are_____ stars that
   form this constellation.

4. This constellation is seen in the _____
   night sky.

5. Using binoculars or a _____ may
   help you see the stars better as you look at the night sky.

6. We do not see the Big Dipper during the daytime. The _____
   is the only star that we see during the daytime.

Bibliography

Look at Me

Cole, Joanna. *On the Bus with Joanna Cole: A Creative Autobiography.* Heinemann, 1996.

Kraus, Robert. *Leo the Late Bloomer.* Dutton, 1971.

Marzollo, Jean. *My First Book of Biographies.* Scholastic, 1994.

Going to School

Baehr, Patricia. *School Isn't Fair!* Macmillan, 1989.

Bourgeois, Paulette. *Franklin Goes to School.* Scholastic, 1995.

Hill, Eric. *Spot Goes to School.* Penguin Books, 1984.

Kalman, Bobbie. *A One-Room School.* Crabtree, 1994.

Kraus, Robert. *Spider's First Day of School.* Scholastic, 1987.

Mayer, Mercer. *Little Critter's This Is My School.* Western Publishing, 1990.

McCully, Emily Arnold. *School.* Harper & Row, 1987.

McMillan, Bruce. *Mouse Views: What the Class Pet Saw.* Holiday House, 1993.

Penn, Audrey. *The Kissing Hand.* Scholastic, 1998.

Pulver, Robin. *Nobody's Mother Is in Second Grade.* Dial Books for Young Readers, 1992.

Schwartz, Amy. *Annabelle Swift, Kindergartner.* Orchard Books, 1988.

Schweninger, Ann. *Off to School!* Viking Penguin, 1987.

Slate, Joseph. *Miss Bindergarten Gets Ready for Kindergarten.* Dutton Children's Books, 1996.

Wiseman, Bernard. *Morris Goes to School.* Harper & Row, 1970.

Friends Forever

Aliki. *Together Again.* Greenwillow Books, 1995.

————. *We Are Best Friends.* Greenwillow Books, 1982.

Kellogg, Steven. *Best Friends.* Dial Books for Young Readers, 1990.

Marzollo, Jean and Claudio. *Ruthie's Rude Friends.* Dial Books for Young Readers, 1984.

Ness, Evaline. *Sam, Bangs and Moonshine.* Henry Holt, 1995.

Pfister, Marcus. *The Rainbow Fish.* North-South Books, 1992.

Turkle, Brinton. *Thy Friend, Obadiah.* Viking Penguin, 1969.

Fabulous Food

Adoff, Arnold. *Eats.* Lothrop, Lee & Shepard, 1979.

Gibbons, Gail. *The Milk Makers.* Macmillan, 1985.

Prelutsky, Jack. *Dinosaur Dinner: Favorite Poems.* Knopf, 1977.

Priceman, Marjorie. *How to Make an Apple Pie and See the World.* Knopf, 1994.

Spier, Peter. *We the People.* Doubleday, 1980.

Clothing

Barrett, Judi. *Animals Should Definitely Not Wear Clothing.* Atheneum, 1970.

Jackson, Mike. *Clothes from Many Lands.* Steck-Vaughn, 1995.

Bibliography (cont.)

Clothing (cont.)

Jones, Charlotte Foltz. *Mistakes That Worked: 40 Famous Inventions and How They Came to Be.* Doubleday, 1991.

Neitzel, Shirley. *The Jacket I Wear in the Snow.* Greenwillow, 1989.

Peek, Merle. *Mary Wore Her Red Dress and Henry Wore His Green Sneakers.* Clarion Books, 1985.

Shelter

Fries, Marcia. *Houses.* Creative Teaching Press, 1997.

Kalman, Bobbie. *Homes Around the World.* Crabtree Publishing, 1994.

Spier, Peter. *We the People.* Doubleday, 1980.

Fabulous Families

Greenfield, Eloise. *Grandpa's Face.* Philomel, 1988.

Hoberman, Mary Ann. *Fathers, Mothers, Sisters, Brothers: A Collection of Family Poems.* Penguin, 1991.

Humphrey, Paul. *In Dad's Day.* Steck-Vaughn, 1995.

_____. *In Grandma's Day.* Steck-Vaughn, 1995.

Johnson, Angela. *When I Am Old with You.* Orchard, 1993.

Johnston, Tony. *Yonder.* Dial Books for Young Readers, 1988.

Levinson, Riki. *I Go with My Family to Grandma's.* E.P. Dutton, 1986.

Lindbergh, Reeve. *Grandfather's Lovesong.* Viking Penguin, 1993.

Polacco, Patricia. *Firetalking.* Richard C. Owen, 1994.

Rylant, Cynthia. *Henry and Mudge in the Family Trees.* Simon & Schuster, 1997.

Say, Allen. *Grandfather's Journey.* Houghton Mifflin, 1993.

Williams, Rozanne Lanczak. *Families Share.* Creative Teaching Press, 1997.

My Community

Florian, Douglas. *City Street.* Greenwillow, 1990.

———. *A Year in the Country.* Greenwillow, 1989.

Grimes, Nikki and Pat Cummings. *C Is for City.* Lothrop, Lee & Shepard, 1995.

Rylant, Cynthia. *Night in the Country.* Bradbury, 1986.

My State

Bock, Judy and Rachel Kranz. *Scholastic Encyclopedia of the United States.* Scholastic, 1997.

Maps and Globes

Boyle, Bill. *My First Atlas.* Dorling Kindersley, 1994.

Fowler, Allan. *North, South, East and West.* Childrens Press, 1993.

Hartman, Gail. *As the Crow Flies.* Bradbury Press, 1991.

It's a Big, Big World Atlas. Tormont Publications, Canada, 1992.

Bibliography *(cont.)*

Faraway Children and Celebrations

Axworthy, Anni. *Anni's Diary of France.* Whispering Coyote Press, 1994.

Bailey, Donna. *Where We Live: Nigeria.* Steck-Vaughn, 1992.

———. *Where We Live: Phillipines,* Steck-Vaughn, 1992.

———. *Where We Live: Russia.* Steck-Vaughn, 1992.

Bailey, Donna and Malcolm Rodgers. *Where We Live: India.* Steck-Vaughn, 1992.

Bailey, Donna and Anna Sproule. *Where We Live: Israel.* Steck-Vaughn, 1992.

Barber, Will. *People Say Hello.* Creative Teaching Press, 1997.

Bulmer-Thomas, Barbara. *Journey Through Mexico.* Troll, 1991.

Cooper, Rod and Emile. *Journey Through Australia.* Troll, 1997.

Cowen-Fletcher, Jane. *It Takes a Village.* Scholastic, 1994.

Greene, Carol. *Holidays Around the World.* Childrens Press, 1982.

Hall, Kirsten. *A Visit to France.* Western Publishing, 1991.

Heide, Florence Parry and Judith Heide Gilliland. *The Day of Ahmed's Secret.* Lothrop, Lee & Shepard, 1990.

Jeunesse, Gallimard, et al. *Atlas of People.* Scholastic, 1994.

Levine, Ellen. *I Hate English!* Scholastic, 1989.

Packard, Mary. *A Visit to China.* Western Publishing, 1991.

Pinkney, Andrea Davis. *Seven Candles for Kwanzaa.* Dial Books for Young Readers, 1993.

Porter, A. P. *Kwanzaa.* Carolrhoda, 1991.

Raffi and Debi Pike. *Like Me and You.* Crown Publishers, 1994.

Spier, Peter. *We the People.* Doubleday, 1980.

Tames, Richard. *Journey Through Canada.* Troll, 1997.

Waters, Kate and Madeline Slovenz-Low. *Lion Dancer: Ernie Wan's Chinese New Year.* Scholastic, 1990.

Thanksgiving

Anderson, Joan. *The First Thanksgiving Feast.* Clarion, 1984.

Arnosky, Jim. *All About Turkeys.* Scholastic, 1998.

Balian, Lorna. *Sometimes It's Turkey—Sometimes It's Feathers.* Abingdon Press, 1986.

Bennett, William J., ed. *The Children's Book of America.* Simon & Schuster, 1998.

Bunting, Eve. *How Many Days to America? A Thanksgiving Story.* Clarion, 1988.

George, Jean Craighead. *The First Thanksgiving.* Philomel, 1993.

Gibbons, Gail. *Thanksgiving Day.* Holiday House, 1985.

Hayward, Linda. *The First Thanksgiving.* Random House, 1990.

Hillert, Margaret. *Why We Have Thanksgiving.* Modern Curriculum Press, 1982.

Lems-Tardif, Gina. *Pilgrim Children Had Many Chores.* Creative Teaching Press, 1997.

Sewall, Marcia. *The Pilgrims of Plymouth.* Atheneum Books for Young Readers, 1986.

Waters, Kate. *Samuel Eaton's Day: A Day in the Life of a Pilgrim Boy.* Scholastic, 1993.

———. *Sarah Morton's Day: A Day in the Life of a Pilgrim Girl.* Scholastic, 1989.

Bibliography *(cont.)*

Traditional Christmas

Barry, Robert. *Mr. Willowby's Christmas Tree.* McGraw-Hill, 1963.

dePaola, Tomie. *An Early American Christmas.* Holiday House, 1987.

_____. *The Family Christmas Tree Book.* Holiday House, 1980.

Diane Goode's American Christmas. Dutton Children's Books, 1990.

Gibbons, Gail. *Christmas Tree.* Holiday House, 1982.

Hall, Donald. *Lucy's Christmas.* Harcourt Brace, 1994.

Henderson, Kathy. *Christmas Trees.* Childrens Press, 1989.

Kelley, Emily. *Christmas Around the World.* Carolrhoda, 1986.

Moore, Clement. *The Night Before Christmas.* Penguin Putnam, 1998.

Raffi's Christmas Treasury. Crown, 1988.

Soto, Gary. *Too Many Tamales.* G. P. Putnam's Sons, 1993.

Wilder, Laura Ingalls. *Christmas in the Big Woods* (Adapted from the Little House Books). HarperCollins, 1995.

_____. *A Little House Christmas: Holiday Stories from the Little House Books.* HarperCollins, 1995.

A Trip to Washington, D.C.

Munro, Roxie. *The Inside-Outside Book of Washington, D.C.* Penguin, 1987.

Hail to the Chief

Bennett, William J., ed. *The Children's Book of America.* Simon & Schuster, 1998.

Giblin, James Cross. *Thomas Jefferson: A Picture Book Biography.* Scholastic, 1994.

Hooray for the U.S.A.!

Bennett, William J., ed. *The Children's Book of America.* Simon & Schuster, 1998.

———. *The Children's Book of Heroes.* Simon & Schuster, 1997.

Cohn, Amy L., comp. *From Sea to Shining Sea: A Treasury of American Folklore and Folk Songs.* Scholastic, 1993.

Robinson, Fay. *Recycle That!* Children's Press, 1995.

Exceptional Explorers

Barton, Byron. *I Want to Be an Astronaut.* Harper & Row, 1988.

Bennett, William J., ed. *The Children's Book of America.* Simon & Schuster, 1998.

Branley, Franklin M. *Rockets and Satellites.* Harper & Row, 1987.

Cutting, Brian and Jillian. *Space.* Wright Group, 1988.

Finch, Spencer. *Famous Americans: Interactive Picture Series.* Scholastic, 1995.

Herman, Gail. *Apollo 13: Space Race.* Grosset & Dunlap, 1995.

Krensky, Stephen. *Christopher Columbus.* Random House, 1991.

Lillegard, Dee. *My First Columbus Day Book.* Childrens Press, 1987.

Maze, Stephanie and Catherine O'Neill Grace. *I Want to Be . . . An Astronaut.* Harcourt Brace, 1997.

Smith, Barry. *The First Voyage of Christopher Columbus 1492.* Viking Penguin, 1992.

Bibliography *(cont.)*

Ingenious Inventors

Bennett, William, J., ed. *The Children's Book of America.* Simon & Schuster, 1998.

Davidson, Margaret. *The Story of Thomas Alva Edison, Inventor: The Wizard of Menlo Park.* Scholastic, 1990.

Finch, Spencer. *Famous Americans: Interactive Picture Series.* Scholastic, 1995.

Fowler, Allan. *What Magnets Can Do.* Childrens Press, 1995.

Hudson, Wade. *Five Notable Inventors* (Great Black Heroes). Scholastic, 1995.

Jeffries, Michael and Gary A. Lewis. *Inventors and Inventions.* Smithmark, 1992.

Nemes, Claire. *Young Thomas Edison: Great Inventors.* Troll, 1996.

Famous Figures in History

Adler, David A. *A Picture Book of Florence Nightingale.* Holiday House, 1992.

Aten, Jerry. *Famous Friends: A Child's First Encounter With Famous Americans* (Outstanding Women) Good Apple, 1987.

Benjamin, Anne. *Young Helen Keller: Woman of Courage.* Troll, 1992.

Bennett, William J., ed. *The Children's Book of Heroes.* Simon & Schuster, 1997.

Donnelly, Judy. *Moonwalk: The First Trip to the Moon.* Random House, 1989.

Finch, Spencer. *Famous Americans: Interactive Picture Series.* Scholastic, 1995.

Gaffney, Timothy R. *Grandpa Takes Me to the Moon.* William Morrow, 1996.

Gibbons, Gail. *The Moon Book.* Holiday House, 1997.

Graff, Stewart and Polly Anne. *Helen Keller: Crusader for the Blind and Deaf.* Dell Publishing, 1991.

Gresko, Marcia S. *Harriet Tubman.* Teacher Created Materials, 1997.

Keenan, Sheila. *Scholastic Encyclopedia of Women in the United States.* Scholastic, 1996.

Lepscky, Ibi. *Pablo Picasso.* Barron's Educational Series, 1992.

Lundell, Margo. *A Girl Named Helen Keller.* Scholastic, 1995.

McMullan, Kate. *The Story of Harriet Tubman, Conductor of the Underground Railroad.* Dell Publishing, 1991.

Monjo, F. N. *The Drinking Gourd.* Harper & Row, 1970.

Parlin, John. *Amelia Earhart: Pioneer of the Sky.* Dell Publishing, 1991.

Szabo, Corinne. *Sky Pioneer: A Photobiography of Amelia Earhart.* National Geographic Society, 1997.

Winter, Jeanette. *Follow the Drinking Gourd.* Alfred A. Knopf, 1988.

Woods, Andrew. *Young Orville and Wilbur Wright: First to Fly.* Troll, 1992.

The Father of Our Country

Bennett, William J., ed. *The Children's Book of America.* Simon & Schuster, 1998.

_____. *The Children's Book of Heroes.* Simon & Schuster, 1997.

Gross, Ruth Belov. *If You Grew Up with George Washington.* Scholastic, 1982.

Healy, Brooks. *It's True, by George! Surprising Facts About George Washington.* Reader's Digest Services, 1978.

Woods, Andrew. *Young George Washington: America's First President.* Troll, 1992.

Bibliography *(cont.)*

Honest Abe

Barkan, Joanne. *Abraham Lincoln and Presidents' Day.* Silver Press, 1990.

Bennett, William J., ed. *The Children's Book of America.* Simon & Schuster, 1998.

———. *The Children's Book of Heroes.* Simon & Schuster, 1997.

Brenner, Martha. *Abe Lincoln's Hat.* Random House, 1994.

McGovern, Ann. *If You Grew Up with Abraham Lincoln.* Scholastic, 1992.

Smith, Kathie Billingslea. *Abraham Lincoln.* Simon & Schuster, 1987.

Woods, Andrew. *Young Abraham Lincoln: Log Cabin President.* Troll, 1992.

Martin Luther King, Jr.

Bennett, William J., ed. *The Children's Book of America.* Simon & Schuster, 1998.

Davidson, Margaret. *I Have a Dream: The Story of Martin Luther King.* Scholastic, 1986.

Jones, Kathryn. *Happy Birthday, Dr. King!* Modern Curriculum Press, 1994.

Marzollo, Jean. *Happy Birthday, Martin Luther King.* Scholastic, 1993.

Mattern, Joanne. *Young Martin Luther King, Jr.* Troll, 1992.

Early American Life

Bennett, William J., ed. *The Children's Book of America.* Simon & Schuster, 1998.

Greene, Carol. *Laura Ingalls Wilder: Author of the Little House Books* (A Rookie Biography). Childrens Press, 1990.

Marriott, Donna. *100 Years Ago.* Creative Teaching Press, 1998.

Wilder, Laura Ingalls. *Christmas in the Big Woods* (Adapted from the Little House Books). HarperCollins, 1995.

———. *Dance at Grandpa's* (Adapted from the Little House Books). HarperCollins, 1994.

———. *The Deer in the Wood* (Adapted from the Little House Books). HarperCollins, 1995.

———. *Going to Town.* (Adapted from the Little House Books). HarperCollins, 1995.

Native Americans

Carlstrom, Nancy White. *Northern Lullaby.* Philomel Books, 1992.

dePaola, Tomie. *The Legend of the Bluebonnet.* Putnam, 1983.

Famous Americans (Interactive Picture Series). Scholastic, 1995.

Goble, Paul. *Buffalo Woman.* Macmillan, 1984.

Martin, Bill, Jr., and John Archambault. *Knots on a Counting Rope.* Henry Holt, 1990.

Martin, Rafe. *The Rough-Face Girl.* G. P. Putnam's Sons, 1982.

McDermott, Gerald. *Arrow to the Sun.* Viking Press, 1974.

McGovern, Ann. *If You Lived with the Sioux Indians.* Scholastic, 1972.

Swamp, Chief Jake. *Giving Thanks: A Native American Good Morning Message.* Scholastic, 1995.

Social Studies Theme Journal for

_____

Name _____

Date _____

Today's theme is_____

_____

_____

_____

_____

_____

_____

_____

_____

_____

_____

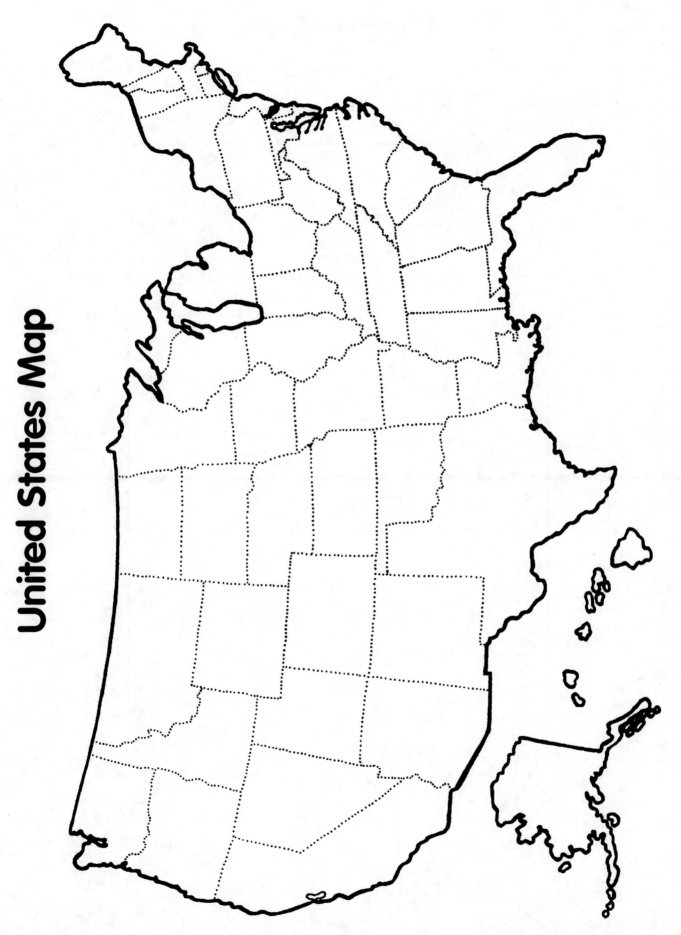

United States Map

World Map

Postcard Format

Front

Back

To: _____

_____

_____

Venn Diagram

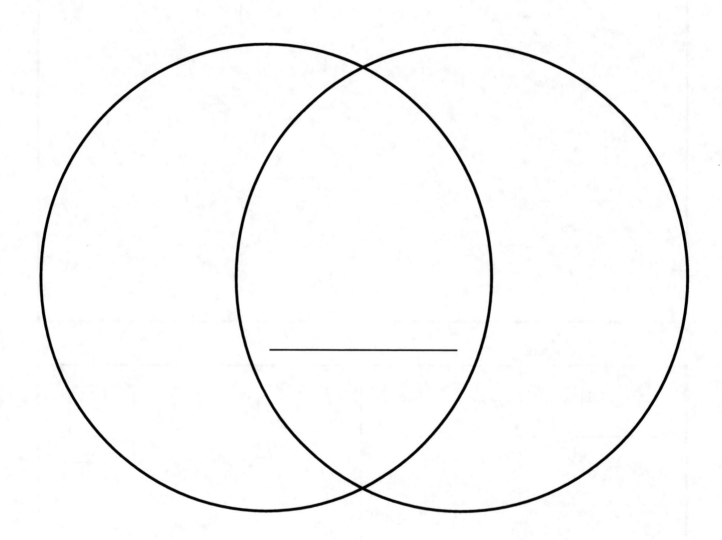

Sample Computer Projects

Some people live in cabins in the mountains.

My favorite part of first grade is getting to work with such a wonderful group of first graders.

Mrs. Rice
5-29-98

CHESTNUT HILL
ELEMENTARY SCHOOL

Note: These projects were made using *Kid Pix Studio.*

Sample Computer Projects *(cont.)*

Things to Do   **Places to See**   **Germany's Location**

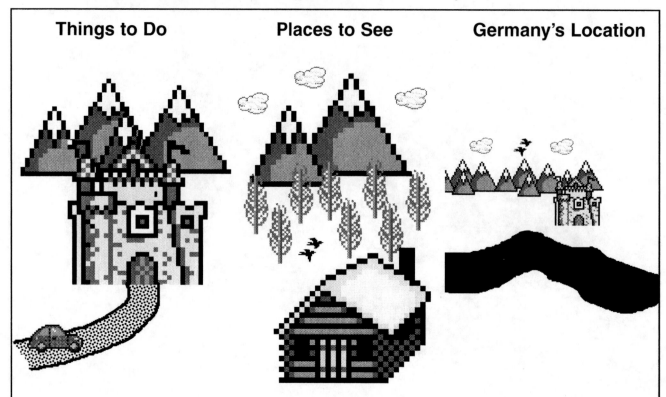

Germany is located in the continent of Europe. It has beautiful mountains and rivers.

Answer Key

Page 79
1. $4.01
2. Brand A is the least expensive.
3. $44.97
4. $17.11 more
5. 11:55 A.M.
6. $16.44

Page 112
The following show "O" on the chart:
  Dad—TV
  Mom—Picnic
  Christina—Shopping
  Jenna—Basketball
  Baroness—Walk

Page 157
1. Wheeler
2. East
3. South
4. Eastman
5. Wheeler
6. Chestnut Hill Drive

Page 184
1. There are four possible menus.
   • turkey, stuffing
   • chicken, stuffing
   • turkey, potatoes
   • chicken, potatoes
2. There are six desserts.
   • pumpkin, whipped cream
   • apple, whipped cream
   • cherry, whipped cream
   • pumpkin, ice cream
   • apple, ice cream
   • cherry, ice cream
3. There are nine snack choices.
   • popcorn, apple juice
   • pretzels, apple juice
   • crackers, apple juice
   • popcorn, fruit punch
   • pretzels, fruit punch
   • crackers, fruit punch
   • popcorn, milk
   • pretzels, milk
   • crackers, milk

4. There are four choices.
   • "Leftovers," "Run, Turkey, Run"
   • "Thanksgiving Parade," "Run, Turkey, Run"
   • "Leftovers," "What's for Dinner?"
   • "Thanksgiving Parade," "What's for Dinner?"
5. There are six choices.
   • plate, glitter
   • plate, feathers
   • plate, sequins
   • bag, glitter
   • bag, feathers
   • bag, sequins

Page 213
1. George Washington
2. James Hoban
3. Oval Office
4. 1600 Pennsylvania Avenue, Washington, D.C. 20242
5. British
6. Potomac

Page 215
1. north
2. east
3. southwest
4. Lincoln Memorial, Washington Monument
5. Arlington National Cemetery
6. north, south (or southwest)
7. Jefferson Memorial
8. east
9. west
10. north

Page 216
1. three years
2. Answers will vary.
3. Answers will vary.
4. Answers will vary.
5. Answers will vary.
6. 25 years
7. Answers will vary.

Answer Key

Page 231
1. Grover Cleveland
2. Bill Clinton
3. John Kennedy
4. Franklin Roosevelt
5. James Buchanan
6. George Washington
7. William Taft
8. Abraham Lincoln
9. George Bush

Page 243
1. 50 stars
2. Answers will vary.
3. Answers will vary.
4. 37 stars
5. Answers will vary.
6. 117 years

Page 249
1. Pledge of Allegiance
2. Mount Rushmore
3. Statue of Liberty
4. The Star-Spangled Banner
5. U.S. Flag
6. Bald Eagle

Page 287
1. Thomas Jefferson
2. John F. Kennedy
3. George Washington
4. Susan B. Anthony
5. Franklin Roosevelt
6. Abraham Lincoln

Page 292
1. north
2. north, south, east, west
3. force
4. repels
5. attracts
6. repels

Page 293
1. no air, no water, no life
2. reflects the sun's light
3. phases of the moon
4. Neil Armstrong and Edwin Aldrin

Page 302
1. Washington, D.C.
2. 36 years
3. obelisk
4. Washington Monument
5. Answers will vary.

Page 307
1. Mount Vernon
2. American
3. first
4. Washington
5. Father of Our Country

Page 318
1. Washington, D.C.
2. There were 32 states when Lincoln died.
3. huge statue of seated Lincoln
4. Answers will vary.

Page 323
1. Kentucky
2. books
3. 1860
4. freed the slaves
5. Answers will vary.

Page 348

	Bonus Questions
1. $3.74	1. $ .77
2. $1.99	2. $11.42
3. $6.50	3. $10.65
4. $ .41	
5. $6.09	

Page 367
1. Meriwether Lewis & William Clark
2. to talk to other Indians
3. Rocky Mountains
4. Shoshone
5. Cherokee alphabet
6. through newspapers
7. giant redwood trees
8. Cherokee

Page 368

1. constellation	4. north
2. the bear (Sky Bear)	5. telescope
3. seven	6. sun